POL POT'S LITTLE RED BOOK

THE SAYINGS OF ANGKAR

HENRI LOCARD

FOREWORD BY DAVID CHANDLER

Silkworm Books

By the same author, with Mœung Sonn:
Prisonnier de l'Angkar (Paris: Fayard, 1993)
Le "Petit Livre Rouge" de Pol Pot ou Les Paroles de l'Angkar
(Paris: L'Harmattan, first edition, 1996)

© 2004 by Henri Locard

All rights reserved. This book may not be reproduced, in whole or in part, in any form without written permission from the publishers.

ISBN 978-974-9575-56-7

First published by Silkworm Books in 2004
Silkworm Books
6 Sukkasem Road, T. Suthep, Chiang Mai 50200, Thailand
E-mail: info@silkwormbooks.com
www.silkwormbooks.com

Photographs: courtesy of Documentation Center of Cambodia
Set in Times New Roman, Stone Sans, and Jayavarman Text

"We shall force them to work with their hands
in order to become new men."
(Mao Zedong, 23 June 1950)

ទុកមិនចំណេញ ដកចេញក៏មិនខាត
No gain in keeping, no loss in weeding out

សូរចាប់មនុស្សច្រឡំ កុំអោយតែលែងច្រឡំ
You can arrest someone by mistake;
never release him by mistake.

តវ៉ាខ្លាំង ប្រឆាំងខ្លោច
He who protests is an enemy;
he who opposes is a corpse!

អ្វីក៏ដោយសុទ្ធតែជារបស់អង្គការ !
Absolutely everything belongs to the *Angkar.*

ត្រូវតែគោរពសមូហភាព !
Respect the collective!

CONTENTS

NOTE ON KHMER TRANSCRIPTIONS	x
ACKNOWLEDGMENTS	xi
FOREWORD	xiii
INTRODUCTION	1
The curtain rises	25

I	IN PRAISE OF THE REGIME	31
	1 Songs and slogans for ceremonies	33
	2 Official slogans for the masses	52

II	MAOIST-INSPIRED SLOGANS	61
	1 The Super Great Leap Forward	69
	2 A clean sweep of the past	76
	3 Relying solely on one's own strength	78
	4 Economizing	82
	5 Rejecting Western consumer goods	85
	6 Fertilizers	88
	7 Reeducation, criticism, and self-criticism	90
	8 Academic diplomas are worthless	94

III	THE *ANGKAR* AND ITS TACTICS	99
	1 The Angkar, *fount of power, awe, and terror*	99
	The Angkar, *source of love and inspiration*	105
	The Angkar, *all-seeing and all-knowing*	110

		The Angkar *demands blind obedience*	114
		The wrath of the Angkar	121
	2	*The tactics of the* Angkar	124
		Secrecy	127
		Deceit	128
		Reeducation	131
		Interrogations	137
		CIA and KGB agents	140
		The proletariat	141
		Children	142
	3	*Watchwords for soldiers and civilians*	144
IV	THE HUNT FOR "ENEMIES OF THE PEOPLE"		155
	1	*Enemies in general*	163
	2	*Clearly defined categories of enemies*	165
		The old favored classes	165
		The clergy and Buddhists	169
		The Vietnamese	175
	3	*Enemies among the ordinary population*	181
		Those who do not adjust to collectivism	181
		The "17 April people"	183
		The sick	186
	4	*Hidden enemies*	194
		The enemy inside the Party	196
		The enemy that wears a mask	198
		He who complains shall die!	204
	5	*The threat of prison*	206
	6	*The wheel of history*	211
V	LABOR		215
	1	*Work hard*	217
		General directives	217
		The warrior laborer	227

2	*Work hard, in the rice paddies especially*	234
	Rice is the source of all wealth	234
	Yields must be multiplied by three	239
	Nature must be defeated	246

VI COLLECTIVISM: THE DISSOLUTION OF THE
INDIVIDUAL   251
  1 Collectivism according to Pol Pot   259
  2 Revolutionary celebrations   262
  3 Male-female relations   264
  4 The collective is the new family   269
  5 The new order   271
  6 The end of individual property   275
  7 The Socialist society   284
  8 The end of individual liberty   293
  9 Forging the new man   298
  10 The monarchy is anachronistic   301

EPILOGUE	303
GLOSSARY	307
NOTES	309
SELECT BIBLIOGRAPHY	323
GENERAL INDEX	327
SLOGAN INDEX	333

Note: Fifty-four sayings are counter-slogans or gibes made up by ordinary citizens to mark their opposition to the regime: 1, 3, 4, 5, 21, 37, 38, 39, 53, 57, 66, 69, 74, 75, 76, 77, 94, 100, 101, 104, 105, 116, 117, 118, 120, 128, 171, 183, 225, 311, 314, 315, 316, 317, 319, 326, 328, 331, 338, 345, 356, 357, 381, 383, 388, 389, 390, 391, 396, 402, 403, 404, 415, 425. These numbers are marked with the letter C (counter-slogan).

Slogans which were very widespread are underlined in the Khmer.

NOTE ON KHMER TRANSCRIPTIONS

The transcription adopted here is the slightly modified and completed system used in *Cambodian Culture since 1975: Homeland and Exile*, edited by May M. Ebihara, Carol A. Mortland, and Judy Ledgerwood (Ithaca and London: Cornell University Press, 1994) and follows the "Franco-Khmer transcription system developed by Franklin E. Huffman in 1983." For easy reading, the transcription here does not use international phonetic symbols. Acute and grave accents from the French language have been added in an effort to partially better transcribe some of the complexities of the Khmer vowels. The symbol /:/ indicates a long vowel.

CONSONANTS

1st register	*2nd register*	*Transcriptions*
ក	គ	k
ខ	ឃ	kh
ង៉	ង	ng[1]
ច	ជ	ch[2]
ឆ	ឈ	chh
ញ៉	ញ	nh[3]
ដ	ឌ	d

1. Identical to the final sound in *sing*.
2. Composed of two phonemes /t+j/, as in the Franco-English *métier*.
3. Prounced /nj/ as in *campaign*.

ប៉	ឈ	th
ណ	ន	n
ត	ធ	t
ថ	ទ	th
ប	ប៊	b
ប៉	ព	p
ផ	ភ	ph
ម៉	ម	m
យ៉	យ	y[4]
រ៉	រ	r
ឡ	ល	l
វ៉	វ	v
ស	ស៊	s
ហ	ហ៊	h
អ	អ៊	'â:[5]

VOWELS

Khmer vowels	1st register	2nd register
า	â	ie[6]
ិ	è	i[7]
ី	ey	i:
ឹ	œ	eu
ឺ	œ:	eu:
ុ	o	u

4. As in *yes*.

5. អ is articulated with a weak glottal plosive and pronounced much like the British vowel sound in /*all*/. When it is subscripted as in ស្ពាត /sa'æ:t/, it is then just pronounced /a/, followed by a palatalized /æ:/.

6. Pronounced /ie/ as in *dear*.

7. These two vowels are very brief.

ឩ	o:	u:
ឩ	ue	ue[8]
ឫ	ae	œ:
ឭ	eue	eue
ឮ	ie	ie
ឯ	é	è
ឰ	aè	è:
ឱ	ay	ey
ៅ	ao	o:
ៅ	au[9]	ou[10]
ំ	om	um
	am	um
ាំ	amm	amm
ះ	ah	éah
ុះ	oh	uh
ិះ	ih	ih
េះ	èh	èh
ោះ	oh	ueh

Archaic characters   Transcriptions

ឱ្យ	aoy
ឧ	u
ឩ	aou
ឪ	aè
ឫ	reu
ឬ	reu:
ឭ	leu:
ឯ	éh

---

8. The diphthong is pronounced /ue/ as in British English *poor*.
9. As in *now*.
10. As in British English *no*.

ACKNOWLEDGMENTS

I am, first of all, infinitely grateful to all the numerous Cambodians without whose helpful memory and generosity this book would never have existed. Many are anonymous, for these sayings of *Angkar* were essentially collected in the provinces, as a side interest while I was identifying the Khmer Rouge prison network that enmeshed the whole country. I must apologize for not having taken note of the persons who reported the sayings, along with the context and the meaning, which was often ambiguous or ambivalent. I was then able to reconstitute these snippets of revolutionary oral parlance. It was a little like collecting the howlers you might find in student papers, so silly and ridiculous to any sensible person. But behind the silliness and the ridicule lurked the incredible inhumanity of the minds that conceived such barbaric words. Those words in actual fact killed, and my witnesses spoke also in the name of the voices that the Khmer Rouge had silenced forever.

I must first of all thank Yung Phalla, and later Haèm Borith, who patiently helped me to transcribe and translate the slogans.

I am grateful to David Chandler who first encouraged me to publish this collection and made suggestions for the translations.

I cannot name all those who helped me by either supplying new slogans or correcting those already found. This book is the result of a collective work: Aèm Poul Hing Nonn, Iv Chan, Kim Yeat Dararith, Kuouy Theavy, Mey Sophy, Mœung Sonn, Monh Sary, Samuth Sokharin, Sék Sophoan, Siv Thuon, Sok Phâl Sorn

Samnang, Saveros Pou, Sim Sorya, Sour Bounsou, Suong Sikœun, Ung Rotha, Vaèn Phat, Y Oy, Youk Chhang.

I am also grateful to people who have been kind enough to look at the manuscript and make suggestions: Claude Boisson, Alain Daniel, Olivier de Bernon, Jean-Luc Domenach, Alain Forest, Russell Hiang Khng Heng, Anne-Marie Locard, William Maley, Damian Morrison, François Ponchaud, Carlyle A. Thayer, Sylvain Vogel.

I am most grateful to all those who helped me with this second and English edition, and in particular: Vin McNamara, Frances Kemmerer, Helen and Alan Jarvis, and Damien Morrison who corrected my English, together with Jakob Cambria, the translator of the original French edition. Andrew Duncan and Alison Sloper have helped me with the index. My gratitude also to Pierre Gillette and Kong Sambo from *Cambodge Soir* who contributed to having the Khmer script retyped. That first edition has been considerably revised and significantly expanded here.

I am grateful to the University Lumière-Lyon 2 which made me benefit from a sabbatical for the academic year 1993–1994, and to the Australian Defence Force Academy, Department of Politics, University of New South Wales, which offered me a research scholarship for the second semester of 1995 to complete this research.

FOREWORD

During their less than forty-five months in power, the Khmer Rouge sought to overturn, transform, and control Cambodian society. They also wanted to undermine people's collective memories and to separate Cambodians from their past. The process involved abandoning most of the time-honored institutions through which Cambodians had looked on the past and addressed the present. These included Buddhist monasteries, schools, newspapers, and books.

Ironically, as M. Locard's absorbing anthology makes clear, a favored method for undermining these institutions was one that was already deeply rooted in Cambodian culture. This involved the oral transmission of edifying sayings, rhymes, and proverbs. Before the revolution these short, commonsensical texts had provided generations of Khmer men, women, and children with diversion and moral guidance. For hundreds and perhaps thousands of years, they had furnished the thought-worlds of ordinary Khmer. They lay at the heart of Cambodian culture. They gently guided people through the ironies, pleasures, and hardships of everyday life. "Don't believe the sky. Don't believe the stars," one proverb tells us. "Don't believe your daughter when she says she has no lover. Don't believe your mother when she says she has no debts." Another warns us, "If a tiger lies down, don't say: 'The tiger is showing respect,'" while a third, cited by M. Locard suggests that "Men always are in need of money, ogres of human flesh, princes of a throne."

The sayings assembled in these pages are much more brutal. Resolutely facing a future that they claimed to have unraveled, the Khmer Rouge used the slogans to identify, attack, and destroy the enemies of the Communist Party of Kampuchea (CPK). In so doing, they sought to subvert what they referred to as "two thousand years" of exploitation. Hearing the slogans repeated incessantly between April 1975 and January 1979, many Cambodians found them lodged permanently in their minds. Twenty-five years later survivors of the Pol Pot era can often recite twenty or thirty of the sayings in this book, even though the regime was responsible for two million deaths and the relevance of the slogans to the survivors' daily lives has disappeared. For true believers at the time, on the other hand, reciting the sayings and making others memorize them induced a state of exaltation and empowerment.

M. Locard has divided the Khmer Rouge sayings into those that glorify the regime, those inspired by Maoist China, those discussing the "Organization" (*Angkar,* i.e. the concealed, all-powerful CPK), and those dealing with the pursuit of enemies, with work, and with collective life, respectively. The last three categories, bizarrely blending triumphalism and paranoia, were *idées fixes* of the Khmer Rouge.

Although the Khmer Rouge claimed to be waging an unprecedented, incomparable revolution with "bare hands," many of the methods they chose and the terms they used to describe it, as Locard makes clear in chapter 2, were imported without alteration from Maoist China. There was no "Little Red Book" of Pol Pot's personal sayings, but many of the adages collected here resemble those in the Chinese anthology. Phrases lifted from the Chinese into Khmer Rouge jargon included "self-reliance," "storming attack," and "great leap forward." Chinese inspiration and patronage were concealed from the people, but Chinese "guests" of the regime were impossible to hide. Over five thousand of them worked in Cambodia in the Pol Pot era, unobtrusively providing the technical expertise that the regime boasted was unnecessary for the revolution to succeed.

As we peruse the sayings collected in this book we can overhear the Khmer Rouge seeking to destroy the social relations, work practices, and cultural activities that had held the society together. We overhear them struggling to start from zero in a country where Khmer-speakers have lived and grown rice for their families for at least two thousand years.

The beneficiaries of government policies, the "masters" of Cambodia and the people overheard on these pages were supposedly the poorest of the poor, the landless, the young, those whom Mao Zedong referred to proudly as "poor and blank." Ironically, however, the sayings are not their own but were written for them—better inscribed onto the "poor and blank"—by a handful of bourgeois men and women who called themselves the Party Center and spent most of the Pol Pot era concealed from view.

Many of these figures (e.g. Pol Pot, Son Sen, Khieu Thirith, Khieu Ponnary, Ieng Sary, Yun Yat, Vorn Vet, and Khieu Samphan; the list is not exhaustive) had been schoolteachers in pre-revolutionary times. They were used to imparting "wisdom" and maintaining order. Their patronage over the "poor and blank" both broke with and resembled pre-revolutionary patterns. The anonymity of the Khmer Rouge teachers and their rejection of the past were new. The reverence that they demanded and received and the relentless moralizing of their teaching, on the other hand, echoed past practices that they were supposedly eager to destroy.

M. Locard's hard work in assembling this collection almost exclusively from survivors' memories throughout Cambodia has been eminently worthwhile. The slogans themselves allow us into the minds of the Khmer Rouge. Locard's detailed discussion of the adages and slogans, reflecting years of study and residence in the country, provides a nuanced and persuasive history of the forlorn, demented era.

I am happy to commend his fascinating book to readers interested in Cambodian history, and to those encountering the Khmer Rouge for the first time.

David Chandler
Melbourne, Australia
December 2003

INTRODUCTION

As in all Communist countries, the political regime of Cambodia used Party indoctrination and propaganda as a fundamental element of control, from the fateful seizure of power by the Khmer Rouge in 17 April 1975 until their fall on 7 January 1979. Yet, for those who have interviewed Cambodians and read eyewitness accounts by people who lived in that society, a universe characterized by almost daily meetings, study sessions, and mutual and self-criticism, it is surprising that the printed legacy of the Pol Pot regime remains so slender.

The written records of the Khmer Rouge pale in comparison with the voluminous writings of a Lenin and the popularity of the *Little Red Book* of Mao Zedong. Why? Because, in a society where oral tradition still holds sway, the political thought of the leadership was reduced to a macabre, bare-bones, "chemically pure" ideology, as Bernard-Henri Levy would say—an ideology of absolute power by a small group, the *Angkar*.[1] The Communist Party of Kampuchea (CPK) publications, such as *Revolutionary Flag,* were only for the Party elite. For, the "little people," as Prince Sihanouk called them in Sangkum[2] days, there was no printed material; instead, slogans were unceasingly drummed into their consciousness, along with revolutionary songs, in order to fashion the New Revolutionary Man.

Furthermore, the Khmer Rouge leaders were convinced believers in traditional rote learning: educate the young by making them endlessly repeat the words of their elders. The slightest deviation from this parrot-like method was suspect. Luminaries of the Democratic Kampuchean regime relied entirely on the most conservative methods of learning and teaching and, by and large, they failed to create the New Man, but only made those youths return to the brute state of millennia long past—if that brute, unfeeling state ever existed. People refused to trust in the force-fed Khmer Rouge dictums.

If the inspiration of this oral propaganda was essentially Maoist, the roots of its rhetoric lay deep in Khmer culture. Often stripped of all pretense, this way of thinking, stretched to the limits of logic, and honed to razor-thin sharpness, became the essence of raw totalitarian ideology. Junior Khmer Rouge cadres functioned as robots, programmed to repeat unceasingly the same phrases learned by heart, which perfectly summed up the thoughts their masters wished to impart. On the other hand, the propaganda of the more orthodox of Communists, in control during the Vietnamese protectorate from 1979 to 1989, had little trouble in portraying such a manipulation of Marxist dogma as "fascism or Red Hitlerism," for those concepts had been caricatured and applied with such outrageous distortion that they had become utterly absurd, if not horrific.

We also have the feeling of entering behind the scenes of the forbidden world of the Khmer Rouge revolution—into the heart of a darkness, which was forever to remain shrouded in mystery. The revolutionaries believed their world would be forever sealed off from outside observers, and far away from itching ears. But now the utter barbarity of this totalitarian cosmos is exposed to the clear light of day. We are hearing echoes of a world to which we should never have been privy. As Michel Heller stressed, the slogan is the foundation of totalitarian language. It has a "monosemantic character, excluding any different reading," and "leaves little place for doubt." In the Soviet Union, language was the stake in the struggle for power. "Power lent words meanings; it had ultimate say over the life and death of words."[3] This "newspeak" expresses fallacies and presents reality as fake. The slogans initiate us into a universe of "paralogical thought, into a logocracy, where power is at the tip of the tongue." We are squarely at the center of an Orwellian universe "where words are entirely autonyms," that is, they are their own referent.[4] The Pol Pot-ian *sahakor* (សហករណ៍), like the Soviet *kolkhoz*, was not a cooperative farm, but, in fact, according to Alain Besançon,"a slave plantation, under the control of a bureaucracy and the watchful eye of a repressive system." Such a description clearly defines the universe of collectives under Democratic Kampuchea.

Yet, a number of these sayings peculiar to revolutionary jargon, with metaphors borrowed from a Khmer environment, are, in theory, admirable maxims. In practice, they were utterly deformed with Machiavellian cunning. They are good examples of Orwellian doublethink. They say admirable things, and signify, in truth, terrifying reality, in the manner of Christian lore in which the Prince of the Angels changes into Satan. These amphibolous slogans truly show us how the road to hell is paved with good intentions. Other slogans, however, show the regime's hand, and constitute the rhetoric of sheer violence. From the mouths of those who held an entire people in a reign of terror, they are but the expression of the violence of blows, arms, and torture. They form the counter-model of sayings which could very well be those of a government intent on the welfare of its own people: thus, we have here, the negative of the democratic society to which we all aspire.

If the message of these slogans is foreign to Khmer culture, its rhetoric and imagery belong to the centuries-old oral, didactic, and rhythmic literary tradition of Cambodia. The Khmer Rouge knew how to use to their advantage a past which they pretended to have swept away. Indeed, from time immemorial, adages, proverbs, maxims, and aphorisms that could easily be committed to memory were an important teaching tool in the education of youths in Buddhist monasteries. According to Dr. Saveros Pou, who has analyzed this type of literature, it had basically two forms: the *bhasit* or *subhasit* and the *chpap*.[5] The first were "adages and proverbs," or more precisely, "sayings of the ancients." This worked well for the revolutionary *Angkar*—the Organization, or the Party—that pretended to be the "father and mother" of every Cambodian, and thereby substituted itself for tradition. The second, the *chpap*, are short versified texts easily committed to memory in stanzas. Possibly composed in the mists of time, they were put to paper during the Middle Khmer era, round about the fifteenth century. They are like fables—short, coarse, earthy tales full of local expressions and reflective of country life; they describe all the moral and social virtues, and thus, are "a mirror of the collective Khmer soul." We can, without doubt, and in a certain measure, say that the *subhasit* are the condensed, concentrated form of the *chpap*, for their terse and metaphoric language contains the kernel of a short tale—as do a number of Pol Pot slogans.

Let us take as an example, a saying known by all Cambodians and chosen by Dr. Saveros Pou:

ឆ្កែនឹងអាចម៍ស្ដេចនឹងរាជ្យ

chkaè ning ach sdach ning riech

Every dog is drawn to its own droppings,
a prince is attracted to a kingdom.[6]

Another traditional saw develops an identical idea:

មនុស្សនឹងប្រាក់ យក្សនឹងសាច់ ស្ដេចនឹងបល្ល័ង្ក

monuh ning prak yéak ning sach sdach ning balanq

Men are always in need of money, ogres of human flesh,
princes of a throne.

Dr. Saveros Pou remarks that Khmer adages often are "frank, direct and very pithy" and "do not shy away from using a note of cynicism." That note of cynicism prevails among a majority of revolutionary slogans. If this traditional literature demonstrates how the Cambodians absorbed "Indian philosophical ideas," the

Khmer Rouge showed that they could combine and use forms of belief and practice from Maoist China. But with a slight nuance! In this instance, it was not a question of founding a new civilization, but rather—deceptively—of destroying an older one. They posed as true patriots as they put to death a country and a culture; they tried to plant the parasitic plant of Maoism on Cambodian soil, one which would be quickly uprooted. For the leadership, the real goal was the mental enslavement of an entire people or the robotization of a whole society: every individual became a cog in an enormous machine—the *Angkar*—possibly the most totalitarian state of the twentieth century.

The sayings noted above are classical in style, but certainly not in content, for, as Dr. Saveros Pou remarked, rare are proverbs that speak of political reality. Some contemporary politicians have tried to "compose high sounding *subhasit* in order to arouse patriotic fervour." Their attempts often failed and their slogans "were swept into the dustbin of history along with their creators."[7] Khmer Rouge slogans are an excellent illustration of this.

The entire doctrine of Pol Pot and his entourage—or at least as it was perceived by ordinary Cambodians—is to be found in the slogans in this book. They immediately bring us into the center of the Khmer Rouge universe. This ideology is so rudimentary and simplistic that it could, in the end, only convince the totally ignorant and illiterate emerging from the deepest forests. These slogans were denounced as a sham by the vast majority of Cambodians, who were not duped. But, it was better for them to keep quiet, make believe that they believed these false truths, and in their inner hearts reject them.

1 C
ដើមកំណើតអង្គការកើតចេញពីសង្គមស្វាធំ

daem komnaet angka kaet chénh pi: sangkum sva thom

The Angkar *originates from the society of apes.*

So ran a counter-slogan that, in itself, is a final condemnation of Pol Pot-ism: while claiming to make Cambodians leap into a new society which would be the prototype of the coming world, *Angkar* only managed, in many ways, to take Cambodia back to the dawn of humanity.

Perhaps, children or ignorant adolescents, from outer provinces and completely manipulated by the *Angkar*, could find comfort and meaning in them. This suited the leadership well, since they prided themselves on being the spokespersons for men and women from this stratum of the population. In fact, these youths became the henchmen of a group of fanatics hungry for absolute power, utterly cut off from national and international economic realities, as well as the real, centuries-old culture of their own country. Great was the consternation and puzzlement of certain militants, whose devotion was faultless, when they found themselves facing their torturers in S-21[8] or other prisons, and were compelled to confess to treacheries they had never committed. How could the Party they had served with their whole heart and soul, and for which they had sacrificed all human happiness, turn against them and accuse them of treason? For all others, this ideology produced a sinister bewilderment, from which they could protect themselves only through contempt and ridicule. You had to have the irrepressible vitality and humor of the Khmers to be able to laugh at those infinitely tragic circumstances in a society that, it seemed, had banished laughter.

All decisions were taken in the name of the *Angkar*, and many slogans referred to it. *Angkar* literally means "organization" in Khmer. It was the Communist Party of Kampuchea, its Standing Committee, as well the state security apparatus, represented in every social cell of Khmer Rouge society. Everyone was under surveillance, even those in high Party positions. But—and this was a specifically Pol Pot-ian contribution to Communist rule in the East bloc—the power of the faceless *Angkar* could also be invested in a group of local leaders who zealously followed Party orders. They would arrest, torture, and "destroy" all opponents—real, potential, or imaginary. In fact, they were forced to do so. If they did not, they would be suspect, and, they, too, would be arrested and executed. There were also those isolated cadres who took it upon themselves to speak and act in the name of the *Angkar* when they wanted to kill an "enemy" or simply have one of those poor peasants in rifle range perform some chore.

Although there was no personality cult outside Party circles, the *Angkar* was above all Saloth Sar, better known as Pol Pot, who, since 1962 (and the mysterious disappearance of Tou Samouth, the secretary of the Cambodian Communist Party), had always led from behind the scenes the small group of fanatics and faithfuls, under the watchful protection of several Khmer *Loeu* bodyguards. These Montagnards, or ethnic minorities from the Northeast, remained steadfastly loyal to the leadership. In Party documents, Pol Pot was also referred to as no. 870, which was the code number of the Party center, or simply the *Angkar*. In the strategic position of Party secretary, he was number one in all fields, "responsible for Party and Military affairs," and in charge therefore of defining Democratic Kampuchea policies.[9] He was surrounded by a small group of the most faithful who were members of the Standing Committee of the Central Committee of the Communist Party of Kampuchea (CPK).

Next was Nuon Chea, Pol Pot's eternal second in command, a man even more mysterious than Saloth Sar and who might have been more directly involved, for instance, in the horrors committed at S-21. He was deputy secretary, officially responsible for education and propaganda, health, social welfare, culture and indoctrination. In fact, he belonged to the inner circle of Khmer Communists, a movement he had joined as early as 1950, and played a leading role in the CPK's policies of extermination.[10]

Son Sen, the meticulous bureaucrat in charge of Party staff, ex–vice rector of the Faculty of Pedagogy in the fifties and sixties, through which so many future cadres of the CPK passed, had turned into strategist of the people's war as head of the National Defense. In a regime where the civilian and the military wings of the Party were hardly distinguishable, the man was in a key position. Although Son Sen was one of his most faithful associates from his early 1967 days in Ratanakiri, Pol Pot nevertheless decided, on 9 June 1997, that Son Sen, along with his wife Yun Yat (also a "minister" under DK), and twelve other members of their family were traitors. He had them butchered before being himself arrested and "tried" by his peers in Anlong Veng in July 1997.

It was Ieng Sary, the foreign minister and the smiling face of *Angkar* for the rest of the world and the People's Republic of China's man, who relayed Party lies for outside consumption. More specifically, it was his bland rhetoric about the need to serve the revolution that beguiled thousands of overseas Khmers to return home; two-thirds of them were exterminated in so-called reeducation camps.[11]

Khieu Samphan, a Central Committee member, the intellectual of the regime and master of indoctrination in charge of educating cadres, was the nominal head of state, after Sihanouk's resignation in early 1976. In 1977, he was promoted to the chairmanship of "Office 870," which "operated as a form of Cabinet for the CPK Central Committee.[12] The flag bearer of the revolutionary movement from 1968 to 1998 and the death of Pol Pot, he denies any responsibility in decision making and therefore in the killings. He who had told his students in the sixties that Cambodia needed to be swept clean of corruption and evil foreign influences gave a sort of keynote to Khmer Rouge ideology. The following slogans probably bear witness to his style of thought and moral ruthlessness.

Ta Mok (Chhit Chhoeun) was a professional revolutionary since the fifties and the days of the Indochinese Communist Party founded by the Vietminh in the days of the First Indochinese War. He was, by 1978, deputy secretary of the Standing Committee of the CPK, in charge of rural base areas and agriculture. As head of

Introduction 9

the Southwest region (the *niredey*) since 1968, he was notorious for conducting ruthless extermination campaigns in his region and in the East in 1978, and placing cadres from his region throughout the country after the last purge among Party ranks before the fall of the regime. He remained head of the Khmer Rouge army until his arrest by the royal government in 1998 after Pol Pot's death. He had put on his best suit to come to Phnom Penh and pay homage to Hun Sen when he was arrested.

Those were the core members of the *Angkar*, but, like a nebula, it was a seething maelstrom of rising and declining fortunes. For instance, Ney Saran, a pioneering member of the group in the late sixties in Ratanakiri, was purged in 1976, bluntly refusing to admit to treachery. Sao Phim, also a revolutionary by profession since the fifties and in charge of the Eastern region, was forced to commit suicide in early 1978, knowing full well what was awaiting him in S-21. Vorn Vet, minister in charge of the economy, was purged in late 1978, while Kae Pauk, a notorious exterminator in his region, the North, later to include the Center as well, not only survived the demise of the Khmer Rouge movement but gained a generalship in the present Royal Army of the Kingdom of Cambodia. He died in 2002.

Ieng Sary, in a written statement to the press on 8 September 1996, at the time of his rupture from Pol Pot and his close associates (Nuon Chea, Son Sen, Khieu Samphan, and Ta Mok), gave us the following portrait of the aging revolutionary—after almost half a century of intimate collaboration with him, beginning with their Paris days in the early fifties:

> All Pol Pot has ever done has been exclusively done to bolster his dictatorial power, because he has always considered himself as an incomparable genius in military strategy, in the economic field, in health, in the composition of songs, in music, in dance, in culinary art, in fashion, in everything, without forgetting the art of lying. He is a god on earth. All the editorials he has written for the radio

of Democratic Kampuchea have always been signed: "the nation and the people of Kampuchea."[13]

The author of this portrait forgets to mention here that it was he himself who was in charge of propagating these lies to the outer world. This goes towards explaining why international opinion was so slow in realizing what was really happening inside the country. Still, these words must contain much truth since it is an established fact that Pol Pot composed at least the words of the two national anthems found in this collection and also the major national slogans that defined overall Democratic Kampuchea policies.

Pol Pot had understood that there could not be absolute power, nor absolute control of people's minds, unless his person remained shrouded in mystery. Therefore he could not exactly present himself as the Khmer Mao Zedong, even though he played the role of absolute autocrat. Not wishing to arouse, for his own person, all the affection, veneration, and adoration Mao knew how to call forth from all corners of the world, he instead fused his own persona into the *Angkar*, about which his own "subjects" had not the slightest shred of information. Instead, to the people of Cambodia, this entity enshrined at one and the same time not only all the principles of charity and love, but also of terror and horror, creation and destruction, something akin to Shiva in the Hindu godhead. The *Angkar* was equally the all-seeing eye who watched over everyone and probed every heart and soul: love transformed into complete dread!

However, the ordinary citizens, even though they knew nothing of these subtleties and subterfuges, were not fooled. For them, the word *Angkar* was without precise definition, as general as it was specific. Who and what was the *Angkar*? It was not Orwell's Big Brother, whose face was plastered on every street corner in *1984*. If, in the inner councils of the Party, Pol Pot was called by this name, បងទីមួយ (*bong ti muey*) "Brother Number One," or even straightaway បងធំ (*bong thom*), literally "big brother," hardly anyone knew Pol Pot or had seen his face. These names, and especially the pairing of *bong* with *thom*, are not found in Cambodian tradition, for *bong* already carries the connotation of "big or elder brother." This association of words is no more than a tautology, or a stab at hyperbole. In this case, we have an example of borrowing directly from the Chinese and the Vietnamese. Although Pol Pot dropped his mask in the five-hour speech he delivered on 27 September 1977, announcing that the revolutionary *Angkar* was indeed the Communist Party of Kampuchea led by him, few were those that heard or understood his message. Further, the general population had not the foggiest clue as to the identities of its leaders. For them, the *Angkar* might very well have been that messenger dressed in black, a *krâma*[14] around his neck, pedaling in haste on his bicycle to deliver a message from the local collective leader to the authority up above. First and foremost, it was the supreme psychological weapon these terrorists used to hold an entire people in a state of fear and abject submission. Moreover, this word was the symbol that the space between a purely violent human and the commonest of mortals, the space normally reserved for the rule of custom or law, had been totally displaced by a totalitarian cosmos. During the three years, eight months, and twenty days of the *Angkar*'s reign, not one law was voted on or decreed, except the constitution of January 1976. The *Angkar* was also the symbol of fragility, a regime condemned to self-destruction.

Besides several categories within the Communist Party hierarchy, the Pol Pot-ists had divided society into two distinct castes: the *mulethans* and the "17 April people." I use "castes" and not "social classes" for, in the manner of Indian society, the frontiers between the two universes were almost impassable. Besides, for the Khmer Rouge promoters of the so-called pure Khmer peasant revolution, the city dwellers or the "17 April" were often of Sino-Khmer origin. *Mulethan* means "base people," those who composed the Khmer Rouge's rear base and were supposed to become the beneficiaries of the revolution, that is to say, the rural people progressively won over by the guerrilla fighters between 1970 and 1975, and who had not fled to the towns for refuge, as the guerrilla forces advanced.

On the other hand, the "17 April" or "new people" were, in the eyes of the Khmer Rouge, privileged social strata of the former Republican government, who were living in towns at the moment of "victory" on 17 April 1975. These Cambodians bore the mark of Cain, and were forever branded for their transgressions. They had committed a crime: that of flight, if they were from the countryside and took refuge in town. They were guilty of treason, if, despite the repeated urgings of the rebels and Sihanouk, they had not joined the resistance between 1970 and 1975. And, worse, some had even fought against the revolution, and thus had become accomplices of the American bombardments! This simplistic stratification was an aberration because it often did not correspond to any real social distinction. It did not conform to Party ideology, which, on paper, seemed closer to Marxist orthodoxy.

According to Laura Summers' analysis, the Khmer Rouge divided Cambodian society into six large classes (feudal, capitalist, small entrepreneurs, workers, peasants, and a special class—Cambodians living abroad on 17 April 1975), and these six were further subdivided into twenty-one sub-classes.[15] We shall spare our readers the details of these wild categorizations. According to Michael Vickery (and his source, Mat Ly, who related the same things to me), the Khmer Rouge ideologists had divided Cambodian society into three big groupings: 1 ពេញសិទ្ធិ *pénhsèt* "Full Rights," 2 ត្រៀម *triem* "Candidates," 3 ផ្ញើ *phnhae* "Depositees."[16] Yet, in fact, this Marxist language was nothing but a cover to describe a reality, which, in practice, had its origins in ancient Southeast Asian traditions: the victor had the right to make an entire people his prisoners, and reduce them to what amounted to some sort of slavery. With Pol Pot, these poor citizens, stripped of their rights, became at one and the same time the victims of totalitarian methods learned in the West, and perfected in the Far East.

The people, as a whole, knew only the binary distinction—that is, people who had kept away from the revolution in the towns (new people) and people who, more or less voluntarily, had been sucked into the maelstrom (base people). I was mainly concerned with gathering the body of Khmer Rouge ideology such as it was transmitted to ordinary people in the collectives. I have also selected a few of the most popular watchwords spread among Party cadres during interminable study sessions, atheistic retreats, and seminars, first in the forest and then in the solitude of Phnom Penh after 17 April 1975.

It is important to recall that mass killings in all Communist regimes mainly have social and ideological causes, not racial, and thus have to be distinguished from Nazism. The only ethnic group or nationality suffering the wrath and punishment of the Pol Potists was the Vietnamese. Still, we can perhaps say that this important minority—already reduced by half by pogroms and expulsions during Lon Nol's time—sustained much less loss and damage than other categories of Cambodians, for they simply had the luck of being almost all expelled at the beginning of the Pol Pot regime. It would be interesting, though, to know how many died along the route of exile and how many stayed behind in spite of orders.

Pol Pot's and his group's revolutionary solidarity with "elder brother" Communist Vietnam had changed its character between 1966 and 1973 to seething hatred. That was between Saloth Sar's long sojourn in China at the outset of the Cultural Revolution and the American decision in 1973 to gradually "Vietnamize" the war and by degrees leave Indochina to its own devices. Aid from the world's most populous country was no doubt more sizeable, the prospects of absolute power for the leaders of the Khmer Communist Party more believable, and above all, the guarantee of complete respect for the territorial independence, sovereignty, and autonomy of the Cambodian revolution more solemnly affirmed. Mao and Chou Enlai were very clever flatterers who lulled the Khmer Rouge, as they had earlier lulled Sihanouk, into believing they would provide protection to their regimes without ever interfering with their internal affairs. Still, they pulled many a string to manage their liegeman Pol Pot, while asserting that he and his revolution were absolute masters of Democratic Kampuchea. The towering figure of Sun Hao, the Chinese ambassador and dean of the so-called diplomatic corps in Democratic Kampuchea days, could, with his benign and smiling face, march through celebrations of the Party as if he were lording over conquered territory.

Some have also sought to show that the Chams, the Malay Muslim minority, were specifically targeted for repression. I am not so sure, and indeed, I have found no slogans that specifically point to this minority as being part of the "enemy" to be eliminated. I am not surprised by this, and I share Michael Vickery's analysis in *Cambodia 1975–1982* that "there was never a central policy to destroy them."[17] In fact, this minority was not specifically targeted for punishment as a community sharing certain characteristics essentially religious in nature. If, indeed, they suffered more at the hands of the Khmer Rouge than the rest of the population, it was because they offered more resistance to the new regime. They, in particular, had a hard time accepting that they no longer had the right to daily worship—a right also denied the Catholic minority, for instance. They were, however, not always forced to eat pork; besides, generally, there was little if any meat in collective meals. And pork was served only at Party fêtes: there, the Chams, like the rest of the population, could throw themselves on this proscribed flesh like famished dogs—proof of how hunger had become the major obsession of the people.

The Khmer Rouge, by bringing collectivization into almost every nook and cranny of social and personal life, politicized every action and every thought of every individual. The following slogans and adages of the *Angkar* embraced every aspect of political, economic, social, and private life: it was an all-intrusive ideology, leaving no space of human life empty. The public sphere had grown into a cancerous tumor that was devouring every human being. This is by essence death-giving; any transgression of the *Angkar* rules, any hint of opposition, and any lack of enthusiasm for the revolutionary line as defined by the Standing Committee in Phnom Penh was considered a political error and severely punished.

***

Some specialists of Democratic Kampuchea could take exception to this collection of slogans for not considering the various political lines or power struggles as reflected in the slogans. Although the repression may have worsened by the beginning of 1976, and the radical policies may have been relaxed during the last few months of the regime, there were few echoes of those apparent shifts in the watchwords heard in the collectives. Few were the slogans linked to a clearly defined shift in DK policy during this, happily, very short-lived regime. Whenever this is a link, it is stated clearly. However, recollect that after the more or less brutal mass evacuation of *all* cities and towns, there was amazing consistency in the way the regime carried out its horrific repression and inflicted untold suffering on all its people throughout the country. In the emptying of towns, though, certainly there was a significant difference between one provincial capital and another in the degree of brutality in carrying out the evacuation orders.

After the complete collectivization of meals—generally at the beginning of 1976 following the first harvest, which led to widespread hunger, famine, or food shortages almost everywhere in the country—these three final years were uniformly barbaric for the people's communes. Government policy, as defined at the top by the *Angkar Loeu*, did not vary one iota during the nearly forty-five months the Khmer Rouge held power. That amounted to a Great Leap Forward in production (agricultural and industrial), the construction of an irrigation system throughout the country in order to triple crop yield, together with the relentless witch hunt for enemies of the revolution. The 1978 change in political line brought about a very controlled opening to the outside world and the complete replacement of officials at Boeung Trabek and Dey Krahom, the two main reeducation centers for intellectuals who had returned home from abroad, but this found little echo on state farms throughout Cambodia. Thus, we can state that *all* the slogans, in *all* their barbarity, were fully enforced *everywhere* and *all the time*. Nevertheless, this does not mean that the Khmer Rouge were *all* robots without heart, or pity, such as the *Angkar* envisioned. No, everywhere, some showed kindness, and alas, often at the risk of their own lives!

It remains for us to ask who could have written these slogans. Were they, like traditional saws, the work of unknown authors? Some, the most known, were heard on Democratic Kampuchea's official radio. Thus, we could deduce that they were the work of the propaganda services of the Ministry of Information and Culture, under first Hu Nim, and then, Yun Yat, Mrs. Son Sen. In fact, a source from the Khmer Rouge leadership who wishes to remain anonymous claims that these main slogans were indeed concocted by the Standing Committee of the CPK. This justifies the title chosen for this collection: *Pol Pot's Little Red Book* or *The Sayings of Angkar*, since indeed that is what these slogans were in actual life because Pol Pot dominated the *Angkar*. They strikingly expressed DK policies. We can imagine that they were then circulated during those large orientation sessions at the top, or during the study sessions in Phnom Penh that the highest ranking cadres had to attend more or less regularly. These grand watchwords, known by all Cambodians, were no more than about thirty in number; they will be pointed out, and underscored. From these grand themes, local potentates (or *kamaphibals*, as they were called) could elaborate on them any way they chose, according to the richness of their imagination.

Among the top leaders of Democratic Kampuchea, one, apart from Pol Pot himself, was much like a revolutionary preacher during these reeducation seminars—Khieu Samphan, the nominal head of state. The ex-deputy of the National Assembly in Sangkum days who also gave some lectures at the Law and Economics Faculty had told his students, before fleeing into the maquis (the underground resistance movement) in 1967, "Khmer society needs to be cleansed and purified." Apparently, he was not a member of the Standing Committee and therefore took no part in major decision making—or so he claims. Still, he was seen in many a propaganda and official cadre meeting, where he was a regular speaker. His numerous speeches were broadcast on DK radio. He was a moralist and a dogmatist and must have given to the revolutionary movement its trenchant and puritan flavor. Among Khmer Rouge notebooks collected in the Documentation Center of Cambodia in Phnom Penh, researchers of the center have singled out "Twenty-six Precepts of Brother Khieu Samphan Theory."[18] These display how the Khmer Rouge were able to manipulate traditional lore in order to extend the absolute power of a tiny clique. Here are a few of the most revealing of their reeducation methods:

ចាបដល់ពេលអរុណរះ ចាបតែងតែហើរទៅរកស្រែចំការ
គឺមិនដែលស្រែចំការហើរមករកចាបទេ

chap dâl pél arunréah chap taèng taè hae tou rok sraè chomka
keu: men daèl sraè chomka hae mok rok chap té

At dawn, birds fly towards the fields;
never do fields fly towards the birds.[19]

គេលុញដីពុំផ្ដុំ នៅពេលវានៅទន់
ké lunh dey et nou pél vie nou tun
Clay is molded while it is soft.[20]

សំលៀកបំពាក់បិទបាំងរាងកាយបាន
តែមិនអាចបិទបាំងពូជអំបូរបានទេ

sâmlik bompéak bet bang rieng kay ban
taè men ach bet bang puch ambô ba:n té

Clothes can hide the body, but they can't hide the origin.[21]

> បើទុកជាចកស្វត្រធម៌ទាំងយប់ទាំងថ្ងៃយ៉ាងណាក៏ដោយ
> កកូនពពែនៅតែមិនទុកចិត្តដែរ
>
> bae tuk chie châchâk sothoa téan jup téang tngay yan na kâ daoy
> kâ kôn popè nou taè men tuk chet daè
>
> The wolf can say prayers night and day;
> the kid will not trust him.[22]

> ចិត្តមិត្តមិនមែនដូចជាជង្គង់
> ដែលគេបត់បែនបានដូចបំណងនោះទេ
>
> chet met men mèn doch chie chungkung
> daèl ké botbaèn ban doch bâmnâng nuh té
>
> The heart, comrade, is not like the knee,
> which can bend at will.[23]

These few examples reveal to us the Khmer Rouge ideological think tank's techniques of persuasion. They not only aped the rhetoric of traditional saws, but they also exploited the very words of the old sayings, emptying them of their established meanings to make them fit the new revolutionary society. Orwell explained to us in *1984* how, in that totalitarian society, words are to be drained of sanctioned meanings in order to make individual free thinking unthinkable. He takes the instance of the adjective "free" which has no longer any figurative meaning, but only practical meaning as in "a garden *free* from weeds." Its wider and of course political significance would have evaporated. Those so-called "Sayings of Khieu Samphan"[24] show us that the sayings of the *Angkar* fall basically into two categories: the first is composed of the purely political slogans, like those concerning the "Super Great Leap Forward," which were entirely concocted by the Party worthies. The second category, concerned with society in general, is composed of either variations of traditional adages, or aphorisms given a new revolutionary meaning. Cadres in study sessions, such as those run by Khieu Samphan, were stuffed with these clichés, with which they could cram their lengthy evening speeches in the collectives, so that each Khmer, deprived of citizenship, could become a docile servant of the *Angkar*.

The main watchwords, known by absolutely all Cambodians who lived under DK, were devised by the Standing Committee of the Party, like all the main pieces of literature produced by the Party. We have, for instance, Khieu Samphan's testimony for this. As to the counter-slogans, only a very few were well known, the majority being whispered among trusted friends. These must have therefore been innumerable and this collection has gathered only some samples. The counter-slogans are in italics, to distinguish them from the Khmer Rouge catechism. They are a sign of undaunted opposition to the regime by the vast majority of the population.

Further evidence that slogans were elaborated by the top leadership are the vast number of learned words of Pali and Sanskrit origin. But some words, directly connected with revolutionary ideology, had to be created. The poorly educated local cadres would find them difficult to utter, and relocated townspeople would love to ridicule them for it. Here are a few examples:

បដិវត្តន៍ ➔ បក្សនិវត្តន៍
padévoat ➔ pak nivoat
revolution ➔ *party of the retired*

កុម្មុយនិស្ត ➔ គុម្មួយនេះ
kommuynih ➔ kum muey nih
Communist ➔ *this clump of trees*

ប្រតិកិរិយា ➔ ប៉េតិកិរិយា
prâ:tékériya ➔ peyté kériya
reactionary ➔ *enthusiastic temperament*

វណ្ណៈអធន ➔ វណ្ណៈ អត់ធន់
vannak ak thun ➔ vannak ât thuen
proletariat ➔ *the class that does not persevere*

On the other hand, the population delighted in distorting the Khmer Rouge jargon. On a humorous note:

កងចល័ត → កងសាឡាដ
kâ:ng chalat → kâ:ng salat
front-line brigade → *carry salad in the arms*

And on a more tragic note:

សង្គមនិយម → សង្គមនេះយំ
sângkumniyum → sângkum nih yum
socialism → *this society that weeps*

This pun must have been quite widespread since it is noted in the account of a prisoner's interrogation at the torture execution center of Krang Kra Chan, in Tramkak district, Takeo province.[25]

Similarly, in the days of UNTAC (United Nations Transitional Authority in Cambodia) in 1992–93, the then fading Khmer Rouge component, which had been forced by their Chinese protectors to sign the 21 October 1991 Paris Agreement, were determined not to implement the accord and not to abide by their signature. For them:

UNTAC → អន្ទាក់ → snare
antéak

The stereotyped language of the slogans was incorporated into the speeches of local cadres, and, along with revolutionary songs and educational playlets, they constituted the corpus of ideological teachings inflicted day and night on the population. By and large their crude methods of persuasion were modeled on the Chinese Cultural Revolution. The indoctrination worked only with the very young and very innocent, provided they had no previous formal education whatsoever. For the city children, it was just a load of nonsense.

Introduction 21

***

Again, some could also argue that a number of maxims assembled here are not truly slogans but simple, stereotypical expressions of any number of events in daily life under the Khmer Rouge. For example, in the revolutionary theater the *Angkar* had begun producing, edifying scenes of daily life were strung together with these clichés, which, from beginning to end, taught a moral and political lesson of sorts, especially aimed at the country's young people. Many slogans expressed the same ideas, and thus appear redundant. But, by definition, Pol Pot-ism is highly repetitive, and taken as a whole, the phrases of this volume represent the web of speeches spun out at night, before exhausted listeners, by local political commissars.

This collection has essentially been constituted from oral sources from many provinces. Very few originate from printed books, and when this has been the case, I checked with a number of witnesses that they had indeed heard those sayings in DK times. This will be pointed out in the notes. I have been careful to compile a corpus of ideological teachings of the Khmer Rouge as spread at grass-roots levels, and not in study sessions for Party cadres.

These slogans have been grouped into six sections. The first contains expressions of triumph and self congratulation, launched from the regime's beginning, and found in all official speeches but fooling fewer and fewer people as time went on. This shameless triumphalism lulled the ruling caste itself into being enamored with its own hyperbole, even on the eve of the arrival of Vietnamese troops in January 1979. The second section sounds a note in a major key of this ideology—a fundamentalist Maoism. Try as they might, the Khmer Rouge, self-proclaimed patriots and true Cambodians, invented nothing and slavishly copied policies which had already failed twice, on a massive scale, in the People's Republic of China. They recycled twice-failed Maoist formulae (from the Great Leap Forward and the Cultural Revolution), and, with a perverseness which characterized them, employed once more with diligence these disastrous watchwords—disastrous except for the *Angkar*, who had absolute power over the hearts and minds of Cambodians. Then, we shall look at slogans about the *Angkar*, its tactics and methods; next, we will see the hunt for so-called enemies, and categories of citizens considered vermin to be exterminated: here, we touch on the very essence of all Communist regimes, which divide society into "comrades," and "enemies" to be wiped out. Finally, we will look at those sayings dealing with work and the collective daily life.

One of the problems in translating Khmer is that personal pronouns are often omitted, and this is true in the majority of slogans. Given the fact that these saws were addressed to the general population, I therefore take it that the speaker was the *Angkar*, and the addressee the average citizen. Thus, they are usually directed to the group, except when they are manifestly aimed at the individual, in which case they can be punctuated with the ritual appellation, "comrade"!

This collection does not pretend to be exhaustive. It would be an incredible boast to claim so. Yet, these slogans form a cohesive body of Khmer Rouge ideology, such as it was perceived by the ordinary Cambodian. They also offer the reader a "guided tour" of everyday Cambodia during those eventful years. In the chaos and diversity, they reveal a unity of thought, and several large, dominant themes. Everything reflects the three major characteristics of the *Angkar*: Machiavellism, barbarity, and finally, distressing stupidity! The proof: even today every time Cambodians hear a Khmer Rouge slogan, they smile—a sure sign of utter contempt!

***

Finally, let us note that, during the regime replacing the Khmer Rouge, from 1979 to 1989, the years of the People's Republic of Kampuchea, Heng Samrin's government propaganda equally relied on slogans; they played a role in educating the "masses," a traditional Khmer way of learning. This regime, in spite of the wagging tongues which dubbed it "Khmer Rouge II," was very different in nature, since a number of rights were restored and the Vietnamese-backed regime set the country on the long road of reconstruction. I have systematically omitted them, for they belonged to a different era: the essence of the Pol Pot-ist regime was the sudden, ruthless evacuation of towns and cities, followed by a countrywide system of collectivization and repression without equal in the history of Communism. The new regime allowed farmers to go back to their villages and most city dwellers to eventually return to their towns, when they did not choose to take refuge abroad. However, there was no freedom of movement without official authorization and the Party exercised complete control over the population, even in the countryside. Here are some examples of slogans during the Vietnamese occupation. People were told:

បីមិនមួយរាយការណ៍ :
មិនជឿខ្មាំង មិនលាក់ខ្មាំង មិនស្ដាប់ខ្មាំង
bey min muey rieyka:
min cheue khmang min lèak khmang min sdap khmang
There are three, not one, prohibitions: don't believe the enemy,
don't hide the enemy, don't listen to the enemy.

But the enemy at this time undoubtedly had a more objective existence, for it was all those who resisted the presence of Vietnamese troops on Cambodian soil—the Khmer Rouge, and their new allies, the FLNPK[26] and FUNCINPEC.[27]

Throughout the decade that the Vietnamese were in Cambodia, the authorities never missed an occasion to repeat to all and sundry the horrors of the Pol Pot-ist regime, exposing them as "self-genocidal" so that the well-intentioned, Vietnamese "elder brother's" occupation would appear less onerous in comparison. Thus, we come across new official slogans that mock Democratic Kampuchea:

បំបាត់នាយទុន	បញ្ចេញអង្គការ
bombat nieytun	banhchénh angka:
បំបាត់ពន្ធដារ	បញ្ចេញវិភាគទាន
bombat punda	banhchénh viphiektien
បំបាត់អ្នកមាន	បញ្ចេញអ្នកក្រ
bombat néak mien	banhchénh néak krâ:
បំបាត់ពណ៌ស	បញ្ចេញពណ៌ខ្មៅ
bombat poa sâ:	banhchénh poa khmau
បញ្ចេញអ្នកខ្លៅ	បំបាត់អ្នកចេះដឹង
banhchénh néak khlau	bombat néak cheh dœng
បើបំបាត់ម្លឹងៗ	មាននឹយយ៉ាងម៉េច
baœ bombat mleung mleung	mien ney yang méch

Wipe out the capitalists, and build the Angkar.
Abolish taxes and solicit contributions.
Destroy the rich and create the poor.
Ban the color white, and honor the color black.
Exterminate the educated and increase the number of ignorant.
If you destroy all this, what does it signify ?

On the other hand, here are some examples of slogans the pro-Vietnamese regime concocted to arouse popular enthusiasm:

បង្កើតក្រុមសាមគ្គី បំបាត់អង្គការ
ba:ngkaet sameki:, bombat angka:
Form solidarity groups, destroy the *Angkar*!

បំបាត់ពន្ធដារ បង្កើតវិភាគទានស្ម័គ្រចិត្ត
bombat punda, bâ:ngkaet viphiektien smachet
Abolish taxes, create voluntary contributions!

Cambodians protested under their breath against the new Party dictatorship. In particular, they expressed their anger at having to go to clear forests along the Thai border in order to construct what was called a "bamboo curtain," in order to deny routes of infiltration to Khmer Rouge guerrillas from bases within Thailand. A very large number of Cambodians died in this heavily mined area:[28]

ទៅជិះឡាន មកវិញជិះចាន !
tou chih la:n, mo:k vinh chih cha:n !
You leave inside a lorry, you return inside a funeral urn!

To denounce the inequalities and injustices of the Vietnamese protectorate, the people whispered among themselves, for example:

កូនអ្នកក្រធ្វើទាហាន កូនអ្នកមានធ្វើនគរបាល
កូនកម្មាភិបាលទៅបរទេស!
ko:n néak krâ: thvœ: tiehien, ko:n néak mien thvœ: nokobal,
ko:n kamaphibal tou bâ:rotéh !
Children of the poor become soldiers,
children of the rich enter the police force,
children of Party cadres go abroad!

កូនអ្នកមានជាប់ដុកទ័រ កូនអ្នកក្រជាប់គ្រូ !
ko:n néak mien choap dokto, ko:n néak krâ: choap kru:
Children of the rich become doctors,
children of the poor become teachers!

THE CURTAIN RISES

Even before the Khmer Rouge seized power, they used slogans in their propaganda to win the hearts and minds of the Cambodian people—above all, the people in the hinterlands, for whom it was customary to say: Prince Norodom Sihanouk was the incarnation of the god-king. Raising high the banner of the former sovereign contributed significantly to the victory of the revolutionaries.[29] This alliance was purely tactical, and the guerrillas in the maquis disrespectfully called Sihanouk "fat-so"! In truth, almost to a man, the Cambodians, especially those in the countryside, had not the slightest clue as to meaning of the revolutionaries' Marxist jargon.[30] Chhit Do, an ex–Khmer Rouge cadre interviewed in the region of Angkor for a television documentary revealed that fooling Sihanouk was deliberate Party policy:

> The Khmer Rouge leaders told us that important cadre like us were Communists, but the people believed in Sihanouk. They said that we who had joined the Party should not believe in him. Starting with the candidates for Party membership, there was this kind of education. No one should have faith in Sihanouk, but they still allowed the people to believe in him. You see, there was public education and covert education. If we still believed in Sihanouk, they explained, there was no point in our making the revolution. Sihanouk and the revolution, they told us secretly, were enemies of each other.
>
> If at any time the Khmer Rouge had not aligned themselves with Sihanouk, they would have been unable to carry on their fight, they would not have been able to challenge Lon Nol. That's why they got Sihanouk on their side and put him up front. They made him front man because his subjects had admired and respected him for so long.[31]

2
ជយោ ! សម្ដេចឪ! អ្នកណាមិនទៅខ្ញុំទៅហើយ!
cheiyo: samdech œu ! Néak na min tou, khnhom tou haey !
Long live Samdech Euv! You're not going? I've gone already!

Every fresh recruit in the Khmer Rouge's guerrilla forces was supposed to shout this rallying call to resistance, thereby inviting his fellow citizens to do the same. *Samdech Euv* was the usual form of address for Prince Sihanouk and literally means "Monsignor-Papa." The new combatant, thus, did nothing more than respond to the appeals of the prince on the air waves from Beijing, កូនចៅ សូមមកតាមឳ ឪនៅចាំក្នុងព្រៃម៉ាគី (*ko:n chau, som mok tam ou, ou nou cham knong prei maki:*), "My children, my grandchildren, come and join your Father, your Father who awaits you in the forest-maquis."

This entreaty found concrete form in the royal couple's visit to the revolutionaries inside Cambodia in February/March 1973. Norodom Sihanouk, accompanied by his wife, Princess Monique, traveled hundreds of kilometers along the Ho Chi Minh trail, escorted by Ieng Sary, the eyes and ears of the CPK in Beijing. After going through the border, they crossed the Mekong at the symbolic historical site of Thala Bariwatt just south of Stung Treng. There, they drove close to one of the ultra secret headquarters of Pol Pot at the time, located slightly north of the confluence of the rivers Tonle Se Sann and Tonle Sre Pok. Then, the motorcade of some fifteen heavily guarded, air-conditioned vehicles took two nights to reach Phnom Kulen where the royal couple spent five nights. Thus the royal party could safely dash westward along a recently rebuilt piste to Phnom Kulen, at the height of the American bombing of the country. The return trip was just as quick. The expedition in and out Cambodia probably lasted less than two weeks.

The Khmers had entirely rebuilt roads and bridges, which, no doubt, facilitated the speed of the trip and held few or no surprises. The cavalcade traveled without any headlights during the night, lest enemy aircraft radar spot clouds of dust in the dry season. During the day, the travelers rested under the coverage and protection of the forest's foliage, or, for the sake of photographers, pretended to tread, one behind the other, propped on their sticks, the long and perilous guerrilla path. Thus, the Beijing propaganda service had all the time to take photos of these dignitaries to their best advantage, in order to fix on paper and film for posterity this memorable and unlikely escapade. Dressed as a Khmer Rouge member, in black pajamas, with the indispensable red-and-white-checked *krâma* around his neck, giving him a touch of the peasant, with Ho Chi Minh rubber sandals on his feet, Sihanouk was thus no more than the first among the proletarians! Still, some were more equal than others, and Princess Monique remarked in her travel notebook that she and her husband were the object of everyone's most gracious attentions.

The royal pair is supposed to have attended a number of meetings with the Khmer Rouge leadership, the revolutionary soldiers, and "the masses," together with a cultural revolutionary show to give them a foretaste of Democratic Kampuchea. They were abundantly photographed on those occasions and also in front of Kulen's famous waterfall among CPK worthies. They were supposed to have visited Banteay Srey and Angkor Wat as well. Since all those photographs have been retouched by the Beijing Party propaganda services, it is impossible to determine which are genuine and which are fakes. However, if it is absolutely certain that Sihanouk and his wife did go as far as the safe haven of the dense forest of Phnom Kulen, it is possible that they also ventured into the temple complex of Angkor. It was quite close to the battlefront at the time.

And, the weight of the prince's personality and authority gave great prestige and importance to the precarious fortunes of the Khmer Rouge. He could not have undertaken this adventurous journey without careful and detailed planning and collaboration between the three Communist movements—in fact, the last time they collaborated closely. This involved the Khmer Rouge army on the ground, the protection of the Vietnamese military, and above all, the Chinese authorities, whose propaganda services gave his visit the widest and heaviest coverage from Beijing, once Sihanouk was safely back there. The shadow play of events consisted of bringing to center stage the "Three Ghosts"—Khieu Samphan, Hu Nim, and Hou Youn—because they were alleged to have been killed by the prince's own political police at the very moment they had joined the underground in the forests in 1967. In the meantime, in the wings, Saloth Sar and his *Angkar* laughed up their sleeves at the comedy they were putting on for their eternally sworn enemy. And on their side, the Maoist officials in Beijing pulled the strings, expressing joy at their plots, fraught with tragedy, but destined to open Southeast Asia to them by installing their liegemen in places of power.

All this could be seen in the photographs and films of Mao's propaganda services, from the retouched snapshots and the craftily edited documentaries, which took months to produce. This trip had tremendous political impact, serving to cover over the cracks within the Communist movement, as well as internally, in the ranks of the Khmer Rouge, between the "three ghosts"—former ministers of the Sangkum and considered to be intellectuals with blood-free hands—and the Pol Pot-ists. Ghost number one, Khieu Samphan, whom many a commentator wished to characterize as an idealist without any real responsibility, was in fact the public face of Pol Pot, whose least commands he duly and loyally carried out. Ghost number two, Hu Nim, who was minister of information in the GRUNK,[32] also devotedly served Pol Pot until he was arrested on 10 April 1977. Ghost number three was Hou Youn, perhaps the most idealistic of this trio and reputedly the one who had drawn up plans for developing cooperatives (and not Pol Pot's state-run agricultural and production units). At the time, he held no office of real power, for he was the only one who dared stand up to Saloth Sar—Pol Pot. For that, he was executed in 1975 in the region of Chamcar Loeu, at Kompong Cham, being spared the agony of Tuol Sleng. At the moment of Sihanouk's trip, he probably had no more authority than, say, Prince Norodom Phurissara, the so-called minister of justice.

Saloth Sar was always in the background in official photographs but controlled all revolutionary activity inside his Kampuchea. Sihanouk was denied all direct access to the "little people" for whom he had great affection by the double wall of Vietnamese-Chinese advisors and the Khmer Rouge army, thus savoring a foretaste of what would be his lot after the seizure of power by the revolutionaries. The second fault line, which split the Khmer Rouge and the Vietnamese Communist Party, only became official at the end of 1977 though it had already occurred on the ground in 1973. The Pol Pot-ists were set to purge those faithful to Hanoi and had started to set up a network of prisons and execution centers which they extended countrywide after their 17 April 1975 victory.

More importantly, Sihanouk's brief stay transformed a small group of ruthless, utopian, revolutionaries with little credibility into a movement of national liberation, fighting "an imperialist invasion" in order to put an end to corruption and create a fairer society. Thousands of idealists and/or naive individuals, the young and not so young, rallied to the call of their "king" in whose person resided legitimate authority against the irrational policies of Lon Nol. With each passing day, the movement swelled in number as new recruits rushed to join.

3 C
ជយោ ! សម្តេចខ្ញុំអ្នកណាមិនទៅដុតផ្ទះចោល !
cheiyo: samdéch ou! néak na min tou, dot phtéah chaol !
Long live Samdech Fuv!
Whoever doesn't go, his house will be burnt to ashes!

4 C
ជយោ ! សម្តេចខ្ញុំអ្នកណាមិនទៅកាប់ចោល !
cheiyo: samdéch ou! néak na min tou, kap chaol !
Long live Samdech Euv!
Whoever doesn't go will be smashed to pieces!

These two threats were no doubt uttered by the opponents of the revolutionaries in order to denounce the extremely violent forms of recruitment into the guerrilla movement. Inside the zones controlled by the FUNK, bloody waves of repression fell on those judged lukewarm in their allegiances, and above all on those hostile to the revolutionaries. Many recruits, among adolescents in villages won over by the revolutionaries, were press-ganged to join the guerrillas, as François Bizot explains in his memoirs, *The Gate*.[33]

Chapter I

IN PRAISE OF THE REGIME

Two themes—both fallacious—dominated all proclamations glorifying the regime: one, that the victory of 17 April 1975 was the highest peak in Cambodian history in the past two thousand years, greater even than the building of Angkor; the other, that the revolutionary regime had put an end to corruption and exploitation once and for all.

Concerning the constant reference to the Angkor era in Khmer Rouge mythology, we should note how bizarre it is for a regime that proclaimed itself proletarian to refer constantly to a triumphant absolutism by divine right. But there also, the analogy is dualistic: the reference to Angkor went hand in hand with unceasing reminders to the valorous Khmer people who, for two millennia, had fought against what was improperly termed "feudal" oppression and colonialist incursions onto Khmer soil. This struggle had never ended in victory—or so the Khmer Rouge propaganda claimed— not only because the people had been betrayed by their leaders who colluded with foreign conquerors, but also because their centuries-old will to vanquish their enemies had not, until now, found its proper leadership apparatus. That was to be at long last embodied by a "Revolutionary Organization, the present far-sighted *Angkar*."

In such a scheme of things, what becomes of the Angkor period and the Indianization of the Southeast Asian peninsula, the bedrock of Cambodian civilization? It is obvious that the Khmer Rouge retained the reference to the mighty builders of Angkor, their ability to raise monuments of pharaonic grandeur and to manage a sophisticated water supply system in order to make the relocated people dig vast irrigation networks thus working many victims to death. In doing so, they also vindicated their inordinate chauvinism.

On the other hand, Pol Pot and his entourage always mentioned the figure of two thousand years, because they must have found their model for the Marxian, so-called primitive, Communism among the Khmer *Loeu* or ethnic minorities living in the Northeast of the country. This was where they set up hidden bases (the ubiquitous *munty 100* or "Office 100"[1]) years before seizing power in Phnom Penh, among the minorities who still, to a large extent, live the same centuries-old lifestyle today. It was also in those mythical regions of the wooded and mountainous periphery that Pol Pot mysteriously died on 28 April 1998, mainly among his original devoted and incorruptible Montagnard bodyguards at Along Veng.[2] The principal characteristic that all these minorities shared was to have been untouched by the Indianization of Cambodia, which began around two thousand years ago. The ultimate objective of Pol Pot-ism, in destroying contemporary property, institutions, and mores, was to coerce the modern Khmers—from the cities, in particular—to become wandering tribes under their totalitarian sway and thus to return to the bronze age.

We find a striking example of these two apparently contradictory themes side by side in Pol Pot's famous five-hour-long speech on 27 September 1977:

> During more than 2000 years, our people have lived in complete destitution and the deepest despair [. . .] If our people could build Angkor Wat, they are capable of doing anything.[3]

As for the second fallacy, the abolition, once and for all, of corruption, it is very tempting to believe that the Khmer Rouge leaders led a Spartan life, if we take as examples the "three ghosts," those so-called paragons of unselfishness: Khieu Samphan, Hou Youn, and Hu Nim. However, if we look at the facts, we see that, from the very first hours of the regime, soldiers looted the citizenry, carrying off private belongings of all kinds that they coveted, such as watches and radios. During the years the regime held power, all the property of those who were continuously relocated was gradually confiscated, whether for the benefit of the cadres themselves, or in order to barter for necessities at the Thai borders, or to be warehoused. After the regime's fall, what the Khmer Rouge could not carry with them for personal use on their flight constituted a huge booty for the victorious Vietnamese army.

We should also be aware that most of the higher cadres ate very well, usually on the sly, whilst their fellow Cambodians were starving to death. For instance, among the Khmer Rouge cadres who were responsible for Sihanouk's security, one admitted to me that he had put on twenty kilos during his two years in office between 1976 and 1978. How many hundreds of thousands of Cambodians starved to death during the same years? Does this not suggest an especially evil form of corruption? In the end, is not the corruption of absolute power over life and death still worse than the corruption linked to money and property and gifts?[4]

1—SONGS AND SLOGANS FOR CEREMONIES

The songs and slogans for ceremonies in this category are slightly different in nature from those that follow in this collection. They are examples of official slogans heard on ceremonial occasions and during governmental gatherings in Phnom Penh and broadcast over Radio Democratic Kampuchea. They are the very ones which Sihanouk, for example, would have heard over the radio in his golden prison, the Royal Palace, and which he mentions in his memoirs.[5] They differ somewhat from those heard daily on collective farms and other work sites.

We need to know of the total and complete divide between the general population and the political drama that played itself out around the *nomenklatura* in the capital. The average Cambodian did not have the slightest idea of what was transpiring in Phnom Penh—nor, for that matter, even what was happening at the zone (*dambon*) or regional (*phumpea*) levels—and was hardly ever given the chance to listen to the radio. At the time, foreign observers of the Khmer Rouge could tune in on these official dithyrambs, of which the very echoes rarely reached the people's communes.

Conversely, apart from the Standing Committee of the Party itself, the Khmer Rouge bureaucrats in Phnom Penh knew very little about what was actually happening in the collectives—in particular, that hundreds and thousands of people were being arrested, while many were actually starving to death. This is why they have been able to claim since Pol Pot's death and the total collapse of the revolutionary movement that, as they knew nothing, they were not responsible for anything.

As we have pointed out, slogans and revolutionary songs played an essential role in Party rituals. The Khmer Rouge did away with all traditional festivals. Similarly, they had banned all traditional festivities and rituals of the non-Indianized ethnic minorities at the periphery. They filled the vacuum with a new revolutionary calendar of events during the course of a year. On the other hand, local cadres usually celebrated whenever it pleased them (at least, so it seemed to ordinary people), and at least once a month, out of public sight, eating copious meals away from the curious.

Officially, there were three major revolutionary holidays: 17 January, 17 April, and 29–30 September and 1 October. The 17 January celebrated the anniversary of the launching of the civil war by Nuon Chea from Phnom Penh, on 17 January 1968, "the first day of armed struggle". The CPK dated the creation of the Revolutionary Army back to that day. Cleverly, the Khmer Rouge substituted the foremost Cambodian celebration, the traditional New

Year on 13 April, with their own celebration on 17 April, the date of their victory, which fell almost on the same day. Not only was there a big meeting at the Phnom Penh stadium, but three days of celebration in the people's communes as well. Everyone sated his hunger, even if it meant that some poor souls died on the occasion from unaccustomed gluttony!

As to the celebration of the anniversaries of both Mao's and Lenin's violent seizures of power around October, those dates corresponded by and large to the traditional Pchum Ben ceremonies in Cambodia—or celebrations of the deceased. The Khmer Rouge, while celebrating the anniversary of the creation of their own revolutionary party in 1960, regarded the defunct heroes of their revolutionary struggles as demigods to be worshipped.

On such occasions, the people, with fists raised, would invariably have to break into "L'Internationale," using the French title. One can presume the majority of the people, the young in particular, would not have a clue as to the meaning of the word. In fact, the Khmer Rouge revolution was so inward looking and chauvinistic that Pol Pot, the presumed translator, failed to render the word "international," អន្តរជាតិ, which is at the core of Marxist and revolutionary ideology. The song is instead entitled: "Society of the Future": the singers are thus catapulted into utopia. Besides, the so-called revolutionary internationalism of the regime was in fact a mere façade. While the *Angkar* begged technical advisors, weapons, commercial favors, and cash from abroad, in particular from the People's Republic of China, in actual fact it considered itself the master of the way it would use those resources.

The original French song was composed by the worker-poet Eugène Pottier in September 1870, before the *lutte finale* of the *Communards* in May 1871. Then, the last heroic and utopian workers turned soldiers from the Paris Commune died under the bullets of the *Versaillais* before the *Mur des Fédérés* at the Père Lachaise cemetery. The words and the music, which were to travel round the world, were composed by Adolphe Degeyter, a worker from

Lille. The "Internationale" became the national anthem of the Soviet Union until 1944.

L'Internationale

Debout! les damnés de la terre!
Debout! les forçats de la faim!
La raison tonne en son cratère:
C'est l'éruption de la fin.
Du passé faisons table rase,
Foule esclave, debout! debout!
Le monde va changer de base:
Nous ne sommes rien, soyons tout!

Refrain
C'est la lutte finale:
Groupons-nous, et demain,
L'Internationale
Sera le genre humain.

In the Democratic Kampuchea version, only the first stanza and the chorus (refrain) have been translated, with revealing adaptations to Khmer Rouge ideology. The first three lines of the stanza have approximately the same meaning, although the volcano metaphor has disappeared. But there are major changes thereafter. For instance, Pol Pot's line four reads: "From today, death or life, no matter," which is quite different from the original. The French text suggests that, with the coming revolution equated to a volcanic eruption, exploitation would abruptly come to an end and this would be the dawn of a new world. The "end" was not an end to life, but an end to hell on earth. While the Khmer leader is prepared to sacrifice any number of revolutionary fighters, the French *Communards* are merely wishing to bring an end to exploitation.

Similarly we can note the significant addition of "at once" to the now famous aphorism about "making a clean sweep of the past." This is what the Khmer Rouge literally did with the forced and abrupt evacuation of all the cities on 17 April 1975.

But the most surprising, and even astounding change is that the French notion about a new world to be constructed on new foundations was radically transformed by the Khmer Rouge into the new dogma: the leap into the future can only be achieved by restoring the grandeur of the past. And it is not the grandeur of Angkor days, but as we already pointed out, it pre-dates the Indianization of the sub-continent. It is a return to the primitive Communism of the ethnic minorities of the Northeast, unsullied by degenerate foreign influences, starting with the Indians. Pol Pot's "Internationale" tells us that Cambodia must leap back two thousand years! "Tomorrow, our new regime will be restored." "Restored," as if a similar regime had ever existed in the past! The utopia is to be found in pre-Indianized Kampuchea. "Our," because the *Angkar* regards itself as the only legitimate leader of the Jarais, Tampuons, and other Kroeungs today, and the only enlightened guide the Khmer nation has ever had over the past two thousand years! Such a self-centered view of Cambodian history passes all understanding!

At the end of the stanza, we note the oft-repeated idea, again not found in the original, that the Cambodians can now work like beasts of burden, since they will enjoy all the fruits of their labor.

In the refrain, as in the title, the major component of French revolutionary ideology has vanished into thin air, that is, the international solidarity of mankind. *Le genre humain*, "humankind" has become "the society of the future." Once again it is repeated that Cambodia is launched into a timeless experiment to achieve the ultimate utopia.

The Society of the Future
សង្គមអនាគត
sangkum anakut

ក្រោកឡើងអស់អ្នកខ្ញុំគេទាំងប៉ុន្មាន
ក្រោកឡើងអស់អ្នកតោកយ៉ាករាល់ប្រាណ
ក្តៅណាស់ចុកណែនស្ទើរប្រេះដើមទ្រូងឆ្លាយ
ត្រាម្ដងនេះស្លាប់រស់មិនស្តាយ
របបចាស់យើងបំផ្លាញឱ្យអស់ឆាប់
អស់អ្នកខ្ញុំគេក្រោកណរឡើងទៅ
ថ្ងៃស្អែករបបថ្មីផងយើងបានវិញ
ប្រយោជន៍ប៉ុន្មានឆ្នាក់បានដៃយើង

បន្ទរ

តស៊ូនេះត្រាចុងបំផុតរួមគ្នាមកដល់ថ្ងៃមុខ
L'Internationale គឺជាសង្គមអនាគត
តស៊ូនេះត្រាចុងបំផុតរួមគ្នាមកដល់ថ្ងៃមុខ
L'Internationale គឺជាសង្គមអនាគត ។

Stand up all the slaves!
Stand up the wretched of the earth!
We suffer cruelly, we stifle, our chest is about to burst!
From today, life or death, no matter!
Let us at once make a clean sweep of the past!
Crowds of slaves, stand up!
Tomorrow, our new regime will be restored:
We shall be masters of all the fruits of our labor!

Refrain
Now this is the final struggle:
Let us all band together and tomorrow
The *Internationale* will be the society of the future!
Let us all band together and tomorrow
The *Internationale* will be the society of the future!

In Praise of the Regime

The "Internationale" preceded Pol Pot's famous 27 September 1977 speech. He then revealed to the world that the *Angkar* was the Communist Party of Kampuchea and gave his version of Khmer history. This was in front of the Party faithful in Phnom Penh. The speech was broadcast on the Democratic Kampuchea radio on the 29th, while the general secretary cum prime minister was received with great pomp in Beijing and later in Pyongyang.

The internationally renowned revolutionary song—Pol Pot's version—was followed by the national anthem, "The Red Flag of the Revolution," before introducing the new January 1976 constitution, which was then followed by "The Dazzling Victory of 17 April." The former was the official revolutionary hymn before the seizure of power; the latter, less of a direct copy from Maoist dogmas and more nationalistic, became the national anthem after the solemn proclamation of the new constitution of Democratic Kampuchea on 2 April 1976. This was what persuaded Norodom Sihanouk to give his resignation and sever his links with the revolutionary movement. Steeped in blood metaphors like the French "Marseillaise," (a model for the author, one cannot fail to notice), both were most likely composed by Pol Pot himself, just as he had himself translated "L'Internationale," with deliberate mistranslations to fit his wild revolutionary fantasies:

The Red Flag of the Revolution
ទង់ក្រហមបដិវត្តន៍
tung krâhâm padévoat

ឈាមក្រហមឆ្អៅ ក្រាលនៅលើប្រថពី
ឈាមដែលពលី វីរជនអស់ប្រជាជន
ឈាម កម្មករ កសិករ បញ្ញាជន
ឈាមយុវជន ព្រះសង្ឃហើយនិងនារី
ឈាមគ្លុចអណ្តែតត្រសែតលើមេឃា
ប្រែក្លាយជា ទង់ក្រហមបដិវត្តន៍

បន្ទរ

ទង់ក្រហម អណ្តែតហើយ
មិត្តយើងអើយពុះពារសំរុកវាយខ្មាំង
ទង់ក្រហម ទង់ក្រហម អណ្តែតហើយ អណ្តែតហើយ
កំហឹងគ្មានស្មើយបក់បោកដូចព្យុះសង្ឃរា
ទង់ក្រហម ទង់ក្រហម អណ្តែតហើយ អណ្តែតហើយ
កុំទុកឡើយចក្រពត្តិប្រតិ
កិរិយាកំទេចអោយអស់ពកម្ពុជាពុះពារសំរុក
សំរុកយកជ័យជំនះ ! ជ័យជំនះ ! ជ័យជំនះ! ។

Glittering red blood blankets the earth,

Sacrificial blood to liberate the people:

Blood of workers, peasants and intellectuals;

Blood of young men, Buddhist monks, and young women.

Blood that swirls away and takes flight, twirling on high into the sky,

Turning into the red, revolutionary flag!

Red flag! Red flag! Now floating on high! Now floating on high!
O comrades, seethe with anger in order to destroy the enemy!
Red flag! Red flag! Now floating on high! Now floating on high!
Let our fury swoop down like a tornado!
Don't spare a single reactionary, a single imperialist!
Make a clean sweep of the Kampuchean soil!
Seething with anger, let us move into the attack!
Let us wipe out all enemies of Kampuchea!
Let us grasp the Victory! The Victory! The Victory!

Those words define the state of mind the *Angkar* wanted its guerrilla fighters to possess in the course of the ruthless civil war between 1970 and 1975. Those words were to become a self-fulfilling prophecy, the very discourse of the absolute destructive violence engineered by the Khmer Rouge at the time.

At the level of the composer's (Pol Pot's) mind itself, they are the ultimate sign of the metamorphosis of the smiling and benign Saloth Sar of the Paris and Phnom Penh days, from 1949 to 1963, into a merciless and savage Pol Pot, along with his special advisor Nuon Chea. His paranoiac delirium soars into the air, carried by the innocent voices of the young singers in the youth groups. The impalpable tones of the music transmute aesthetic emotion into coarse brutality, a striking example of Communist mental manipulation. Beyond the socialistic aspiration to complete equality, sheer violence becomes the universal value that encompasses the apocalyptic Pol Pot-ian universe.

The words of this national anthem fit the revolutionary fight for power and the war communism installed by *Angkar* after 17 April. But a few details, like the allusion to the "Buddhist monks," had become irrelevant. So, along with a new constitution, a new national anthem had to be devised. On 5 January 1976, Sihanouk was presiding at Khemarin Palace over his so-called last Cabinet meeting of the revolutionary "government," chaired by the so-called prime minister, the faithful Penn Nouth. Pol Pot had mysteriously disappeared from the scene for a couple of months and the new constitution, along with the national flag and the new national anthem were presented to His Majesty. All that was too much for Sihanouk to swallow, in particular the gory red national flag adorned with three golden towers of Angkor (exactly where the star stands in the Vietnamese version). There and then the ex-king must have decided to hand in his resignation, which was not to be officially accepted until April.[7]

If the bloody metaphor still floods the mental universe of the *Angkar*–Pol Pot, "workers, peasants and intellectuals . . . young men, Buddhist monks and young women" of the first song have been replaced by the "worker-peasant" phrase, which was the Pol Pot-ian translation of "proletariat," as the word did not exist in Cambodian vocabulary. We note also that the entire Democratic Kampuchean policies are put in a nutshell: the nationalism, the determination to bring affluence through sheer hard work and self-sufficiency, in the context of the Super Great Leap Forward. However, the theme of destruction and annihilation of enemies, the major plank of their government action, goes unmentioned.

The Dazzling Victory of 17 April!
១៧មេសាមហាជោគជ័យ

dâb prampi mésa moha cho:kchey

ឈាមក្រហមច្រាលស្រោចស្រពក្រុងវាលកម្ពុជាមាតុភូមិ
ឈាមកម្មករ កសិករដ៏ឧត្តម ឈាមយុទ្ធជនយុទ្ធនារីបដិវត្តន៍
ឈាមប្រែក្លាយជាកំហឹងខ្លាំងក្លាតស៊ូមោះមុត
១៧មេសាក្រោមទង់បដិវត្តន៍ឈាមរំដោះផុតពីភាពខ្ញុំគេ
ជយោ! ជយោ! ១៧មេសាជោគជ័យ
មហាអស្ចារ្យមាននន្ធំធេងលើសសម័យអង្គរ
យើងរួបរួមគ្នា កសាងកម្ពុជា និងសង្គមថ្មីបវរ
ប្រជាធិបតេយ្យសមភាព និងយុត្តិធម៌
តាមមាគ៌ាម្ចាស់ការរឹងរាជ្ជរឹងមាំ
ឡេ្ដាដាក់ខាតការពារមាតុភូមិ
ទុកដីឧត្តមបដិវត្តន៍រុងរឿង
ជយោ! ជយោ! ជយោ! កម្ពុជាថ្មី
ប្រជាធិបតេយ្យសំបូរថ្កុំថ្កើង
ឡេ្ដាជ្រោងត្រវ៉ទង់បដិវត្តក្រហមខ្ពស់ឡើង
សាងមាតុភូមិយើងឱ្យចំរើនលោតផ្លោះ
មហារុងរឿង មហាអស្ចារ្យ !

Glittering red blood which blankets the towns and countryside of
the Kampuchean motherland!
Blood of our splendid worker-peasants!
Blood of our revolutionary combatants, male and female!
Blood that was transmuted into seething fury, into fierce struggle,
On 17 April, under the revolutionary flag!
Blood that has liberated us from slavery!
Long live the dazzling victory of 17 April!
More grandiose, more meaningful than the Angkor era!

In Praise of the Regime

> Let us all band together to build Kampuchea,
> And a radiant new society,
> Democratic, egalitarian and just,
> Absolutely determined to rely only on our own forces!
> Determined to defend our country at all costs!
> Our wonderful land, our glorious Revolution!
> Long live! Long live! Long live! new Kampuchea!
> Democratic and gloriously prosperous!
> Let us be determined to wave always higher the red banner of Revolution!
> Let us build our homeland to achieve a Great Leap Forward,
> A gigantic, a glorious, a prodigious Leap Forward!

One can easily recognize Pol Pot's pen here—he whom Ieng Sary, his close associate since Paris and Ratanakiri days, ironically calls "an incomparable genius [. . .] in the writing of songs."[8]

***

The following counter-slogan is a telling illustration of how, in their heart of hearts, ordinary citizens might have felt when hearing the national anthems:

5 C

ឈាមក្រហមទុំកូនយំនៅក្នុងពោះម៉ែ
កូនកើតបីខែម៉ែៗធ្វើបដិវត្តន៍

chhiem krâhâm tum ko:n yum nou knong pueh maè
ko:n kaet bey kaè maè maè thvœ: padévoat
*"Red blood" is the tears of the baby in its mother's womb
and when it is three months old—
this means its mother has worked for the revolution.*

Did unfortunate mothers whisper this when they had to give birth during those fatal years? Each mother was doing her revolutionary work: producing a child for the *Angkar*. Why the reference to three months? Because traditionally in Cambodia, if a baby reaches that age, it has a fair chance of surviving.

6

ជយោ ថ្ងៃ១៧ មេសា មហារុងរឿងមហាសំបូរសប្បាយ!

cheyo: thngay dob prampi mésa moha rung reueng moha sambo: sabay!

Long live the most glorious 17 April,
[day] of super-abounding joy!

As we pointed out, there were two other big official holidays. One was 17 January, reputedly the date of the founding of the Revolutionary Army in 1968. In actual fact it commemorated, within the revolutionary mythology, the onslaught of the ethnic minorities in Ratanakiri, secretly directed by the *Angkar* (then essentially Saloth Sar, Ieng Sary, and Son Sen), against the royal national army of the Sangkum Reastr Niyum, led at the time by General Nhiek Tioulong.

The other was the three days of celebrations on 29–30 September and 1 October marking the anniversary of the foundation of the Communist Party of Kampuchea (CPK), allegedly in 1960.[9] Let us point out that this last holiday falls almost on the same date as Mao's seizure of power in Beijing in 1949. September 1976 was not only marked by the funeral ceremonies for the Great Helmsman, but, also, at that moment, Pol Pot wanted it officially noted that the *Angkar* was Communist and owed a particular debt to the thoughts of the "departed, great, loved one." We must also bear in mind that the late September and early October period is symbolic of the Moscow October revolution, the mother of all Communist uprisings in the world.

***

Revolutionary songs were accompanied by a string of slogans such as:

7

ជយោ! អង្គការបដិវត្តកម្ពុជាដ៏មហាឈ្លាសវៃ
មហាភ្លឺស្វាង មហាអស្ចារ្យ!

cheyo: angka: padévoat kampuchie dâ: moha chliehvey
moha phlœ: svang moha âhcha!

Long live the revolutionary *Angkar*,
utterly wise and clear-sighted and ever glorious!

8

បរាជ័យ! ចក្រពត្តិអាមេរិក និងបរិវារ!

parachey! chakrâpoat amérik ning bâriva:!

Down with the American imperialists and their lackeys!

9

បរាជ័យ! ពួកអាយ៉ងព្រៃនគរ
និងពួកអាក្បត់លន់ នល់ ខ្ញុំកញ្ជះដាច់ថ្លៃ!

parachey! puek ayong prey noko:
neung puek akbot Lon Nol khnhom konhchéah dach thlay!

Down with the Prey Nokor[10] puppets,
the Lon Nol traitors and their running dogs!

10

ជយោ! ប្រជាជនកម្ពុជាមហាធំធេង មហាអស្ចារ្យ!

cheyo: prâchiechun kampuchie moha thomthéng moha âhcha:

Long live the great and glorious people of Kampuchea![11]

The general population had to repeat these four slogans ritualistically during the festivities marking the great victory of 17 April 1975, in mass meetings throughout the country.

11

ជយោអង្គការបដិវត្តកម្ពុជាមហាឈ្លាសវៃ
និងភ្លឺត្រចះត្រចង់!

cheyo: angka: padévoat kampuchie moha chhliehvey
ning phlœ: trâchah trâchong

> Long live the ultimate wisdom and foresight
> of the Revolutionary Organization of Kampuchea!

Another often used qualifying adjective in official jargon, was ដ៏ត្រឹមត្រូវ (*dâ: treumtrov*), meaning correct, and pointing out the right path to follow. The *Angkar Padevoat* was replaced, in September 1977, by the Communist Party of Kampuchea (CPK). It is worthwhile to underscore here that while this was true for the grand, public demonstrations in Phnom Penh, it was *not* so in the people's communes where the word *Angkar*, a synonym for the powers that be, would continue to be used. Before the fall of the regime in January 1979, hardly anyone knew the name of Pol Pot. It is significant that the *Angkar*, in the paeans of the Party, took the place of honor in the droned litany of praise, the more especially because it personified a god for revolutionaries.

12

ជយោ បក្សកុម្មុយនីសកម្ពុជាដ៏ត្រឹមត្រូវ និងភ្លឺស្វាងមហាអស្ចារ្យ!

Cheiyo: pah comunis kampuchea dâ: trœmtreu ning phlœ: svang moha: ocha

> Long live the correct and extremely clear-sighted
> Communist Party of Kampuchea!

This slogan would replace the previous one after 26 September 1977, when Pol Pot proclaimed that the *Angkar* was in fact the Communist Party of Kampuchea (CPK). The proclamation corresponded to the period of the Pchum Ben (ភ្ជុំបិណ្ឌ), the feast of the dead and a major festival in the Khmer calendar.

13

ជយោ! កងទ័ពបដិវត្តកម្ពុជាដ៏ក្លាហានភ្លឺត្រចះត្រចង់!

cheyo: kongtoap padévoat kampuchie dâ: klahan, pheu: trâchah trâchong

In Praise of the Regime 47

Long live the courageous,
magnificent Revolutionary Army of Kampuchea!

14
ជយោ! កងទ័ពបដិវត្តកម្ពុជាដ៏ក្លាហានមិនអាចបរាជ័យ!
cheyo: kongtoap padévoat kampuchie dâ: klahan, min ach parachey
Long live the courageous,
invincible Revolutionary Army of Kampuchea!

On the occasion of the so-called tenth anniversary of the founding of the army of Democratic Kampuchea, on 17 January 1978, the above three slogans were shouted. And the third was repeated three times by Pol Pot, at the end of his speech to a mass meeting of workers and peasants who had come from people's communes around the country.

We need to underline here the special place that the Revolutionary Army held in the Khmer Rouge regime. Contrary to the tradition in democratic countries where the army and its officers cannot exercise any direct political authority, and even more than in other Communist countries, this Revolutionary Army was the personal instrument of power of the tight soviet that was grasping the country. In closely controlling the Central Military Commission, as Mao had done in China, this small group was able to impose its utopian vision of society through violence and terror. This army was, then, the heart and soul of the regime, and it can be suggested that the true nature of Khmer Rouge society was a totally militarized social order. Official speeches, moreover, never missed the opportunity to praise "the most faithful tool of the dictatorship of our Revolutionary Organisation and our poor masses,"[12] or "the purest instrument of execution of the dictatorship of the proletariat."[13] Without its strong arm, the *Angkar* would have been unable to exert its authority.

15
ជយោ កម្ពុជាប្រជាធិបតេយ្យដ៏រុងរឿង!
cheyo: kampuchie prâchiethepethay dâ: rungreueng
Long live glorious Democratic Kampuchea!

This was more frequently heard than the almost identical:

16
ជយោ កម្ពុជាប្រជាធិបតេយ្យដ៏មហិមា!
cheyo: kampuchie prâchietepathey dâ: mohimie
Long live the resplendent Democratic Kampuchea!

17
ជយោ កងទ័ពបដិវត្តកម្ពុជាដ៏អង់អាចក្លាហាន
និងខ្លាំងពូកែម៉ហាអស្ចារ្យ
cheiyo: kongtoap pdévoat kampuchie dâ: ong ach khlahan
ning khlang pukaè moha ochia
Long live the Kampuchean Revolutionary Army that is most
courageous and most efficient and grandiose!

18
ជយោ មាគ៌ាបដិវត្តកម្ពុជាដ៏មហាភ្លឺស្វាង
ឯករាជ្យម្ចាស់ការរឹងប៉ឹង
និងជាម្ចាស់ពិតប្រាកដរបស់ជោគវាសនាប្រជាជាតិ!
cheyo: miekie padévoat kampuchie dâ: moha phlœ: svang
aèkriech mchah ka: reungpang
neung chie mchah pit prakât roboh cho:kviesna prâchiechiet
Long live the extremely prescient line of Kampuchea's revolution:
only count on your own force and be resolutely
and completely master of the motherland's destiny!

This was more often heard than the similar slogan:

19

ជយោ នយោបាយឯករាជ្យភាព សន្តិភាព
អព្យាក្រឹតនិងមិនចូលបក្សសម្ព័ន្ធណា
របស់កម្ពុជាប្រជាធិបតេយ្យដ៏រុងរឿង!

cheyo: noyobay aèkriechphiep sontephiep
apiekret neung min cho:l paksompoanna
roboh kampuchie prâchietheptey dâ: rungreueng

Long live the policy of independence, peace, neutrality,
and non-alignment of the glorious Democratic Kampuchea!

These last two watchwords sum up the official foreign policy of Democratic Kampuchea. Moreover, it had already been the official policy of the FUNK, headed by Sihanouk, at the time of its creation in Beijing in 1970. This line signified for the Cambodian people the rejection of all foreign aid, at least officially, since the regime could not have survived without substantial aid from the People's Republic of China and North Korea, particularly military assistance, and the active participation in the Non-Aligned Bandung Movement. And Democratic Kampuchea received unfailing, verbal encouragement from numerous revolutionary and dictatorial governments, from Idi Amin and Emperor Bokassa to Ceauçescu and Ne Win; these last two were, in fact, officially welcomed on state visits during the last phase of the regime.

More disturbing for its Southeast Asian neighbors was the wish expressed by the revolutionary leadership that all ASEAN countries were going to fall, in turn, under the sway of Maoist revolution. This was probably nothing more than rhetoric, for the weak Cambodia of Pol Pot was hardly capable of seriously aiding terrorist movements in the region. It was discovered, however, at the fall of the regime in January 1979, that a number of foreign terrorist groups were actually being trained within Democratic Kampuchea borders. If such rhetoric could arouse fears in chancelleries, the Cambodian people were left in complete ignorance as to the stakes. All they knew was that, in the name of sacrosanct self-sufficiency, everyone had to make superhuman efforts in daily labor.

***

Among the above slogans, six were introduced at a mass meeting marking the second anniversary of the 17 April victory in 1977. We suggest that they were repeated in similar celebrations in the provinces. Participants, standing tall, had to raise clenched fists to the sky, repeating each slogan twice and in unison, the better to express the determination of each and every one to go forward to snatch new victories along the path to socialism.

During official visits of foreign delegations, special slogans were composed for the occasion. Thus Comrade Jacques Juquet, secretary general of the minute Maoist *Parti Comuniste Marxiste-Léniniste Français* (PCMLF), the first Frenchman to be officially received by the regime, from 9 to 16 September 1978, intoned at the end of his speech during a banquet in his honor:

> Long live the glorious Cambodian revolution!
> Long live the great people of Kampuchea
> Who have a 2,000 year tradition of struggle!
> Long live the heroic Kampuchean Revolutionary Army!
> Long live glorious Democratic Kampuchea which has no
>   ambition to annex any country and which has several times
>   proclaimed this stand!
> Long live the fraternal Kampuchean Communist Party!
> Long live the Central Committee of the CPK and Comrade
>   Pol Pot!
> Long live the unanimity of views on ideology and the struggle
>   which bind together the CPK and the PCMLF!

The banquet proceeded in a warm and fraternal atmosphere permeated with profound sentiments of revolutionary friendship.[14]

The presence of Jacques Jurquet in Phnom Penh was no coincidence: it was part of a grand scheme, in 1978, on the part of the Democratic Kampuchea leadership to expand the number of its foreign friends in view of the now very well-documented threat of

Vietnamese invasion. Amid the Maoist networks in France, which were for the most part "libertarian and jolly," as Christophe Bourseiller underlined in his study, *Les Maoïstes: la folle histoire des Gardes rouges français*.[15] Jacques Jurquet (along with the *Gauche prolétarienne* of Beny Lévy, alias *Marc Victor*) shared the same vision of a world conspiracy theory as Pol Pot and his group. They both believed they played a role on the world stage. At the time, however, the PCMLF barely included about one hundred supporters! They regarded themselves as "the members of a new resistance, while the occupying forces were the capitalists who bled the French people to death."[16] Jurquet had a taste for the secret, for conspiracy, and he longed for a movement that was well disciplined, militarized, and ready to use all forms of violence. Unlike his French compatriots, he had fully mastered the lessons of Mao and his chief advisor Kang Sheng, head of the People's Republic of China's secret services and in charge of relations with fraternal foreign parties.[17] Kang Sheng was Jurquet's patron and benefactor during the latter's many stays in the heartland of the Asian revolution. Fortunately, that potential violence remained only confined to their publication, *L'Humanité nouvelle*, of which Beijing bought ten thousand copies at a preferential rate. However the journey through Democratic Kampuchea left Jacques Jurquet and his two French companions very mystified. Jurquet declared to the *Provençal* daily after his return to France:

> We've not come across hard evidence that mass murders have taken place in Cambodia. But we have no evidence to the contrary either. Still, the present political line of the Cambodian Communist Party excludes all recourse to violence.[18]

***

Pol Pot, on the occasion of his last official speech broadcast from Phnom Penh on 5 January 1979, launched a few slogans at the end of his impassioned oration, to encourage his compatriots to fight to the finish against foreign Vietnamese invaders:

Long live the valiant and correct Kampuchean Communist Party!
Long live the powerful Kampuchean revolution!
Long live the great Kampuchean people!
Long live the valiant and invincible Kampuchean Revolutionary Army!
Long live glorious Democratic Kampuchea![19]

2—OFFICIAL SLOGANS FOR THE MASSES

The Khmer Rouge were past masters of the art of manipulating political jargon, first learnt from the Vietnamese and later the Chinese. As Sihanouk sarcastically remarked in *Prisoner of the Khmer Rouge*, the regime never stopped praising themselves, with all the more grandiloquent flourish as their policies became more and more criminal.

20
បដិវត្តន៍ភ្លឺត្រចះត្រចង់ !
padévoat phlœ: trâchah trâchong
The radiant revolution shines in all its splendor!

This describes better the leadership's mindset than the daily nightmare of the Cambodians.

The people whispered among themselves, to mock the Khmer Rouge:

21 C
បដិវត្តន៍ភ្លឺត្រចះ បានភ្លឺស្រឡះពាក់ស្បែកជើងកង់ឡាន
padévoat phlœ: trâchah ban phlœ: srâlah péak sbaèk chœ:ng kâng lan
*The revolution shines in all its splendor in a society
radiant with joy,
and we wear sandals fashioned out of automobile tires.*

In Praise of the Regime

The soles of Ho Chi Minh sandals were cut from old car tires, and the straps from inner tubes. Yet, these sandals, the badge of revolutionaries, could have also very well been stamped out at the Takhmau tire factory in Phnom Penh, a plant which operated during the Khmer Rouge era with Chinese technicians and engineers since the Khmer Rouge had purged competent Khmer workers and cadres.

22
អង្គការម្ចាស់ទឹកម្ចាស់ដី
angka: mchah teuk, mchah dey
The *Angkar* is master of the waters, master of the earth.

This slogan was heard, as fabulous accounts of agricultural production figures were reported over the air waves. But this further attribute of the *Angkar* is also in its own way the equivalent to "king" in the Cambodian language, royalty bearing the title of "masters of the territory" ម្ចាស់ផែនដី (*mchah phaen dei*). So, like God in the book of Genesis and like the Khmer monarchy in its traditional semi-divine status that had symbolized power over the earth and waters, the *Angkar* had become an all-powerful transcendent metaphor. We should not lose sight that the center of Cambodia lies on the banks of the Mekong and Tonle Sap; thus, this myth takes on a reality of its own, for earth and water confront each other during the monsoon rains. Harnessing—or not—the rise of the waters so that bumper crops of rice could be assured has always been at the origin of the grandeur and decadence of Cambodian civilization. The Khmer Rouge used this tradition to their benefit.

23
យើងជាទេវតាទឹក
yœng chie tévoda teuk
We are masters of the waters!

This was proclaimed by Ta Chham (តាឆាំ), well-known leader in Zone (*dâmbon*) 3, while the vast Komping Puey (កំពីងពួយ) dam southwest of Battambang was under construction. This vast water reservoir constructed at the cost of countless human lives in the Khmer Rouge regime has been renovated in 2002.

The same lyricism found in the previous slogan was employed to describe the dreamed-of new society where the duality of master and slave, worker and proprietor, will have been abolished, the proletariat having become full owners of the means of production:

24
កម្មករទាំងមូល ជាម្ចាស់រោងចក្រទាំងមូល
ជាម្ចាស់ឧស្សាហកម្មទាំងមូល

kamekâ: téangmul chiemchah rongchah téangmul
chiemchah uhsahakam téangmul

**The entire working class is the master of factories,
master of all industries.**

This slogan addressed the working class, while the following addressed the peasantry:

25
នៅក្នុងកម្ពុជាប្រជាធិបតេយ្យទាំងមូល កសិករ
ទាំងអស់ជាម្ចាស់ទឹកដី ម្ចាស់ស្រែចំការច្បារដំណាំ!

nou knong kampuchie prochietheptay téangmul kâsekâ: téang âh
cheamchah teuk dey mtchah sraè chamka: chba: domnam!

**Everywhere in Democratic Kampuchea, every peasant is
the master of water, earth, rice paddies,
and the vegetable gardens!**

In the Khmer Rouge constitution, presented to Sihanouk on 5 January 1976 and officially proclaimed on 2 April, Article 12 uses the same concept and phraseology. In particular, the following article shows that the totalitarian state alone, by putting an entire population to hard labor, could claim to be able to guarantee affluence for all and, at one and the same time, could sweep under the carpet all forms of unemployment:

> Every citizen of Kampuchea is fully entitled to a constantly improving material, spiritual, and cultural life. Every citizen of Kampuchea is guaranteed a living.
> All workers are the masters of their factories.
> All peasants are the masters of the rice-paddies and fields.
> All other working people have the right to work.
> There is absolutely no unemployment in Democratic Kampuchea.

26

ជយោក្រុមប្រឹក្សា ប្រជាជន ប្រជាពលករ
កម្មករ កសិករ ដ៏ឧត្តម ពលរដ្ឋ បដិវត្តន៍កម្ពុជា !

cheiyo: krom preuksa prâchiechun prochiepulekâ:
kamekâ: kasekâ: dâ: utdom pulroat padévoat kampuchie!

Long live the people's assemblies, the glorious masses of workers and peasants, splendid citizens of revolutionary Kampuchea!

We must note here that these so-called "people's assemblies" never really existed. There was the official "Representative Assembly of the People," elected after the proclamation of the constitution, which was supposed to stand for the legislative power. It only met once for a couple of hours under the presidency of Nuon Chea, in order to unanimously approve this constitution. This was to become in fact the single "law" "voted" under the Democratic Kampuchea regime.

As to "people's assemblies," in actual life they consisted merely of forced meetings either for Party celebrations or on the occasion of the visit of a cadre to a collective. Exhausted and passive citizenry had to sit on the ground being force-fed endless hollow speeches. The other kind of assembly was in the form of conventional, evening, mass reeducation meetings held several times a week. The people were always encouraged to make suggestions or to speak their minds—but at their own risk! For if they dared to, they would be listened to with smiles and sympathy, then culled secretly at a later stage to be taken away and interrogated, then tortured in a prison, to be possibly assassinated as enemies of the revolution.

The revolutionary regime annihilated the plagues of the past:

27

ប្រនាំងដាច់ខាតចំពោះ អំពើល្មើសច្បាប់
ច្រឡើសបើសច្រឡោងខាម អំពើពុករលួយ
សុំសំណូក ស្នូកបាន់ របស់វណ្ណៈជិះជាន់

râchhang dach khat chompuh ampi: lme:h chbap
chrâlehbeh chrâlaongkham ampi: pukroluey
sisomno:k so:kpan roboh vannahchihchoan

Oppose with all our strength all illegal acts, hooliganism, vandalism; reject the corruption and bribes of the exploiting classes.

Now that corruption had disappeared from revolutionary society, Cambodia was completely purified—in theory—for it was this quest for absolute purity (ideological and moral) that led to the tireless and endless search for and elimination of "impure elements":

28

កម្ពុជាប្រជាធិបតេយ្យ ស្អាតស្អំ មិនពុករលួយ
kampuchie prâchiethepethey sa'a:t sâ'om min pukroluey

Democratic Kampuchea is clean and pure: there is no corruption.

The following are a few slogans proclaiming that this new regime is the ultimate embodiment of perfect democracy and independence, and the people have been totally freed from capitalist exploitation:

29

កម្ពុជាប្រជាធិបតេយ្យ មានឯករាជ្យបរិបូរ
សន្តិភាពពេញលេញ អព្យាក្រឹតទាំងស្រុង

kampuchie prâchiethepetay mien aèkriech bâ:ribo:
santéphiep pénhléng apiekrit téang srong

Democratic Kampuchea is complete independence,
perfect peace, and complete neutrality.

30

កម្ពុជាប្រជាធិបតេយ្យ គ្មានអ្នកជិះជាន់
ហើយគ្មានអ្នកត្រូវគេជិះជាន់

kampuchea procheathepethay kmien néak chihchoan
haey kâ: kmien néak trou ké chihchoan!

In Democratic Kampuchea, there is no exploiting class,
and thus no longer any victims of the exploiters.

31

អង្គការមិនត្រាន់តែរំដោះ សមមិត្ត ប៉ុណ្ណោះទេ
ថែមទាំងរំដោះទឹកដី រំដោះ ទ្រព្យធន រំដោះ
សិទ្ធិសេរីភាព ដណ្តើមបាន ឯករាជ្យទាំងមូល
ហើយបានរំដោះ វណ្ណៈទៀតផង

angka: min kroantaè rumdoh samemit ponoh té
thaèmtéang rumdoh teukdey rumdoh troapthun rumdoh
setsereyphiep dondaemban aèkeriech téangmul
haey ban rumdoh vannah tietphâ:ng

The *Angkar* has not only liberated you all, comrades,
but liberated our territory, liberated our riches,
liberated our liberty, gaining complete independence,
and it has equally freed you from the very notion of classes.

Note the paradox of the claim to have "liberated our liberty." In actual fact the Khmer Rouge had radically wiped out all notions of liberty (together with, in reality, all notions of brotherhood and fraternity), to an extreme that perhaps no other regime has ever attempted to achieve.

***

To conclude this chapter, here is one sample of the paeans of praise to the new regime, which, in gathering different strands, could be pronounced by a local official at the beginning or the end of a speech:

32
ប្រទេសកម្ពុជា បានរំដោះទាំងស្រុងហើយមានសេរីភាពឡើងវិញហើយ
ជយោ កម្ពុជាប្រជាធិបតេយ្យ មហាអស្ចារ្យ មហាថ្កុំថ្កើង

prâtèh kampuchie ban rumdoh téang srong haey mien séreyphiep laeng vinh haey

cheiyo: kampuchie prâchietepetay moha âhchah moha thkom thkaeng

Our Kampuchean motherland has been completely freed
and recovered her liberty:
Long live Democratic Kampuchea which has made
a prodigious leap forward, an astounding leap forward.

As good students in their studies in Paris or Beijing, the Khmer Rouge, of course, took to heart the famous words in Marx and Engels' 1848 *Communist Manifesto*: "Workers of the world unite!" But, how could one translate "proletariat"? Here, as we saw in the case of the second national anthem, they ran into two difficulties: first, linguistic, for the word did not exist in the Khmer language; second, societal, for the modern industrial world was only in its infancy in a country made up of small peasants, owners of a patch of land. Therefore, in contrast to the orthodox Marxian chapter and verse, in the Cambodia of 1975 there were very few workers, products of the industrial revolution, or capitalists and bourgeois in the cities and towns, or a landless peasantry selling their labor to large property owners. In truth, historically speaking, Cambodia had nothing remotely resembling the large ex-rural class that had been driven from their land to the unhealthy slums of the industrial towns in the north of England in the 1830s and 1840s to become "appendages" of the new machines. Thus, Khmer Rouge doctrinaires resorted to coupling the two words, "workers and peasants" to come up with the equivalent of "proletariat."

33
កម្មករ កសិករទូទាំងប្រទេសត្រូវរួបរួមគ្នាជាធ្លុងមួយ !
kamkâ: kasekâ: tu:téang prâtéh trou ruep ruem knie chie thlong muey
Worker-peasants unite tightly to make up a single stack!

This translation, again according to traditional Marxism, poses a problem as to the oneness of the working class or proletariat.[20] If it is fragmented, or better still, split in two, it cannot offer a united resistance to its oppressors (bourgeois in towns or feudal in the countryside). Again, in their revolutionary zeal, the Khmer Rouge leaders had much trouble in translating Marxist concepts into Cambodian. They invented another scholarly term for "proletariat"— វណ្ណៈអធន *vannak athun*, which they borrowed from Hindu culture. Indeed, *athun* means "very poor," even "indigent" and "without resources," and *vannak* carries the same meaning as "caste," for at its origins it referred to skin color, then "bloodline," and finally "social class." Hence, theories on the nature of caste, as well as those equally questionable theories of Marx on the "proletariat," are found entangled in this cherished word of Pol Pot-ian creation.

In this revolutionary society where the country had suddenly taken a 180-degree turn after 17 April, all other social classes ceased to exist, for all now had to take on the coloring of a proletarian, including the ex-monarch on his rare excursions outside Phnom Penh:

34
ត្រូវចេះកាន់វណ្ណៈអធន!
trou chèh kan vannak athun
Embrace the proletarian condition!

You enter the proletariat as you enter holy orders. But—and this watchword will take on sinister overtones—for those who could not fit the new profile did it mean they would simply be purged?

Alas, this was to become very much a reality.

Chapter II

MAOIST-INSPIRED SLOGANS

If the watchwords of this collection are inspired by the political philosophy of the Great Helmsman, some are, it seems, literally word-for-word translations of his writings. Like Mao's political line in the wake of the Cultural Revolution, the internal logic of Khmer Rouge ideology was a search for absolute power, not of a single individual, but of a tight soviet constituting the *Angkar*. As in the case of Mao, the pretence to elaborate lofty principles was but a ruse to mask the group's true aims. On the surface, the sayings seem harmless and even ingenuous, while in the context of Democratic Kampuchea politics they represented nothing else than cold and merciless Machiavellism. Those were but the seal on a fallacious and anti-humanist political theory, imagined by Marx and Engels, and put into practice by Lenin, Stalin, and Mao.

If Pol Pot officially revealed only in September 1977 that the *Angkar* was the Communist Party and who its chairman was, the *Angkar* never tried to hide that it was using Communist rhetoric. Over the years, the sole deviation in its political line happened when the revolutionary camaraderie that Saloth Sar and his group felt for the Vietnamese changed to hatred. This break was without doubt partly due to personal reasons: the Vietnamese treated their friends very much like protegés, with utmost condescension and political opportunism. The Cambodians were above all to serve the interests of the Vietnamese revolution and their Indochinese Federation.[1] By contrast, the Chinese not only flattered Cambodian revolutionaries because of their chauvinism, dismissed with such visible contempt as it had been by the Vietnamese, but also guaranteed Pol Pot the right to the absolute power to which he aspired. In exchange for this, he and his group embraced Maoist views of world revolution, controlled from Beijing. Cambodia would serve as a springboard for revolution in Southeast Asia and China would reassert its millennium-long hegemony over the region. This was symbolized by the vast air base of Krang Leou, in Kompong Chhnang province in the very heart of the country. Thousands of Cambodians, relocated from the East region that was being massively purged in 1978, died in the process of constructing two long concrete runways together with secret military headquarters dug into the rock of an adjoining hill. Still, the Khmer Rouge leadership did not always toe the Beijing line. In the last months of the regime the *Angkar* made light of counsels of prudence from its seasoned revolutionary protector, recklessly attacking Vietnam. Ironically, Pol Pot's uncritical acceptance of Mao's thought was being promulgated at the precise time China was initiating a slow process of de-Maoization.

It is therefore logical that this initial submission to Mao had been officially proclaimed well before 1977, but only after the seizure of power; during the civil war and the period of the United Front, the Khmer Rouge had to put themselves forward as locally inspired nationalists. Thus, Pol Pot decided that his Communist Party of Kampuchea had been founded on 30 September 1960, practically on the very anniversary date of Mao's triumphal entrance into Beijing in 1949. Pol Pot's toying with the past made a clean sweep of the history of the Party before that, and particularly of its ties to Vietnam. Of course, the month of October also evokes the images of the October Revolution in Russia, and what's more, Mao had the good grace to die around that same time of the year. In Pol Pot's funeral oration delivered on 18 September 1976, at a mass meeting in Phnom Penh "to weep for the passing of Mao Zedong," he proclaimed, "the demise of Chairman Mao Zedong constituted the most deplorable loss, for he dedicated all his energies to providing us with his multifarious support under all circumstances, in our revolutionary struggle for the nation's and the people's liberation."[2]

Pol Pot, in his panegyric to the memory of his great mentor, recalled that "Chairman Mao had personally led the famous Cultural Revolution, and succeeded in successfully smashing counter revolutionary and anti socialist headquarters of Liu Shao-chi, Lin Piao, and Deng Tsiao-ping." He equally praised the successes of the "Great Leap Forward" in the reconstruction of China, ignorant of, or feigning not to notice, that this buzzword hid a great failure. And, finally, in his stirring elegy, he placed this thinker in the Pantheon of great Communist prophets—Marx, Engels, Lenin, and Stalin: "His Excellency, Chairman Mao Zedong summed up these experiences to be added to the classical literature of Marxism-Leninism, in the form of Mao Zedong Thought, which is most valuable for the Chinese and world revolutions of our time and in the future." After citing no less than a dozen works of Mao (and he must have read them all!), Pol Pot announced that "they illuminate Marxist-Leninist literature and are immortal."[3]

Hyperbole is an important element in the stilted language of Communist rhetoric, and often the unfailing repetition of the same extravagant exaggerations masks the absence of substance in Khmer Rouge discourse. Yet, the Khmer Rouge leader's emotions could not have been feigned. With the disappearance of his protector, Pol Pot lost a father, morally speaking. And he must have felt uneasy for the future of his revolution, and, moreover, of his hold on power. How he must have been relieved and comforted by the sumptuous and enthusiastic welcome that the Hua Guofeng government reserved for him during a visit to Beijing the following year!

On 30 September 1977, at the very moment when the Chinese were celebrating the twenty-eighth anniversary of power in Beijing, Son Sen, minister of defense, recalled, at a gathering at the Chinese embassy in Phnom Penh, that the thoughts of Mao Zedong were always the correct line of the Chinese Communist Party (CCP) in the People's Republic of China.

> We are also extremely happy with the fact that, under the leadership of the CCP Central Committee with Comrade Chairman Hua [Guofeng] as head, the fraternal CCP, the Chinese army, and people have raised the struggle banner to totally smash the vicious and dark activities of the Gang of Four. Due to this victory, the situation in China has greatly improved.
>
> The Chinese people have continued to hold high the great revolutionary banner of Comrade Chairman Mao, to carry on the revolution under the proletarian dictatorship and adhere to the Party's basic line based on class struggle, so they have achieved a great and brilliant victory, thus preventing the return of revisionism and capitalism and strengthening, developing and improving the proletarian dictatorship.

Being minister of defense meant that, under the Democratic Kampuchea regime, he was also in charge of repression, because his post incorporated the two functions of the army: to protect the country from enemies both from abroad and from within. The purges in China are the model for his own purges, S-21 (later Tuol Sleng) being officially under his own responsibility.

Following closely the Chinese line, it is clear that revolution is destined to be eternal, along with the power of the Standing Committee or the *Angkar*. To back up his words, Son Sen quoted from volume 5 of the collected works of Mao, which had been published at the time of the Eleventh Congress of the CCP. Son Sen, in the name of the Khmer Rouge government, declared his undying attachment to the [political] line of the CCP and to "the splendid and pure Mao Zedong Thought. The ties of friendship between the two countries and the two parties will continue to further develop and strengthen forever."[4]

We shall end this anthology of "Mao-latry" in recalling that Pol

Pot was already in the People's Republic of China when his five-hour speech, which proclaimed *urbi et orbi* that the *Angkar* was the CPK and he himself the chief, was broadcast on DK radio. It had initially been delivered on 27 September 1977. He then left for a triumphal journey on the 28th, announcing that 29 and 30 September and 1 October would henceforth be days of great celebration throughout the country, in honor of the seventeenth anniversary of the founding of his party in 1960. As did the feudal lords of times gone by, Pol Pot went to China to perform his act of kowtowing before the new "emperor," Hua Guofeng, the source of all revolutionary and proletarian power and legitimacy for a Pol Pot at the height of his glory. Only the top brass, members of the Party, and the armed forces saw and heard Pol Pot in the flesh in Phnom Penh on D-day. A few days later, while the speaker was already in China, some citizens, among whom were those reeducated in special training camps like Dey Kraham, north of Kompong Cham, had the right to listen to this speech broadcast on DK radio which they interrupted at scripted spots with applause, to accompany the cheers heard over loud speakers.

In recent history, this Chinese fascination on the part of the Khmer leaders dates back to Bandung in 1955 when Sihanouk first met and fell under the charm of the suave Chou En-lai. When the latter came to Phnom Penh for "a triumphant visit" from 22 to 27 November 1956, "he solemnly stated that China will never interfere in the internal affairs of the kingdom."[5] This, for instance, did not prevent the Chinese, at the time of the Cultural Revolution, when they were extending the airfield of Siemreap-Angkor, to make sure all the Cambodian workers were won over to their revolutionary propaganda. When the Sangkum regime came to an abrupt end on 18 March 1970, they all joined the Khmer Rouge maquis.

To go back to Sihanouk, he could never be persuaded to become a Communist, although, he tells us, Mao tried to convert him. However, the ex-king was fascinated by the character and this fascination dates back to 1956 when they first met in Beijing. Mao was expecting his royal host on the steps of his presidential palace and Sihanouk was never to forget this attention. He said to Bernard Krisher that Mao "was not at all dictatorial, even less imperial. In informal situations, one could easily have mistaken him for a hearty village chief."[6] However, a little further down, Sihanouk tells with great insight that, for this revolutionary, haunted towards the end of his life by a wish to see his undertakings become immortal, little Cambodia could have become a perfect laboratory to experiment his utopian vision of total revolution:

> Later, he was to wholeheartedly support the Pol Pot regime. Blind to its excesses, he saw it only as the classical proletarian revolution he had dreamed of personally spearheading all his life. Goal-oriented, he was oblivious to the Khmer Rouge's cruel extremism and coldly indifferent to the human casualties it perpetrated.[7]

In brief, the Maoist revolution, and above all, the "Cultural Revolution," was the revenge of the ignorant over the educated, the triumph of obscurantism, the meritocracy of our own world turned on its head: the fewer diplomas you had, the more power you attained. It is useful to repeat here that, contrary to rather widespread rumors, apart from Khieu Samphan (usually singled out as having had no say in the decision making of the *Angkar),* the principal leaders of the Khmer Rouge hardly had any higher education degrees. This was the case of at least all the main ones: Pol Pot, Nuon Chea, Ieng Sary, Son Sen, Ta Mok, and Kaè Pauk. They were neither peasant, nor technicians, and the most that they could have become in life would have been minor civil servants, or simple primary school teachers. The most notorious of the key leaders, after Pol Pot, is that of Ieng Sary: he was awarded a scholarship to study in Paris, after obtaining his French *Baccalauréat,* part one only, in Phnom Penh. He took the second part after two years' study at a private school in Paris. Registered as a political science student, he never attended lectures nor took any exam. Son Sen had only attended a provincial primary school teachers' training college. He later enrolled as a philosophy student at the Sorbonne, but failed to pass any exam.

As for Saloth Sar, he was a serious student who, according to family and friends, applied himself to his studies. Despite this, the highest degree he ever got could not have been more than a primary school certificate. However, this was not good enough to qualify him to enter Sisowath High School, the only state secondary school in Phnom Penh at the time. Despite all his efforts, he never got secondary, let alone university, diplomas. His only professional qualification was a certificate in carpentry—a career stream of study for the less than promising students—from the Russey Keo Vocational School in Phnom Penh. Yet, he was the recipient of undue favor at every step in his education, which allowed him to tempt fate with a college education. He probably sat for a diploma (the French examination at the end of the first cycle in secondary education) one last time in 1947–48; he was then twenty-three years of age, for he was born in 1924, according to his younger brother Saloth Nhiap, born in 1926, and his oldest brother Saloth Suon, born in 1911, who taught his young brother reading in Phnom Penh. He failed. True, it was a difficult examination for Cambodians since only twenty-seven out of ninety candidates passed that year. All his school life, Saloth Sar persisted in taking examinations which he invariably failed. Despite this lamentable history of school achievements, he who was thought of as a brilliant intellectual by his family back in Kompong Thom never soiled his hands at physical labor in the fields when he regularly returned to his family home during the Cambodian New Year or the long holidays during the monsoon. He was very much taken by his own writings and his books. And, it was he who put his people to work in rice paddies!

Would a personality cult have developed around Pol Pot, of which there were signs in 1978, if the regime had survived? In the collectives, Mao was hailed as លោកប្រធានមៅ (*lo:k prothien mau*), "our leader Mao." He was also called អគ្គមគ្គុទេសក៍ដ៏ឆ្នើម (*akéakméak-kutéh dâ: chhnaem*), words of Pali origin which signify "supreme guide." At the time of his death, in September 1976, flags were put at half-mast and the people had to pay homage to the memory of the great departed.

We must finally be aware that Maoist Chinese were present in the flesh in Democratic Kampuchea in the thousands. No one knows their exact number and historians disagree. What is certain though is that about one dozen disembarked from the first plane landing from Beijing, shortly after 17 April. The foreign community was then still held hostage in the French embassy. They flanked the scores of revolutionary cadres on the stand at the Olympic Stadium to celebrate the victory. The three days of rejoicing ended with the projection of two Chinese films: *The Unknown Island* about the Sino-Japanese War, and another in praise of a great revolutionary hero, Ton Si Yoeun, who laid many mines to blow bridges and sacrificed his life to enable Mao's troops to march to their victory.

The abrupt departure of the Chinese experts in the early days of 1979 was less glorious. They saw the disaster coming, but they expected the Khmer Rouge would be able to stave off the Vietnamese onslaught for a few months. Phnom Penh fell in twelve days. According to Chung Tuang-weng, a member of the Phnom Penh Chinese embassy interviewed by the *Bangkok Post*,[8] who took three months and ten days to walk 270 kilometers and reach the Thai border, "the Chinese Government had sent [to Cambodia] about 15,000 experts in the agricultural, irrigation and military field." Here he omits mention of the Chinese staff in the hospitals in the capital. Did Chung express his government's official view when he deplored Pol Pot as "a doctrinaire whose mismanagement of Chinese aid led to the fall of the regime"? Among other grievances, the Chinese did not understand why the two hundred small tractors that had been sent were left to rust. "When the Chinese sought an explanation for this, Pol Pot and his men answered that men, and not 'iron buffaloes' are the most important resource to be exploited."

The Chinese had also sent two hundred tanks and three hundred armored cars. When the Khmer Rouge sent illiterate young boys aged between thirteen and sixteen to be trained, the Chinese military experts refused.[9]

All this was because, if the Khmer Rouge applied the lessons of Mao, including the most radical ones, to the letter, their fierce nationalist pride incited them to go even beyond the wildest schemes of the Great Helmsman. After victory, they gave their population no rest but soldiered on with the Maoist concept of continuous revolution. This entailed complete ruralization and sweeping destruction of the old society. With the evacuation of all the cities, they abolished money, markets, and salaries, and collectivized everything, even food. By leaping abruptly into absolute Communism, they imagined they had outwitted Mao, enabling them to declare that their revolution was genuinely national and owed nothing, or so they postulated, to anyone.

1—THE SUPER GREAT LEAP FORWARD

35
ខ្យល់មិនបូព៌ាតែងតែឈ្នះខ្យល់ទិសបច្ឆិមជានិច្ច
ktjol tèh bo:pie taèng taè chhnéah ktjol tèh pachem chie nich
The wind from the East
always vanquishes the wind from the West.[10]

This emblematic slogan had a dual meaning. Of course, it is illustrative of the Cold War conflict between the so-called Capitalist bloc and the Communist bloc, but the metaphor of the East wind engulfing the Third World into the revolution was a favorite Maoist cliché at the time. It also meant that in the bitter feud between the two Communist giants—the Soviet Union and the People's Republic of China—the Khmer Rouge revolutionaries were clearly on the side of their friends and supporters.

36
អង្គការមហាលោតផ្លោះមហាអស្ចារ្យ
angka: moha lo:t phloh, moha âhcha:
With the *Angkar*, we shall make a Great Leap forward,
a prodigious Great Leap forward.

Without doubt this was the most often heard slogan during the Khmer Rouge era. It rang out during arduous daily labor in the rice paddies, in the clearing of forests, and in all collective public works projects. It was in the name of this sacrosanct principle that rice output was supposed to triple, from one ton to three per hectare— or even sixfold, a proof of the frantic utopian delirium that knew no end![11] The manufacture of homemade machines, using only locally available resources, was strongly encouraged, a faint stab at imitating the small industries created in the Chinese countryside during the Great Leap Forward from 1959 to 1962. Spectacular economic growth had been projected based on a tripling of rice production, made possible by the clearing of new land, the widespread use of "green" or natural fertilizer, and above all, wide-scale irrigation, thanks to the building of dams and canals throughout the country. On top of this, the extensive use of manual labor was to produce, eventually, at least two or more crops per year.

If one wished to translate the slogan literally, មហាលោតផ្លោះមហាអស្ចារ្យ means simply *a great leap, a prodigiously great leap*. There is not, in the Khmer version of the watchword, any indication that the leap is to be "forward." Thus, the motto could, without changing a single word, become a counter-slogan, indicating that the Khmer Rouge regime meant literally "a super great leap" indeed, but not into progress but into the darkness of a delirious utopia.

Let us take note that, at the same time, the Party also wanted unceasingly to inculcate in the people a spirit of absolute loyalty and obedience to the country's leadership, a leadership which took all credit for what it perceived as the country's phenomenal economic growth. We can take as an example of these extravagant boasts, the words of Khieu Samphan, one of the most utopian thinkers of the Khmer Rouge leadership, who proclaimed these mind-boggling results after the revolutionary regime had taken power. As head of state, the president of the Supreme Presidium could announce such economic miracles to thunderous applause, during a meeting in Phnom Penh on 17 April 1976: "In the period between 18 March 1970 to 17 April 1975, we won great victories of immense significance in an extremely short time. These victories were achieved by great leaps and bounds. [applause and cheers] In these few years, our nation and people leaped forward as far as one would in five centuries [applause] ... In just one year, we achieved in all aspects as much as one would in ten years."[12] The staggering progress of the first year of the regime (one year equals ten) was preceded by a stupefying feast during the civil war (one year of "revolutionary struggle" equals one century!) for Khieu Samphan, who had just been appointed head of state.

This slogan was uttered almost twenty years after the stinging failure of the Great Leap Forward in China; yet it shows how the Khmer Rouge had completely aligned themselves with the most obdurate Maoist hardliners, as if, in their stubbornness, they wished to show, against all evidence, that the Great Helmsman had been right. The revolutionary Khmer Rouge were probably not even aware of the dramatic failure of the Great Leap Forward campaign, as the Chinese Communist Party had never admitted it in their official statements. In fact, in the eyes of the Khmer revolutionaries, any failure was due not so much to the falsity of the policy, but rather because Chinese followers of Mao perhaps did not have the courage of their convictions to carry their radical views to their logical end. Nor did they show the firmness of the Khmer Rouge in repressing all possible refractory elements.

***

Even among those the Khmer Rouger defined as "the people," even among those called "ancient" *pracheachon chas,* or "the base" *neak mulethan*, the new regime was not very popular. It was discretely whispered about with impertinence:

37 C
តែសីុប្រហុកផ្ទាះមិនរួចទេ
taè si: prâhok phloh min ruech té
If you eat prâhok, *you are unable to leap.*

Prâhok is a form of fermented, salty fish paste. Rich in protein, it constitutes the primary seasoning in Cambodian cooking, principally in the countryside. "He who eats *prâhok*," symbol of the country's cuisine, simply means "Khmer peasants."

38 C
មហាលោតផ្ទាះមហាហោះរំលង
moha lôt phlâh moha hâh rumlong
The Super Great Leap Forward, this is a big leap beyond all reality.

The Cambodians were more realistic than their utopian leaders.

39 C
មហាលោតផ្ទាះ មហាអស្ចារ្យ ហុតទឹកបបរផ្លាហូរទឹកភ្នែក
moha lo:t phloh moha âhcha: hot teuk bâ:bâ: thla ho: teuk phnè:k
The Great Leap Forward, the prodigious Great Leap Forward—
this is like swallowing liquid bâbâ, *this is the tears flowing from the eyes.*

Bâbâ refers to a clear rice gruel.

40
កសាងជាតិឱ្យបានជឿនលឿនលើសសម័យអង្គរ
kâ:sang chiet aoy ban cheuen leuen lœh samay angko:
Through rapid development,
our country must surpass the Angkor period.

The saw among the Khmer Rouge leadership was that the great victory [of 17 April 1975] was even more brilliant than the Angkor era, even more brilliant than the Angkor temples.[13] Here, we have a Khmer version of the Maoist Great Leap Forward. It contained all the unbounded ambition common to the Khmer Rouge, as well as the disdain for nature and humanity, also a telltale strain from Khmer tradition. They undertook to build dams, dikes, and canals throughout the country with the sole use of human hands, as had been done during the Angkor period, because the Khmer Rouge refused to use modern machinery to carry out this mammoth public works program. Besides, their chauvinism made them reject the idea of foreign aid.

Machines would only come when production had resulted in a Great Leap forward, when the country would be in a position to buy them. The very idea that the Cambodian people would be capable of accomplishing works of pharaonic proportions has haunted the Khmer imagination. In the end, this slogan also reveals the stupidity of the Khmer Rouge leaders, who wanted to apply to the letter Maoist recipes that praised human labor over machine power. Even in regrouping entire populations in the provinces, as in Mondolkiri, the Khmer Rouge could not control to their own advantage the millions of pairs of arms at their disposal, as Mao had done with hundreds of millions in China. We must not forget either that the Cambodian population was dying off tragically during the Khmer Rouge years of governance.

***

In a visit to the so-called Institute for Scientific Training and Information in Phnom Penh, now the Technological Institute of Cambodia, Elizabeth Becker—accompanied by another journalist, Richard Dudman, and British university lecturer Malcolm Caldwell, a Khmer Rouge sympathizer who was assassinated on the eve of his departure—noted the following slogan written on the walls:

41
ប្តេជ្ញាត្រូវតែប្រកាន់ខ្ជាប់ជានិច្ចនូវការងារដ៏មហាលោតផ្លោះ មហាអស្ចារ្យ!
pdachnha trou taè prâkan khchoap chienich nou kangie dâ: moha lo:t phloh moha âhcha:
Be determined always to carry out work very rapidly
and by leaps and bounds!

This slogan should not come as a surprise, yet we are in December 1978 and thus the last weeks of the regime. One would have thought that the very controlled opening to the outside, as witnessed by the ever-growing number of visiting foreign delegations, should have signaled a slight change in political direction in the country. It is proof that the hard and pure Pol Pot-ist political line still prevailed. Thiounn Mumm, a Khmer Rouge leader with the prestigious diploma of the *École Polytechnique* of Paris, acted as guide for these three.[14]

Here is the second of the two slogans Elizabeth Becker saw in December 1978 on banners at the institute:

42
យើងជាបក្សកុម្មុយនីស្តដ៏ត្រឹមត្រូវ និងភ្លឺស្វាង
yœ:ng chie pak komuynih dâ: trœmtrou ning phleu: sva:ng
We, the Communist Party,
follow the correct and clear-sighted line.

It recalls the similar slogan:

43

អង្គការមហាត្រឹមត្រូវ មហាភ្លឺស្វាង មហាអស្ចារ្យ

angka: moha treum trou, moha phlœ: svang, moha âhcha:

The *Angkar*'s [political] line is perfect and just, and remarkably clear-sighted; it represents an extraordinary leap forward.

In Becker's slogan, "the *Angkar*" has been replaced by the "Communist Party," in accordance with Pol Pot's admission about the identity of the Organization in his 27 September 1977 speech. The change of wording in this slogan about clear vision was not for the sake of eyewash. The school Becker had visited was reserved for the education of the elite, the leadership's children, and hence, was the inner sanctum of the gods: "We, the Communist Party are correct and clear-Sighted." The substitution of the "Communist Party" for "the *Angkar*" was for the benefit of cadres in Phnom Penh and foreign opinion, and not for ordinary people in the collectives. The local leadership still wore the mask of anonymity in the countryside. This is additional evidence of the deep chasm separating everyday life in the people's communes and the center of power in the capital.

The following slogan reasserts the revolution's clarity of vision and further glorifies the revolution, in step with Beijing propagandists:

44

បដិវត្តន៍ភ្លឺស្វាងមហាអស្ចារ្យ

padévoat phlœ: svang moha âhcha:

The clear-sighted and radiant revolution

45

ប្តេជ្ញាត្រវិទង់ក្រហមបដិវត្តន៍អោយកាន់តែខ្ពស់សន្ធោសន្ធៅ

pdachnha krovi tung krâhâm padévoat aoy kan taè khpuh sontho: sonthou!

Let us swear that we shall ever hold higher and higher the flaming red flag of revolution!

This slogan is almost a direct translation from the *Little Red Book* and dates from 1945: "They raised high the revolutionary flag."[15]

2—A CLEAN SWEEP OF THE PAST

The next three watchwords take up the interminably repeated orders of the Cultural Revolution, i.e., every citizen had to renounce all thoughts from former regimes and embrace the radically new ideology. We know that the Cambodians hardly understood this political jargon:

46

លប់បំបាត់ចោលកំអែលពួកចក្រពត្តិសក្តិភូមិប្រតិកិរិយា !
lup bombat chaol komaèl puek chakrâpoat sakedéphum prâtékériya
Completely get rid of all the castoffs from imperialist,
feudal, and reactionary days.

47

ត្រូវជំរុះពាក្យចក្រពត្តិចោល
trou chumruh pieh chakrâpoat chaol
Reject imperialist words.

48

ចូរសមមិត្តជ្រាប÷ ពួកសក្តិភូមិ ស៊ីបំផ្លាញគោ និងសម្បត្តិជាតិ
cho: samamit chriep: puek sakedéphum si: bomplanh ko:
ning sâmbat chiet
Listen well, comrades: the feudal class
devours cattle and national riches.

49

ប្តេជ្ញាជំរុះ និងកំទេចរបបចក្រពត្តិសក្តិភូមិ និងអភិជន
ដែលសុទ្ធតែជាប្រតិកិរិយា!
pdachnha chumruh neung komtéch robob chakrâpoat sakedéphum neung
aphichun daèl sottaèchie prâtékériya

> Dedicate yourselves to renouncing and destroying
> all imperialist, feudal, aristocratic regimes:
> they are all reactionary!

Let us say that in this litany against the spurned regimes denounced in all public speeches—feudalism, capitalism, imperialism, hegemonism, colonialism—the Khmer Rouge never spoke of Soviet revisionism (សេរីនិយម, *saereniyum*), a matter which was very much present in CPK (Communist Party of Kampuchea) documents, just as it inflamed the Chinese Maoists at the time.

50
ជីកស្មៅត្រូវជីកទាំងឫស

chi:k smau trou chi:k téang reuh

When pulling out weeds, remove them roots and all.[16]

This slogan echoes a popular Chinese saying, which the Khmer Rouge infused with sinister meaning: in the hunt for enemies of the *Angkar*, real or suspected, the Khmer Rouge arrested not only the "guilty one", but also his wife and his children. The children were often put in prison and/or massacred along with their parents. Their minds had been irreparably corrupted by them, the revolutionaries thought; besides, the torturers always feared that these children might one day avenge their parents.

In China, however, the Maoists simply kept close tabs on prisoners' families, making their lives most arduous, and even encouraged spouses to sue for divorce.

51
បញ្ឈឹមកុំអង្គៀមខាងលើ ត្រូវវាយខាងក្រោម
ហើយខាងក្រោមត្រូវរៀបចំវាយអោយត្រូវ
កុំវាយប្របិច ត្រូវវាយអោយរបើកទាំងផ្ទាំងៗ

pachœm kom angkiem khang lœ: trou viey khang kraom

haey khang kraom trou riepchom aoy trou

kom viey prâbech tgrou viey aoy robaek téang phtéang, téang phtéang

> West, you must not nibble. You must hit from under.
> And under, you must prepare to hit right on the nail.
> Don't hit on the side; you must hit to destroy absolutely all.

In other words, you must destroy the old society completely and thoroughly.

3—RELYING SOLELY ON ONE'S OWN STRENGTH

We have any number of variations on this ancient Buddhist theme, salvaged by the Khmer Rouge, but which is also the bedrock of Mao's thoughts. China herself, as well as every Chinese, must rely on her own resources. This was one of the driving thoughts of Maoism, proclaimed by the Great Helmsman since 1945. We find an entire chapter in the *Little Red Book* devoted to this theme—"Rely on your own strength, and struggle withstanding all hardship."[17]

> 52
> ខ្លួនទីពឹងខ្លួន
> khluen ti: peung khluen
> Everyone has to rely solely on his own strength.

In the same way, at the first Conference of Non-Aligned, Afro-Asian Nations in Bandung, in the spring of 1955, Kim Il-sung had floated an identical precept in the form of *juche* or "self sufficiency." Moreover, when Hu Nim, minister of information and propaganda, solemnly received a delegation from People's Democratic Republic of [North] Korea, on 27 January 1977, just before his own arrest and imprisonment at S-21 on 10 April 1977, he paid tribute to this doctrine of *juche* as an example of Kim Il-sung's creativity, "the respected and well loved leader of the Korean people."[18] In truth, much like Pol Pot, for whom he was an attractive model, Kim Il-sung did not invent very much compared to Mao. All of that was clever window dressing allowing the Korean leader to free himself from his Stalinist and Maoist protectors, in order to be able to rule his country as he pleased, exactly in the same way Pol Pot and his regime did, first with the Vietnamese, and then with the Chinese. This watchword has equally enabled commentators to assert, and even to offer as proof, that Pol Pot and his group had distanced themselves from the "fraternal solicitude" of Beijing.

Let us finally note that, contrary to the Christian tradition of an eternally, protective God and affectionate Father, Buddhism has little to say about God, teaching rather that enlightenment comes from within oneself.

53 C

ខ្លួនទីពឹងខ្លួន ខ្លួនចាស់ទៅ ខ្លួនសុីអាចម៍ខ្លួន

khluen ti: peung khluen kluen chah tŏu khluen si: ach khluen

Everyone has to rely solely on his own strength.
In other words, it is asking an old man to eat his own shit!

In true Cambodian tradition, with the very earthiness of this counter-slogan the people denounced the real meaning of the previous saying, which flowed endlessly from the mouths of their torturers. The people in the collectives had to survive under the harshest living conditions.

The same fundamental idea could also be expressed as follows:

54

ខ្លួនឧបត្ថម្ភខ្លួនដោយខ្លួនឯង

khluen ŭpathom khluen daŏy khluen aèng

Everyone must minister to his own needs.

55
ប្រកាន់ខ្ជាប់នឹងដៃនូវជោគវាសនាដោយខ្លួនឯង
prâkan khchoap neung day nou cho:k viesna daoy khluen aèng
You have to take a hand in your own future!

56
ឯករាជ្យម្ចាស់ការ
aèkriech mchah ka:
Be masters of your own destiny!

This watchword is one of the regime's most well known. For the Khmer Rouge, it was the ultimate maxim and the justification for all their policies. They passed themselves off as true patriots who had publicly rejected all aid, and hence, all foreign interference in Cambodia's affairs. It represented one of the greatest frauds perpetrated by Pol Pot's regime, for Cambodia then as well as today would find it difficult to survive without foreign aid and advisors and experts. During its rule, the CPK was mainly dependent on Beijing for its doctrine and ideology, material support, and technicians to run the country. Above all, the leadership needed the weapons to repress its own people. Without the CPK's unfailing support, the regime would not have survived long.

The Khmer Rouge, in fact, used this admirable maxim to make every Cambodian work like a field animal, for the theory was that he was working to enrich himself and for his own benefit, not for the advantage of any boss. Once the workmen had become imbued with this idea, the supervisors, who usually did not do any work themselves, could relax their surveillance and take breaks.

Also, this maxim allowed the Khmer Rouge to put the blame on every citizen for problems and difficulties he or she met in daily labor. They could wash their hands of all responsibility for the catastrophic results of their aberrant policies.

Among themselves, the people could mock this adage:

57 C
ឯករាជ្យម្ចាស់ការ ងាប់កប់ខ្លួនឯង
aèkeriech mchah ka: ngoap kâp khluen aèng
Be masters of your own destiny! The dead must bury themselves!

This black humor shows that the luckless devils in the people's communes well understood that they were being forced to do impossible and inhuman tasks. Truly, during the country's sad regime, how many among them had to dig their own graves?

58
ក្បាលនរណា សក់អ្នកហ្នឹង!
kbal no: na sâk néak neung!
Where your head is, only your own hair can grow!

We find here another traditional saying, appropriated by the Khmer Rouge, which, once again, implied that everyone was entirely responsible for his own acts, and thus must take responsibility for the consequences. The cruel irony at the time was that all individual initiative was suspect or outlawed, and few could be responsible for the impossible tasks imposed by the *Angkar*.

For example, if a very young child, driven by hunger, stole some yams, and a Khmer Rouge spy caught him in the act, he could be violently struck or otherwise punished, or even, in the most extreme of cases, murdered. If his parents pleaded for him, their pleas would be answered by this dictum: "only the child is responsible for his acts, and must suffer the consequences." However, the usual punishment was another task to accomplish.

59
ទទួលខុសត្រូវខ្ពស់
totuel khoh trou khpuh
You must have a high sense of your mistakes!

60
ត្រូវចេះថ្ចៃប្រឌិតរស់រវើក !
trou chèh tchnay prodet ruh rovœ:k
Always have a quick and inventive spirit!

As with the Great Leap Forward in China, the Khmer Rouge wanted Cambodians to be self-reliant and to reject all foreign aid— except, of course, that from the People's Republic of China or Kim Il-sung's Korea. But that remained discreet. Artisan manufacture of small machinery in the communes such as threshers, disposal units for vegetable fertilizers, and machinery for irrigation and electricity, was encouraged at the top.[19]

Yet, this strong conviction was contradicted by the very urgent need for blind obedience to the leadership. A completely submissive attitude to authority was ill suited to the spirit of initiative necessary for all innovation.

4—ECONOMIZING

The absolute principle of economy was taught to soldiers during the civil war between 1970 and 1975. This was, above all, applied to villages not yet under rebel control, and thus, not yet collectivized. It was part and parcel of a tactic to win the hearts and minds of its inhabitants.

61
មិនត្រូវប៉ះពាល់ទ្រព្យសម្បត្តិរបស់ប្រជាជន ទោះបីអង្ករមួយគ្រាប់ ម្ទេសមួយផ្លែ ម្ជុលមួយដើមក៏ដោយ!
min trou pah poal troap sombat roboh prâchiechun tueh bey angkâ:
muey kroap, mtèh muey phlaè, mchul muey daem kâ: daoy
Hands off the people's property! Not a single grain of rice, a single chili, a single needle!

Again, here is another admirable piece of advice. But after victory, in a society where all property belonged to the collective, or rather, to the *Angkar*, it meant endless tyranny. This slogan was particularly aimed at all citizens who were forced to scrounge for a leaf of cabbage or some yam or a grain of rice or a banana if they wished to survive. Punishment for these offences, as we have seen, could be drastic. The idea is borrowed directly from Mao: "Do not take from the people a single needle, or a single piece of thread from the masses."[20]

This fundamental directive of the Maoist revolution—economizing on everything—which the Khmer Rouge faithfully adopted as their own, was first stated as a general principle by Mao in 1934. Along with the need for cadres (both civilian and military) to take part in production, economizing later became the subject of an entire chapter in the *Little Red Book*. "Our system of accounting must be guided by the principle of saving every copper for the war efforts, for the revolutionary cause and for our economic construction."[21] In Democratic Kampuchea, the local authorities raised the following warning:

62

ត្រូវចេះសន្សំសំចៃ

trou chèh sonsom somchay
You must economize in everything!

As Mao had said more than forty years earlier:

63

ត្រូវចេះសន្សំសំចៃ បដិវត្តន៍ខ្ពស់បំផុត

trou chèh sonsom somchay padévoat khpuh bomphot
For the most glorious of revolutions, always practice thrift.

This was an admirable maxim, especially for a poor country, a victim of war. This Maoist slogan could be accompanied by an example: "for every measure of rice, we must set aside a handful." We should not eat all of it, and, if we only eat very little, we shall have reserves for a long time to come.

However for the Khmer Rouge, this could mean that anyone who left a grain of rice in the bottom of his bowl was an "enemy" of the revolution. Likewise, when the hour came to execute one of these "traitors," they had to economize on the price of a bullet: more often than not, the victim was knocked senseless on the base of his neck with a hoe.

64
សន្សំសំចៃអោយដល់កំរិត គិតតាំងពីអង្ករមួយគ្រាប់ទៅ!
sonsom somchay aoy dâlmamrit kettang pi: angkâ: muey kroap tou
**Think at all times of saving everything,
even the smallest grain of rice.**

This injunction was particularly common and used unsparingly in the leaders' speeches, in a country where there was a shortage of everything and where people could expect neither financial nor material rewards for incessant hard labor. This imperious need to save everything could be heard, for example, in an editorial on the radio: "We have to strive to save even the smallest grain of rice or speck of salt, and even the slightest bit of wire."[22]

An editorial dated 15 January 1976 developed the same idea, thus showing that, in the Khmer Rouge ideology, everything was related—self-sufficiency, frugality, economy, zeal for work, and most of all, a blind obedience to authority:

> We must continue to struggle for economy. In fact, we must conserve everything . . .
> 1. We must conserve food, including rice, fish, salt, and all other commodities.
> 2. We must conserve arms and ammunitions, fuel, petrol, and kerosene.

3. We must conserve water and agricultural instruments to increase production.
4. At the same time, we must save time and labour, employing them in the most economical fashion.
5. We must also strive to maintain tools and equipment so that they have long life, and thus, avoid spending money on new ones.[23]

The ideas of self-sufficiency, independence, and frugality surely will bring prosperity to Democratic Kampuchea in a short span of time.

5—REJECTING WESTERN CONSUMER GOODS

Related to this sacrosanct principle of self-sufficiency, little Cambodia had to try to produce everything itself. It was one thing to import all manufactured goods (not to mention weapons) from People's China, but it became a point of honor to refuse at one and the same time commodities coming from the old society and from "imperialist countries." In the following slogan, "American" was added—or omitted—as one chose.

65
អង្គការមិនប្រើរបស់របរពួកចក្រពត្តិ(អាមេរិក) និងពួកសក្តិភូមិទេ
angka: min prae roboh robâ: puek chakrâpoat (amérik), ning puek sakedéphum té
Angkar never uses any object from imperialist (American) or feudal society.

The Khmer Rouge thus affirmed, with much conviction, that perfumes smelt bad, or "reeked with the smells of the bourgeoisie or imperialists." City dwellers returned the compliment, for they found that soldiers emerging from the maquis smelt to high heaven.

Most automobiles were cannibalized. Wheels were used for pony carts; tires were cut into soles for the footwear of all Indochinese revolutionaries, the famous Ho Chi Minh sandals; inner tubes were used for sandal straps and belts; aluminum was melted for spoons; different motor parts were recycled for motor repairs; and iron was fashioned into scythes, hoes, plough shafts, and other agricultural instruments.

Many manufactured goods (televisions, refrigerators, washing machines, etc., particularly in Phnom Penh) were simply collected at certain spots and left there to rust. After the routing of the Khmer Rouge at the beginning of 1979, the Vietnamese claimed as war booty much usable material, carrying it off on boats or in lorries, as the Cambodians watched silently and glumly, for they were forbidden to enter the capital many months after their new masters took power. For instance, a Vietnamese made a fortune in Saigon by repairing and selling all the pianos stolen in Cambodia.

In fact, very often, especially during the first months of the new government, this slogan was used to compel the new people to shed all their precious possessions, such as Orient watches or perfumes, gold chains and jewelry, for which the Khmer Rouge had a sweet tooth! Paradoxically, Khmer Rouge soldiers had a fondness for small American objects that they took off the Republican soldiers they killed, such as cigarette lighters, torches, aluminum helmets, or knives "made in the U.S." Others, the true Khmer Rouge who came out of the forests, heard that gold necklaces were henceforth worthless, and so they hung them around horses' necks or on oil lamps!

On the other hand, factories were generally left alone and then were started up with Chinese aid, such as the oil refinery at Kompong Som that was planned to reopen in 1979–80. And, with the exceptions of the books at the Faculty of Law and Economics that were burnt during the evacuation of Phnom Penh, public libraries and the National Museum were left intact—or rather abandoned to a sad fate during the regime's three years, eight months, and twenty days.

Derisively speaking of the cupidity of Khmer Rouge soldiers, the people quietly spread the following slogan:

66 C

ខ្មៅចុះឲ្យតែបានក្រមាក្រហម ដែកើតកមចុះឲ្យតែបាននាឡិកាអូរីយ៉ង់ !

khmau choh aoy taè ban krâma krâhâ:m day kaet kâm choh aoy taè ban nieléka o:riyang

Caring little about their dark skin, so long as they wear a red krâma, *caring little if their wrist is covered with scabies, so long as they wear an Orient watch!*

We should here recall that the *krâma*, the scarf usually of checkered white and brick red (or blue, though the Khmer Rouge only wore red), had ubiquitous use in Cambodia; along with black pajamas, it completed the Khmer Rouge uniform. Traditionally, it was rolled into a turban to protect one from the sun; or used as a loincloth when showering or swimming in rivers, or as a net for fish, a bag for carrying various objects to the countryside, a baby's cradle or hammock, or a stole worn for devotions at Buddhist temples at feasts and ceremonies. For the Khmer Rouge, *krâma* were woven from silk in Phnom Srok, in the north of Battambang province, and served as a symbol of power. They were used in Khmer Rouge security services as handcuffs, or blindfolds at executions before victims were brained with a hoe, etc. . . .

Let us not fail to note the racist odor of this counter-slogan; truly, in Khmer public opinion—and this is still true today—a darker skin is openly and without shame considered a blemish. The Khmer Rouge (many from the distant hinterlands) very often had dark skin, in particular because they were more exposed to the sun's rays than urbanites. And, they were practically accused to their face that they were brazen for not being ashamed of that!

67
សូមស្នើជូនុខកម្មសិទ្ធិសួនតួដូចជា ៖
នាឡិកាអូរីយ៉ង់ អលង្ការ និងប្រេងម្សៅ!

so:m snae chumruh kameset suentue do:chchie
nieléka o:riyang âlangka neung préng msau

**Be so kind as to hand over all your belongings,
like Orient watches, jewels, powders, and oils!**

This expression was simply an excuse for robbery, and was used by Khmer Rouge leaders during the terrible purges of 1977–78, when the *niredey* (និរតី), the Khmer Rouge from the Southwest led by Ta Mok, came to replace purged cadres and killed the *pieyoap* (ពាយ័ព្យ) from the Northwest, for instance. The loot thus could furnish a small fortune to start life over in another country, after the fall of the regime. These watches and jewels, collected at the beginning of the regime or at the doors of prisons, could also be swapped for spare parts at the Thai border. During this trade, it was the Khmer Rouge who were swindled in their turn by their more wily neighbors.

Let us remark that the verb used by the Khmer Rouge ស្នើ (*snae*), means "to be so good as to give gladly," whereas the people, under the barrels of guns, had no choice but to be stripped of their worldly possessions.

6—FERTILIZERS

68
ត្រូវតែសន្សំសំចៃជីលាមក !

trou taè sonsom somchay chi: liemuk

Beware not to scatter the fertilizer of human excrement!

Without doubt, during their training courses in the People's Republic of China, Khmer Rouge leaders had been duly impressed by this Chinese tradition of intensive use of human feces in agriculture, as was also the custom in Vietnam. We can also see the hand of Maoist experts in this very widespread practice in Khmer Rouge Cambodia. The *Angkar* had young children gather leaves and twigs to mix with human excrement, and once the compost matured, had them spread it on fields. It was an essential ingredient, in the absence of chemical fertilizers, to improve the soil, most often impoverished and exhausted in nutrients. In official pronouncements, the storage and collection of this natural fertilizer held a more important place than education or culture![24]

Cambodians who did not relieve themselves in designated areas ran the risk of being labeled "enemies" of the revolution. Such control of natural resources profoundly ran against traditional Khmer customs and was thought of as repugnant by those who had to handle this human compost.

69 C
យោធាអស់អំណាចសែងអាចម៍ដាក់ស្រែ
yothie âh omnach saèng ach dak sraè
Soldiers deprived of their ranks carry feces into the rice fields.

The population here makes fun of soldiers who have been demobilized and made to perform such degrading tasks. In the earlier phase of the regime, they would be soldiers identified as supporters of Sihanouk.

70
មិត្តត្រូវបង្កើនស្មារតី សន្សំសំចៃជីរលេខមួយ
mit trou bângkaen smaredey sonsom somchay chi: lékh muey
Comrades, collect the no. 1 fertilizer!

No. 1 fertilizer was of course human waste. Cambodians had to defecate in special, designated areas for collection of feces, near rice fields, behind small bushes. The women protected their privacy behind a *krâma*. Men had to collect their urine in hollow, bamboo tubes, slung across their backs or chests, in which they usually stored the sugared juice of palm trees. Nothing was to be wasted in order to enrich the impoverished Cambodian soil!

In the later and more repressive period of the regime, "no. 1 fertilizer" could also mean the dead human bodies scattered in fields or in shallow graves under fruit-bearing trees, also to fertilize the soil.

7—REEDUCATION, CRITICISM, AND SELF-CRITICISM

Before ending this chapter on Maoist influences, let us look at two basic aspects of this revolutionary thought—on the one hand, reeducation, along with criticism and self-criticism, and on the other hand, training by manual labor instead of schooling, as the mother of all life's secrets.[25]

71
ត្រូវតែចេះស៊ីយមិតេរៀន មិតេរៀនគ្នា
trou taè chèh svay titien, titien knie
Everyone must know how to do self-criticism
and conduct criticism of one another.

Self-criticism and mutual criticism constituted basic mental exercises in this Communist society. It was practiced in Pol Pot's Cambodia during nightly meetings, the frequency of which varied in time and place. They could be endless, going on day after day, or every other evening, or once a week, etc. How one struggled to stay awake after long days in the fields and short nights! You had to learn how to sleep with your eyes open! The best proof of how everyone managed to sleep while awake was that during the grilling of witness after witness, hardly anyone could remember what had been said. It was always the same—old refrains, the same empty words that everyone has now banished from consciousness with disgust. The routine established a balance between discussing the work of the day and preparing for the work of the morrow. The leaders did everything to continuously improve productivity—at least, that was their goal. The purpose of these regular meetings was to make sure that everyone was both blindly subservient to *Angkar* and working as hard as his or her body could stand. Often too, these nightly meetings were fraught with dire warnings. It was necessary to encourage public denunciations of malingerers, as in the heydays of mass Maoist campaigns in China. It was also necessary to expose "enemies" of the revolution who "plotted in the shadows" to "undermine the extraordinary gains of the *Angkar*." Did not these meetings constitute what Article 9, in the section on justice, in the 1976 Democratic Kampuchea's constitution, defined as "people's courts"? Before such "tribunals," deviant behavior "which menaced the people's state" was supposed to be "corrected through reeducation in the framework of the state's or people's machinery." Accusations, arising almost always from commune leaders, invariably led to arrest, and then to liquidation. How often in public did people confess their wrongs, errors, flaws, or denounce their neighbors, almost always under threat and in fear for their own safety? People did their best to be invisible, lower their heads, and keep their opinions to themselves. Yet, how many times did others throw more oil on the fire to cause trouble! Such methods created an atmosphere of suspicion and hatred, thereby allowing the Khmer Rouge to apply the old adage, "divide and conquer." It is also worth noting that, perhaps contrary to what happened in China, the ultimate goal of these meetings was not to inform the people of the new Party lines or to analyze how to carry out the watchwords from top leadership, but to discuss everyday work. When challenged by the local leadership, workers might condemn themselves or neighbors for lack of enthusiasm for work, or for errors that they might have committed (or seen committed) in not fulfilling daily quotas imposed by the *Angkar*.

In this area, Mao's orders from 1945 as seen in the following examples, were carried out to the letter:

> To check regularly on our work and in the process develop a democratic style of work, to fear neither criticism nor self-criticism, and to apply such good popular Chinese maxims as "say all you know and say it without reserve," "Blame not the speaker but be warned by his words" and "Correct mistakes if you have committed them and guard against them if you have not"—this is the only effective way to prevent all kinds of political dust and germs from contaminating the minds of our comrades and the body of our Party.[26]

We are going to see how these words reveal much about the methods of repression inspired by Mao and carried out by the Khmer Rouge, above all after their seizure of power.

The concept of self-criticism is best exemplified by the following slogans:

72
ធ្វើខុសត្រូវទិតៀន កសាងខ្លួនដោយខ្លួនឯង ត្រូវដាក់ទណ្ឌកម្មខ្លួនឯង
thvœ: khoh trou titien kâ:sang khluen daoy khluen aèng trou dak toanekam khluen aèng
If you committed an error, criticize yourself first,
then punish yourself.

73
រៀនសូត្រពីសមមិត្តគំរូ រៀនសូត្រពីមហាជនល្អ
រៀនសូត្រជានិច្ចកាលនូវរាល់កសារដែលដកដោយអត្ថរស សមាធិ
នូវបប៉ាន់អង្គការនិងវិន័យ និងរាល់កសារទ្រឹស្តី ម៉ាកឡេនីន
ដើម្បីលើកស្ងួយសមត្ថភាព សតិអារម្មណ៍របស់ខ្លួនដោយសកម្ម
rien so:t pi: samamit kumru: rien so:t pi: mohachun lâ'â:
rien so:t chienichkal nou aèkesa: daèl dâk daoy atharueh samathi
nou bompâ:n angka: neng viney neng aèkesa: trœusdey Marks-Lénin
daembey leukstuey samathaphiep sotéarom robâh khluen daoy sakam

Learn from model comrades, learn from our magnificent people, and forever learn from valuable documents, concentrate your mind[27] to increase [your understanding of] the discipline of *Angkar* and the theories of Marx-Lenin, in order to raise your mental competency.

Obviously some of the principles are borrowed from Buddhism. This was from a Khmer Rouge cadre notebook. Formal reeducation as understood in Communist, and in particular Maoist, countries was mainly reserved for cadres. Ordinary people were only treated with bare slogans and standard speeches learned indeed by heart during those reeducation sessions.

The people remained deeply hostile to these "tribunals" and the endless palaver of the Khmer Rouge leadership. They spoke sarcastically in confidence among themselves, as the next three slogans testify.

74 C
ទ្រឹស្ដីហូរដូចទឹក តែគ្មានការអនុវត្ត
treusdey ho: do:ch teuk, taè kmien ka: anuvoat
Theory flows like water, possible applications there are none.

Or, speaking of nightly meetings, they said:

75 C
មានសាលាថាតែគ្មានសាលាធ្វើ
mien sala tha, taè kmien sala thvœ:
There are halls for speeches; there are no halls for action.

Very close in meaning to this counter-slogan, but more metaphorically put, are the following:

76 C
ទ្រឹស្ដីហៀរតែងជាក់ស្ដែងគ្មាន
treusdey hie kaèng chiek sdaèng kmien
Theory overflows to your ankle, concrete actions there are none.

77 C
ទ្រឹស្ដីហៀរដល់កែង ឯការជាក់ស្ដែងនៅលើចុងឈើ
treusdey hie dâl kaèng aè ka: chéak sdaèng nou lœ: chong chhœ:
Theory overflows to your ankles;
concrete actions you find at the top of the trees.

These words were uttered surreptitiously on work sites, but not spoken to group leaders who never stopped offering counsel and giving orders to workers, though they themselves would not bother to soil their own hands in daily labor. The truth, in the Khmer Rouge world, is associated with treetops, because the people knew that everything was relative, depending on which way the wind blew.

8—ACADEMIC DIPLOMAS ARE WORTHLESS

In the wake of the "Great Proletarian Cultural Revolution," the Khmer Rouge thought that the return to production and physical labor was the essence of all training, education, and correct thought as Mao had proclaimed: "Where do correct ideas come from? Do they drop from the skies? No. They come from social practice and from it alone; they come from three kinds of social practice, the struggle for production, the class struggle and scientific experiment."[29]

The Khmer Rouge applied this advice to the letter—except that they forgot the third kind of social practice, scientific experiment—and stretched it to its most inane conclusions.

78
គ្មានសញ្ញាប័ត្រមានតែសញ្ញាឃើញ
kmien sanhabat, mien taè sanha khœ:nh
There are no more diplomas, only diplomas one can visualize.

In other words, what matters is not the diploma you may show, but what you can actually do with your hands. Here, we find a play on the words សញ្ញាប័ត្រ, *sanhabat*, "diploma" and បាត់, *bat,* which means "to lose," and on ឃើញ *khoenh*, which means both "to see" and "to find."

We are looking at one of the major slogans of the regime, endlessly repeated during the entire period of power. It represented the Khmer Rouge's way of thinking and how they envisioned the organization of society. This slogan constituted the logical conclusion of the grand maxims of the Cultural Revolution. Accordingly, at the time, universities and schools were closed so that the youth could participate in the revolution. Diplomas had lost all value, if not done away with outright. All schools—from elementary to university—which had been established throughout the country from the time of Sihanouk, were shut. Manual labor—essentially, work in rice paddies—became the only form of education for the Khmer Rouge. All degree holders were suspected, hunted out, often arrested and executed. Almost the only ones with degrees that the Pol Pot-ists allowed were the Chinese advisors! The slogan's inspiration came from Mao of course, but its radicalized form (with the absence of science altogether) is emblematic of Democratic Kampuchea. The top leaders (e.g., Pol Pot, Nuon Chea, Ieng Sary, Son Sen) would claim they had foregone higher education to devote all of their lives and energy to the revolution. They expected everyone to do the same. The leaders who had gone through and completed their courses in France were either purged (like Hou Youn and Hu Nim), or possibly marginalized (like Thiounn Mumm) if they were totally docile and proved useful.

The same idea could be expressed in a more concrete way:

79

ចបជាដងស្ដាបបាំការរបស់អ្នក វាលស្រែជាក្រដាស់សរសេរ
châp chie dâ;ng slap paka: roboh néak, viel sraè chie krâ:dah sâ:sé
The spade is your pen, the rice field your paper.[29]

80

ត្រូវចេះអនុវត្តបីជំហាន
ទៅហើយទើបឃើញ ឃើញហើយត្រូវធ្វើ ធ្វើហើយទើបដឹង
trou chèh anuvoat bey chumhien
tou haey tœ:p khœ:nh khœ:nh haey trou tvœ: tvœ: haey tœ:p dœng

You must do things in three steps: once you are on the spot,
you see; once you see, you must do; once you do, you know.

Obviously, with the Khmer Rouge, you learn only through practice. This educational principle is typical of the way the revolutionary cadres treated the population that was there to do their masters' bidding. Each morning, the people were led to the work site like a flock of sheep. They must at once set to work with hardly any explanations. The *Angkar* would repeat this slogan, as the "17 April people" were not familiar with these harsh manual tasks. The command was modeled on the old saying: ចេះពីរៀនមានពីរក (*chèh pi: rien mien pi: ro:k*), "you know by learning, you become rich through effort."

In the same vein, the Khmer Rouge roused high school students with:

81

បើចង់បានបាក់អងបាក់ឌុបត្រូវទៅយកនៅទំនប់ប្រឡាយ
bae chong ban bak ung bak dub[le],trou tou yo:k nou tumnup prâ:lay

If you wish to pass your Bac, part one and part two,
you must build dams and canals.

Cambodia had adopted the Baccalaureate, the diploma a student receives after completing secondary education in France, and before 1975 it consisted of two parts—part one, general knowledge, and part two, specialized subjects.

Addressing the country's youth in his famous speech cum program of 27 September 1977, Pol Pot urged:

> You should learn while working. You must not be afraid of work or to be particular about it. The more you work, the more you learn and the more competent you become . . .
>
> . . . Theory should be learnt at the same time it is being applied to actual work. Our people study and at the same time directly serve the production movement. To implement this, schools are located mainly in the co-operatives and factories.[30]

82
អង្គការយកម្លប់ឈើជាសាលារៀនជាកន្លែងធ្វើមីទ្ទិញ
angka: yo:k mlup chhœ: chie sala rien, chie konlaèng thvœ: mi:tinh
*The Angkar takes the shade of trees as schools,
as well as political meetings.*

One of the most widely publicized pictures of this revolutionary society was that of attentive villagers sitting on the ground under a large tree, eyes lifted to a cadre dressed in black who is explaining a lesson. These people who listened with utter admiration to the words of the *Angkar*—or seemed to listen—could very well be the symbols of a society where all thought was absolute and descended from on high. The Khmer Rouge had made a complete confusion of education and propaganda. These meetings could also have a very ordinary, practical purpose, such as explaining how to plant or farm this or that vegetable.

83
បើមិត្តមានជំហរបដិវត្ត មិត្តធ្វើអ្វីក៏កើតដែរ
bae mit mien chumhâ: padévoat, mit, thvœ: avey kâ: kaet daè
*If you have a revolutionary position,
you can do anything, comrade.*

Once again, the idea of a correct revolutionary spirit able to realize all is taken from Mao's *Little Red Book:*

> There is an ancient Chinese fable called "The Foolish Old Man Who Removed the Mountains." It tells of an old man who lived in Northern China long, long ago and was known as the Foolish Old Man of North Mountain. His house faced south and beyond his doorway stood the two great peaks, Taihang and Wangwu, obstructing the way. With great determination, he led his sons in digging up these mountains hoe in hand.
>
> Another grey beard, known as the Wise Old Man, saw them and said derisively, "How silly of you to do this! It is quite impossible for you few to dig up these two huge mountains." The Foolish Old Man replied, "When I die, my sons will carry on; when they die, there will be my grandsons, and so on to infinity. High as they are, the mountains cannot grow any higher and with every bit we dig, they will be that much lower. Why can't we clear them away?" Having refuted the Wise Old Man's wrong view, he went on digging every day, unshaken in his conviction.
>
> God was moved by this, and he sent down two angels, who carried the mountains away on their backs. Today two big mountains lie like a dead weight on the Chinese people. One is imperialism, the other is feudalism. The Chinese Communist Party has long made up its mind to dig them up. We must persevere and work unceasingly, and we, too, will touch God's heart. Our God is none other than the masses of the Chinese people. If they stand up and dig together with us, why can't these two mountains be cleared away?[31]

For the Khmer Rouge, the "angels" were the arms of an entire people forced to accomplish the works of titans, and very often, useless works because they were so poorly conceived. In actual fact, the fable of the foolish old man was taught at Party reeducation sessions for cadres.[32]

Chapter III

THE *ANGKAR* AND ITS TACTICS

Ambiguity is at the very heart of the concept of the *Angkar*. Concealing the identity of the leaders was indeed the supreme stratagem, but how could the leaders induce allegiance, and even affection, among a population from whom they demanded so many inhuman sacrifices? While the cipher favored absolute power, and confounded any form of opposition, the rise of a devotion and cult for that invisible leadership was impossible. What a contrast with the worship of Mao or the fervor of Chinese crowds!

Failing to induce adoration and submissiveness, the *Angkar* could only generate hatred. If concealment was the ultimate ploy for the leadership, it backfired and whipped up abhorrence in a context of total revolution. This might be one of the explanations why repression assumed proportions unknown in other Communist countries. The mask of the *Angkar* was a good tactic to grab power, but it proved disastrous in government.

1—THE *ANGKAR*, FOUNT OF POWER, AWE, AND TERROR

For Maoists and other Communists, as for Pol Pot-ists, the Party was the fount of all power and revolutionary strategy: all orders and slogans were issued in the name of the *Angkar Padevoat*, the Revolutionary Organization. As we have seen, the Party, along with all its members, was more or less a synonym for the *Angkar* among the Khmer Rouge and ordinary people in the collectives. However, perceiving the use of this term on all and sundry occasions as an abuse of power, the *Angkar* (in this case Son Sen and Pol Pot) issued an instruction reminding local cadres that the entity represented only the upper leadership and not the local cadres themselves:

INSTRUCTIONS ON USING THE TERMS "ANGKAR" AND "PARTY"

We have observed that some people and organisations become confused in using the words "Angkar" and "Party." Also, in other places, there are bad elements and enemies burrowing inside that use the term "Angkar" to cheat and destroy the Party and the revolution.

In addition, our Party recognises that the word "Angkar" is often used to denote individual people, which is not beneficial to building correct political, ideological and organisational stances, and is in sharp contrast to this stance of socialist revolution of our Party.

The Party's Central Committee thus would like to give some advice to all bases, Ministries and Departments, and units as follows:

1 - The word "Angkar" and "Party" are to be used for organisations only, not individuals.

2 - When addressing a person, we say "Comrade," calling the person by his or her name, position, or "Comrade representative" of this level or that level. For instance, we say "Comrade Teng, Comrade Secretary, Comrade Representative of regional Angkar"
. . .

Please, Angkar-Party members of all ranks, guide and educate on this problem to allow comrades [in the top ranks] and our comrades [in the lower ranks] to impregnate themselves with and implement correctly [this directive].

    C/c: All Divisions and regiments,
    All Departments for implementation.
    With highest revolutionary fraternity,

24/07/77   11/07/77
Khieuv [Son Sen]   Committee 870 [Pol Pot][1]

However, there is little evidence at the grassroots that the directive was ever implemented. Was the order, signed by both Son Sen (in charge of the army together with internal security, that is, repression) and Pol Pot (Mr. 870), just one ploy for these top brass to pass on responsibility for criminal activities to their underlings? At the time of arrests, local cadres always claimed this was done in the name of the "*Angkar*." If they could no longer use the generic name as an umbrella, it would mean the *Angkar Loeu* washed its hands of responsibility for the worst abuse of human rights. At the same time, it was also clear that they demanded from their subordinates never to tire of cracking down on those they perceived as or suspected of being their arch "enemies." A proof of the authors' duplicity or, at least, incoherent thinking is to be found in the contradictions of the above document. The authors claim that this instruction aims to ban the abuse of the word "*Angkar*" at the local level by individuals, but at one and the same time, it requires "Angkar-Party members of all ranks" to spread this instruction among all cadres. So *Angkar* addresses its instructions to *Angkar*. This means every Party apparatchik was indeed the *Angkar*—no mistaking it!

The image that government propaganda in China and Democratic Kampuchea wanted to project was similar. Thus, as Francois Godement very rightly observed in his *La renaissance de l'Asie*:

> To persuade and to force, to terrorise and to educate, to transform and to control this duality of objectives and methods was at the very heart of the movements Mao Zedong initiated.[2]

This description is applicable to the methods of the *Angkar*, and to the awesome image that it attempted to instill in the minds of Cambodians—of love and terror at one and the same time. And like some antique deity, the *Angkar* desired to be both a force of seduction and a source of threat, to give with one hand and to strike with the other! Soth Polin says quite rightly that for the Khmer Rouge "gentleness entwines with cruelty to the point where they become confused."[3] This was, according to witnesses, also a good description of Pol Pot's own personality. There is no mistake, however, that as early as 1973, during the struggle for power at the village level in the zones controlled by the Khmer Rouge, the people knew the true meaning of "*Angkar*":

> We knew that the word Angkar did not refer to persons, we knew it meant "death" if we caused trouble. There were two possibilities: death or the prison (in pagodas or in schools).[4]

In his notorious speech on 27 September 1977, Pol Pot revealed to the world the true colors of the regime, and admitted that the *Angkar* was the Communist Party of Kampuchea, the CPK. He then developed his vision of Khmer history and his conception of power. He spoke of the dialectics of obedience and command, of absolute submission and absolute power. Before shouting the traditional slogans of triumph and glory to the regime, he broached a key concept—complete obedience to Party-*Angkar*'s orders. Pol Pot ended his five hours of *apologia pro vita sua* with "very dear wishes to all the comrade workers, peasants, and fighters present at this meeting. May you enjoy very good health, great strength, and complete success in carrying out the tasks that the Party has confided to you."[5] Still, the speech was only broadcast two days later for the solemn opening of the three-day celebration in praise of the Party, on 29 and 30 September, followed by the symbolic third day of 1 October. By then Pol Pot and his entourage had already flown to Beijing, the Mecca of total revolution, to celebrate with Hua Guofeng, communing with the soul of the Great Helmsman, who died a year earlier, the twenty-eighth anniversary of Mao's grabbing of power in 1949. By a sleight of hand, this had also miraculously become the seventeenth anniversary of the triumph of Pol Pot as well. Thus, this rewriting of the history of the Communist Party of Cambodia put the founding of the Party in late September 1960, instead of 1951, at a first secret meeting of revolutionaries, who were later to form the core of the *Angkar*, in a back room of the Railway Station in Phnom Penh.

Absolutely nothing changed after this revelation for the very miserable members of people's communes—except that for three days they ate to their hearts' content, feasting abundantly on meat and other goodies banned from their daily diet. They had only a very hazy idea that the Organization's rituals were linked to the Trinity of the twentieth century—Marx, Lenin, and Mao. Moreover, among the ordinary people, no one had ever heard of Pol Pot. When Elizabeth Becker arrived in Pochentong, in the company of Malcolm Caldwell and Richard Dudman, on 9 December 1978, she did take note that in Pol Pot's Kampuchea, "nothing happens unless the Angkar orders it."[6] By the very end of the regime's fateful years in office, only the name of *Angkar* was known by the non-Party members.

The parallelism is striking between the Khmer Rouge's three principal virtues—poverty, chastity (imposed above all on the "little people," but, without doubt, practiced less and less the higher one climbed in the revolutionary hierarchy), and obedience, and the vows of Catholic religious orders. Is there a link between the grand Pol Pot-ist virtues and the traditional Christian education that Saloth Sar had at the devout *École Miche*, under the supervision of the Christian Brothers, and attended by the children of the bourgeoisie and Vietnamese community in Phnom Penh from 1932 to 1938? Of these three, "obedience" meant essentially "submission" to the inane orders of the *Angkar*. The reader may object that it is useless to look into Catholicism for something which was, for the Khmer farmer, connected to a fatalism reinforced by Buddhism, and particularly to belief in *karma*, from which there was no escape. He submitted to the *Angkar*'s authority, as he had to authority since time immemorial. Yet, it is interesting to stress that Pol Pot-ism, a virulently atheistic belief, functions like a sort of a perverted form of religion. Is not that the very definition of an ideology?

In Pol Pot language, this particular virtue—obedience/submission—is called *chat tang* (ចាត់តាំង), "to command," literally "to designate [such and such] a task," signifying the need to obey without hesitation. The Khmer Rouge considered submission or *docility* as the cardinal virtue, the criterion by which everyone would be judged. Consequently, it showed that the sworn goal of the *Angkar* was absolute power—the course of action of a totalitarian organization—over a hapless people. Thus, in an editorial aired on DK radio on 29 December 1977, on improvement in the education of cadres, you could hear: "The capable cadres are those who fully and clearly understand all aspects of the Party's stand, including its conception and application . . . They are responsible for inculcating the Party's lines among the people with high responsibility to the Party."[7]

Blind obedience was expected on the part of cadres who acted as links with the people. Thus, the most inane orders were slavishly followed, whatever the results. The *Angkar* was presented in the slogans in the following ways.

THE *ANGKAR*: SOURCE OF LOVE AND INSPIRATION

84
អង្គការជាប្រលឹងបដិវត្តន៍
angka: chie proleung padévoat
The *Angkar* is the soul of the revolution.

85
អង្គការជាប្រលឹងប្រទេសជាតិ
ângka: chie proleung prâtéhchiet
The *Angkar* is the soul of the motherland.

The party incessantly attempted to evoke patriotism. In actual fact, its narrow chauvinism destroyed a nation.

It remains curious that a revolution proclaiming to be antireligious characterized the Party leadership as a "soul," by definition an invisible, supernatural, and godlike essence. The *Angkar* indeed fulfilled the function of a deity—or at least the close-knit gang at the top wanted the people to believe so.

To impose its will, the Khmer Rouge leadership, at first, took a gentle approach, using sweet words to dull distrust and engender blind loyalty, a tactic more productive with uneducated country youth.

86
ត្រូវស្មោះត្រង់ និងស្រលាញ់អង្គការ
trou smâhtrâng ning srâlanh ângka:
Love the *Angkar,* sincerely and loyally.

Another, almost identical version conveys the same thought:

87

ត្រូវតែស្រលាញ់អង្គការដោយគ្មានព្រំដែន

trou taè srâlanh ângka: daoy kmien prumdaèn
Your love for the *Angkar* must be boundless.

The Khmer-Maoist revolutionaries strove to arouse deep affection for the *Angkar* even as Mao had. Mao-*Angkar* was a god, and a source of love and eternal, radiant happiness.

These slogans were often found in the words of many revolutionary songs, accompanied by gestures, which were endlessly repeated for children, in particular the then-famous song "We-I,[8] the youth love Angkar with no limits."

88

អ្នកស្រឡាញ់វណ្ណៈទេ? អ្នកស្រលាញ់ពូជសាសន៍ទេ?
អ្នកស្រឡាញ់អង្គការទេ?

néak srâ:lanh vannak té néak srâ:lanh pu:chsah té
néak srâ:lanh ângka: té
Do you love your class? Do you love your race?
Do you love the *Angkar*?

It is worthwhile noting that, among these all-embracing categories that the Khmer Rouge used to define societal relationships within the new revolutionary mentality, the family disappeared—a sweeping revolution in Asia indeed. Still, the family was not abolished but fragmented and reduced to a large extent to its minimum reproductive function. The *Angkar* was placed at the pinnacle of the pyramid, while classes were reduced to one, the proletariat comprising everyone, since everyone had to be absorbed into groups of workers or peasants. The notion of race, positioned in between class and the *Angkar*, fundamentally means "nation."

89
អង្គការជាមាតាបិតារបស់កុមារាកុមារី និងយុវជនយុវនារី

angka: chie mieda: beyda: robâh koma:ra: koma:rey
ning yuvéachun yuvéanieri:

The *Angkar* is the mother and father of all young children,
as well as all adolescent boys and girls.

This flatters the listeners with honey-sweet words. In the name of this principle, babies were looked after by older women in the daytime to allow mothers to join their work teams. From the age of about five or six, young children were taken from their family (first during the daytime only, then for longer periods), and brought up in *mondolkoma* មណ្ឌលកុមារ, sort of work camps for children. The only general "intellectual" education was a very summary indoctrination, made up of slogans backed up by revolutionary songs. Sometimes, however, the Khmer alphabet was taught, together with basic reading and writing and children attended these primitive schools about two hours in the mornings. The rest of the day they mainly tended cattle and collected dung and leaves to make up the much-needed compost. Some local leaders even took the initiative, for example in some areas of the province of Kratie for instance, to really teach children how to read and write. But with the sinister appearance of the *niredey* cadres from the Southwest, at the beginning of 1978, these few traces of intellectual training disappeared from that region.

In the meantime in Phnom Penh, there were special institutions for the leaders' children, who received a much more formal revolutionary education. The first school textbooks were devised by a special team of educators in Phnom Penh, but, unlike the currency that was printed but never distributed, school books were neither printed nor distributed apart from a few copies.

The normal and natural affection children have for their family now had to be transferred to the *Angkar*, and in turn, the parents became strangers to their own children, if they belonged to the "17 April" group. The *Angkar* thus played the symbolic role of mother and father for a docile youth, to remain "unsullied" by the old ideologies. But the *Angkar* had grand plans to develop education before its abrupt expulsion from power.

Before the seizure of power, the *Angkar* was able to persuade some young people, during training and indoctrination courses in the forests, that their parents had been killed by American bombings, even if this was pure invention. Thus, after victory, young Khmer Rouge soldiers could no longer "recognize" their own parents, since they had become glorious martyrs to imperialism. This might be an explanation for the utter cruelty of these young, fanatical soldiers, even toward their own family. At times, therefore, love for the *Angkar* would, and did, replace the very strong bonds of family solidarity.

However, reality generally gave the lie to the utopian schemes of the Khmer Rouge. As family members were exterminated by ever-growing bloody repression, bereaved individuals found solace in finding one an adoptive mother, another an adoptive son, the third an adoptive grandmother. The *Angkar* could not be a substitute for real human beings. Even the Maoist Chinese, in their attack on the family unit, were never as radical. Thus, Y Phandara, during his imprisonment at Boeung Trabek, refused to forsake his own paternal sentiments, because he knew that, in the People's China, filial feelings were also praised by the government, even if attachment to the Party came first.[9]

90
អង្គការថ្នាក់ថ្នម បងប្អូន ពុកម៉ែ
ângka: thnak thnâ:m bâ:ng pâ'o:n puk maè
The *Angkar* tenderly looks after you all,
brothers and sisters, mothers and fathers.

91
បើម៉ែឪវាយដំកូន បាននិយថាមើលងាយអង្គការ
ដូច្នេះអង្គការមិនប្រណីឡើយ

bae maè ou viey dom ko:n ba:nney tha: mœ:l ngiey ângka:
do:chnèh ângka: min prâ:ney laey

If parents beat their children, it is a sign they despise the *Angkar*.
Thus the *Angkar* will have no compassion at all for them.

Like God for Christians, the *Angkar* was the incarnation of perfection:

92
មិនបាច់ប្រើការពិចារណាទេព្រោះអង្គការមានការ
ត្រឹមត្រូវស្អាតបរិសុទ្ធ

min bach prae ka: picha:rena: té pruh ângka: mien ka:
trœm trou sa'a:t bâ:risot

Useless to argue, for the *Angkar's* motives are perfectly pure!

With the rule of the *Angkar*, it was better not to waste one's time in subtle arguments, better not to think at all! All were expected to have unreserved confidence in the Party.

This slogan's key word was *bârisot*, "pure." For Cambodian revolutionaries, one of their *idées fixes* was the notion of purity: sexual purity first and "sexual misdeeds" were among severely punished "crimes" (quite contrary to Khmer traditions), although the rule was apparently not so strictly applied among the higher echelons of Party hierarchy. Concern with "racial purity" on the part of the leadership was not an explicit policy, although lighter-skinned educated people were exterminated more massively than the darker peasant communities. Purity was above all an ideological concept. Let us recall that the major preoccupation for Khieu Samphan, the head of state, was to "cleanse" Cambodian society, an obsession that was quickly shared by all the leaders, the sign of what looked like a collective paranoia.

THE *ANGKAR*, ALL-SEEING AND ALL-KNOWING

93
អង្គការមានផែនការថ្មីជានិច្ច
ângka: mien phaènka: thmey chie nich
The *Angkar* is always making new plans.

This slogan means that the structure of power was strictly vertical, all initiatives coming from the top, and that the Party would solve all problems.

94 C
អង្គការថាហើយមិនធ្វើ រាស្ត្រល្ងើវេទនាដូចសត្វ
ângka: tha: haey min thvœ: ries lngœ: vétenie do:ch sat
The Angkar *speaks but does nothing:*
bewildered citizens suffer like beasts.

The *Angkar* is represented in the collectives by the various local chiefs who, now one, now the other, give contradictory orders to the people. Sometimes they must proceed with one task, at other times with another, leaving many unfinished. Still, everyone must slavishly obey the one who spoke last and toil like beasts of burden.

As in all Communist countries, the *Angkar* proclaimed itself not only the voice of the people, but pretended to know and articulate their innermost thoughts, the theory being:

95
អង្គការជាខួរក្បាលរបស់ប្រជាជន
ângka: chie khue kba:l robâh prâchiechun
The *Angkar* is the people's brain.[10]

People, therefore, did not have to think at all anymore. Indeed, as in other Communist countries, citizens had seen their brains blown out, as it were.

96
អង្គការឈ្លាសវៃ
ângka: chhliehvey
The *Angkar* is full of cleverness.

We feel all the ambiguity of this statement, behind which lies a faintly veiled threat from the all-seeing *Angkar* god.

97
បើអង្គការមិនឆ្លាត ម្ល៉េះសមអង្គការមិនអាច
យកជ័យជំនះពីចក្រពត្តិអាមេរិកដែលមាន
សំភារៈសឹកនិងដុល្លាដ៏ច្រើននោះទេ
bae ângka: min chhla:t, mlèh sâm ângka: min a:ch
jo:k chey chumnéah pi: chakrâpoat a:mérik daèl mien
sâmphieréaksœk ning dolla dâ: chraœn nuh té
If the *Angkar* had not been clear-sighted,
it could never have vanquished the American imperialists
who had quantities of arms and dollars.

This assertion, in all its variations, was repeated unceasingly in all speeches in all parts of the country, after the "great 17 April victory." It literally went to the head of Pol Pot and his group, persuading them that they controlled an invincible war machine, just as it did the Vietnamese leadership with their vast army. Later, it was this conviction that propelled small, weak Cambodia to attack Vietnam, at its own peril, slaughtering the entire population of villages within reach of the border. The slaughter was further driven by the profound conviction that Vietnam had brutally invaded its weaker neighbor in the later months of 1977 and moved up to fifty kilometers inside the revolutionary and restless neighbor's territory to teach them a lesson. Vietnam was to emerge victorious within two weeks when it massively invaded its neighbor on Christmas night 1978. Pol Pot and his ominous army were indeed a paper tiger.

As to "defeating Americans," it would be closer to the truth to state that neither the Khmer Rouge nor the Vietminh ever really vanquished the Americans forces as they have made everyone believe. Rather, it was the Americans who progressively withdrew from all three Indochinese countries, under the pressure of their own public opinion, horrified by the mounting death toll and war crimes. Despite the *Angkar*'s declaration of victory over the Americans, the U.S. never maintained a permanent army in Cambodia.

Here now are two slogans; the first serves as an introduction to the second, which is one of the most meaningful and best known Khmer Rouge slogans:

98

យើងជាបក្សកុម្មុនីស្ដដ៏ត្រឹមត្រូវ និងភ្លឺស្វាង

yœng chie pak komunih dâ: trœm trou ning pleu: sva:ng

We, the Communist Party,
we follow the correct and clear-sighted line.

99

អង្គការផ្នែកម្នាស់

ângka: phnè:k monoah

The *Angkar* has [the many] eyes of the pineapple.

This says everything. It is the nature of Pol Pot-ism, and what Robert Jay Lifton, speaking of the Cultural Revolution, calls, with reason, "totalism."[12] Totalism is a "totalistic" revolutionary ideology that attempts to control everything, every human being in his entirety. The *Angkar* was an omnipresent being, fount of all power and all authority, with the attributes of a god. This slogan, purely Khmer Rouge in rhetoric, served as a warning. It played the same role as another saying in other times, when Christian parents would say to children, "be good, for the little Lord Jesus sees and hears everything!"

In the political sphere, we also have here a Khmer Rouge version of Orwell's famous aphorism: "Big Brother is watching you." But the Khmer Rouge leadership was more wily, since the *Angkar* had no face and there were no posters of Pol Pot on village or town walls as there are in *1984*. And still, Pol Pot, as we have seen, let himself be called "Number One Brother" (បងទីមួយ or *bong ti muey*), or more to the point "Big Brother" (បងធំ or *bong thom*), at least among the Khmer Rouge, it goes without saying, since the ordinary people did not know him! Besides, the expression in Khmer is a tautology, since *bong* already means "elder brother." Saloth Sar's political culture—first, Franco-Soviet, then "Vietminh-Maoist"—was no doubt too limited for him to have read *1984*. And yet Orwell described a number of means of population control thirty years before the Pol Pot-ian society came into being—which is not surprising since the Khmer Rouge form of control of revolutionary society was largely inspired by Stalinism. The *Angkar* passed itself off as the substitute for the omniscient god of the great religions and was the center of all power. We understand better why the regime could not tolerate the least remnant of belief or religion. It was a matter of eliminating a competitor.

One can imagine that the previous slogan of only three words referring to the pineapple was an excellent metaphor for the *Angkar*'s strategy and undoubtedly the object of much sarcasm, since the nodes of pineapples are by definition blind, although they are called "eyes" in the Khmer language. Here are two further examples:

100 C

អង្គការភ្នែកម្នាស់តែគ្មានប្រស្រី

ângka: phnè:k monoah, taè kmien prâsrey

The Angkar *has the many eyes of a pineapple, but none of them has an iris.*

101 C
អង្គការភ្នែកម្នាស់បានជាមើលមិនឃើញប្រជាជន

ângka: phnè:k monoah, ba:nchie mœ:l min khœ:nh prâchiechun

The Angkar *has the many eyes of a pineapple;
this is why it is unable to see the people.*

THE *ANGKAR* DEMANDS BLIND OBEDIENCE

102
ត្រូវរាយការណ៍ជូនអង្គការ !

trou rieyka: chu:n ângka:

Report everything to the *Angkar!*

Every doubtful action and dubious gesture and suspicious word had to be reported to authorities following the strictly prescribed hierarchical order. Everyone spied on everyone else, a much more honed system of surveillance than Maoist neighborhood committees. The Khmer Rouge, in essence, used children, as well as teenage soldiers, called *chhlops* or "militia," for spying. The latter, always recruited among the so-called old people, were the *Angkar*'s eyes in people's communes.

103
ត្រូវចេះតាមដានគ្នាទៅវិញទៅមក !

trou chèh ta:m da:n knie tou vinh tou mo:k

Secretly observe the slightest deeds and gestures
of everyone around you!

This enabled the local cadres not to have to watch people all the time during working hours, since reporting on others was systematically encouraged, with its trail of personal vengeance or hatred. During these nightly meetings everyone was expected to report the lapses in *Angkar* discipline that he had witnessed that day.

Paradoxically, ordinary citizens—and particularly the "17 April"—also had to know when to keep quiet when they were witnesses to, or victims of, wrongdoings or abuse by the leaders, such as illicit trading, theft, forbidden sexual liaisons, or even rape. In this case, one heard:

104 C
ត្រូវចេះដាំដើមគ

trou chèh dam daœm ko:
Know how to plant a kapok tree.

In Khmer, the kapok គ *(ko:)* is a homonym for គ *(ko:)*, meaning "mute." This slogan simply says "you should know when to hold your tongue." For the "17 April" especially, this was essential, if they did not wish to draw the authorities' attention to themselves. Moreover, they had to know how to hide their past, especially if they had been neither farmers nor simple workmen. Some, in fact, owed their very survival to the fact that they had feigned muteness.

This is actually a traditional Khmer saying that the Khmer Rouge gave a different drift to. If this is, in effect, a counter-slogan in the framework of a repressive society, it could, under certain conditions, become a friendly counsel on the part of local Khmer Rouge leaders to protect those under their charge. Thus, it is an indication of the collusion that could exist between village or group heads and inhabitants in order to escape the *Angkar*'s wrath.

105 C
រក្សាស្មារតីបួនយ៉ាងគឺ មិនដឹង មិនឮ
មិនឃើញ មិននិយាយ

réaksa: sma:rodey buen ya:ng keu: min dœng min leu:
min khœ:nh min niyiey
Stick to the four precepts: do not know, do not hear, do not see, do not speak.

This recommendation is equally ambiguous. It is the golden rule of a totalitarian society. In the case of danger or questions, it was better to keep the lowest profile possible. Thus, if you were an involuntary witness to an arrest or to an act of violence, better make believe you saw nothing at all. From the mouth of a sympathetic local official, it could very well be a discreet warning to avoid making trouble for yourself and thus serves as proof of hidden opposition among leaders.

But, at one and the same time, this watchword, when uttered by the *Angkar*, was indeed a strict order for the local leadership. It meant that ordinary citizens had better turn a blind eye and a deaf ear to the numerous forms of misconduct from revolutionary norms on the part of cadres—such as eating surreptitiously "socialist" food, storing "imperialist" knick-knacks (like radios, watches, perfumes, and jewelry) for personal use, and worse, committing rapes. Those deviant behaviors were to be ignored.

Historically, these four prohibitions date back to the First Indochinese War (1946–54), when the Vietminh forbade the peasant population to report any details about their secret bases and whereabouts.

The aforementioned saying contradicts the following dictum of the *Angkar:*

106
យើងត្រូវស្មោះត្រង់ចំពោះអង្គការ!
ye:ng trou smâh trâng chompuh ângka:
Be sincere with the *Angkar*!

In fact, this exhortation was endlessly repeated by Khmer Rouge torturers and took on further significance during the numerous questioning sessions to which everyone was subject. You had to tell everything about your past and present life to the *Angkar,* with the utmost sincerity. Those who did not have the correct social or professional "pedigree" faced a cruel dilemma as to how to save

The Angkar and Its Tactics

their lives when interrogated and tortured: was it better to tell the truth or lie?

107
យើងខ្ញុំទាំងអស់គ្នាសូមប្តេជ្ញាដើរតាមតាំអង្គការ!
yœ:ng khnhom téang âh knie so:m pdachnha: dae ta:m miekie ângka:
Let us all together commit ourselves
to follow the way of the *Angkar*.

Here is the first of a dozen or so short injunctions, stressing the pressing necessity to obey blindly and immediately all orders from the *Angkar*. Obviously, they are synonymous, but their very number speaks to the vital role they played in the regime. The most common were:

108
ត្រូវគោរពអង្គការចាត់តាំង!
trou ko:rup ângka: chattang
People must respect the assignments of the *Angkar*!

109
អង្គការចាត់តាំងត្រូវតែអនុវត្ត
ângka: chattang trou taè anuvoat!
The *Angkar* orders, execute!

110
ត្រូវមានអង្គការវិន័យ!
trou mien ângka: viney
Maintain the *Angkar*'s discipline!

111
អង្គការដាក់ទិសត្រូវតែគោរពវិន័យ!
ângka: dak teuh trou taè ko:rup viney
When the *Angkar* gives an order, obey it with complete discipline!

The same idea must have been repeated in many variations, according to the locality and at the discretion of local leaders. Such an injunction was a shorthand message of a fundamental governmental directive to the base people: every cell of the fabric of society had to submit to the regime's iron discipline.

Thus, in a series of orders addressed to the usually young interrogators at S-21, now Tuol Sleng Museum, called "Lessons for the Communist Youth of Kampuchea" and dated September 1976, we see that the first lesson was "to respect the discipline of the Young Communist Organisation unconditionally and with high morale."[13]

This slogan reiterates the previous slogan:

112

ប្ដេជ្ញាគោរពអង្គការវិន័យ អង្គការចាត់តាំង

pdachnha: ko:rup ângka: viney ângka: chattang

Let us pledge to respect the *Angkar*'s discipline and obey the *Angkar*'s assignments!

113

អង្គការដាក់ទិសត្រូវអនុវត្តឱ្យបានសំរេច !

ângka: dak teuh trou anuvoat aoy ba:n sâmrach

When the *Angkar* gives orders, carry them out to the letter!

These peremptory orders of the *Angkar* had to be executed even when they were totally irrational, or even when the one executing them was very weak from illness or starvation.

114

អង្គការដាក់ទិសត្រូវតែធ្វើ !

ângka: dak teuh trou taè thvœ:

When the *Angkar* tells you what to do, you do it!

115
អង្គការថាយ៉ាងម៉េច ត្រូវធ្វើយ៉ាងហ្នឹង !
ângka: tha: ya:ng méch trou thvœ: ya:ng neung
When the *Angkar* prescribes a task, you must comply with the order!

116 C
អង្គការដាក់ទិសនេះ គឺថាដើម្បី...ដើម្បីគឺថា
ângka: dak teuh nih keu: tha: daembey ... daembey keu: tha: ...
The Angkar *gives you an assignment,*
it is for you to . . . it is to do for you . . .

By this counter-slogan the people mocked local authorities that stammered, unable to find the right words, when they tried to give detailed orders. It is an indication that as purges weeded out the ranks of the Khmer Rouge, people's communes came to be led by completely ignorant and uneducated individuals.

In addition, during nightly meetings, petty leaders rattled off speeches learned by heart during study sessions for Party cadres. Often, it so happened that they lost the thread of their thoughts, repeating unceasingly the same phrase, in the hope that their failing memory would somehow pick up the rest. In actual fact, as purges cleared the ranks of Party members and cadres, new and uneducated ones were picked up for their ability to easily memorize those long speeches. Pol Pot's North Korean models, it seemed, were past masters in the art of repeating, word for word, Kim Il-sung's speeches, after only hearing them once.

117 C
តាំងពីអង្គការបំភ្លឺខ្ញុំមក ខ្ញុំកាន់តែភ្លើឡើងៗ
tang pi: ângka: bâmphleu: khnhom mo:k khnhom kan taè phlœ: laeng phlœ: laeng
Since the Angkar *has enlightened me,*
I've become more and more of an idiot!

The Cambodian of Chinese origins found it difficult to pronounce the complex Khmer vowels and confused the sound [eu:] of ភ្លឺ "light," with the sound [e:] of ភ្លើ "idiot." The rest of the Cambodian population turned their flattery to ridicule—while recognizing their mispronunciation had hit the nail on the head.

The people, to voice their contempt and to show that they understood nothing at all of the jumble of nonsense of Marxist theory, would whisper among themselves:

118 C
ពាក្យសំដីរបស់ប្រធានៗស្ដាប់ទៅដូចចាក់ទឹកលើក្បាលទា

piek sâmdey robâh prâthien prâthien sdap tou do:ch chak teuk lœ: kba:l tie

Listening to the words of leaders
is like pouring water onto a duck's head.

In the introduction we defined the *Angkar* as an abstract and invisible entity, allowing any minor official to say that it was not *he* who ordered this or that, but the *Angkar*—as indeed in any administrative system. This ploy had become so widespread that the *Angkar Loeu*, or the "*Angkar* up above" (in fact Pol Pot and Son Sen), signed a decree to put an end to this abuse of authority among their underlings. To no avail! Here is a slogan that translates this reality:

119
ចំពោះបុគ្គលខ្ញុំមិនអោយបងប្អូនពុកម៉ែគោរពទេ
បងប្អូនពុកម៉ែគោរពតែអង្គការចុះ

châmpuh bokkul khnhom min aoy bâ:ng pâ'o:n puk maè ko:rup té bâ:ng pâ'o:n puk maè ko:rup taè ângka: choh

It is not to myself as an individual that you all, brothers and sisters, fathers and mothers, owe respect and obedience, but to the *Angkar*.

Every order, therefore, was in the name of the *Angkar*. As if that would not suffice, all family ties, the only ties traditional Khmer peasants truly knew, had to be obliterated before this unique incarnation of authority. Is Saloth Sar, the dutiful little pupil of the Christian Brothers at the *École Miche*, here echoing the Gospels, or even the Buddha's renunciation?

THE WRATH OF THE *ANGKAR*

But people were not fooled by the all-seeing, all-knowing *Angkar*. In their minds, the *Angkar* was a fierce demoniac deity:

120 C
ត្រាន់តែពួកឈ្មោះអង្គការញាក់សាច់
kroan taè leu: chhmuh angka: nhéak sach
Just hearing the name "Angkar" gives us goose flesh.

The leadership, however, was prepared to pass the blame for terrorizing the population on to the victims themselves:

121
អង្គការកាចតែចំពោះបុគ្គលណាដែលធ្វើអោយកាច
ângka: ka:ch taè châmpouh bokul na: daèl thvœ: aoy ka:ch
The Angkar is ferocious only with those who provoke its wrath.

122
ឃើញអង្គការស្លូត
កុំចង់ធ្វើអោយអង្គការកាំចណាំ !
khœ:nh ângka: slo:t, kom châng thvœ: aoy ângka: ka:ch na:
You see that the Angkar is gentle;
be careful not to make it ferocious!

The *Angkar*'s smile gave way to a threatening, angry look, much like an adult acts with a very young, restive child. The general population was treated like a group of retarded people. That, alas, was but a continuation by the Khmer Rouge, of a tradition rooted in the country's history. Too often, the French thought that they could not confide posts of responsibility to these smiling children, and thus heavily relied on the Vietnamese as overseers or civil servants in the colonial administration. Sihanouk, in his relationship with his "subjects," had always cut himself into the role of a father who watches over the well being of his "children" and "grandchildren."

123
កុំលនឹងអង្គការ កុំហ៊ានឹងកំអែលចក្រពត្តិ!
kom lo: neung ângka: kom heu:ha neung kâm'aèl chakrâpoat
Don't try it out and see with the *Angkar*,
flaunting the trappings of imperialists!

The Khmer Rouge tracked down every ornament or article of clothing that could remind them of the West.

124
មិត្តមិនបាច់តថ្លៃទេ !
mit min bach tâ: thlay té
Comrade, useless to discuss the price!

125
អត់តថ្លៃ !
ât tâ: thlay
No bargaining!

These last two terse formulae show, in their brevity and brutality, that in Khmer Rouge society all discussion was prohibited when receiving orders or when an accused was pleading to a judge/

torturer. The *Angkar*'s orders fell like the swish of the guillotine's blade.

126

ដឹងគុណអង្គការ

dœng kun ângka:
Be grateful to the *Angkar!*

These were stereotypical words continually cropping up in the leadership's lexicon in order to justify all hardships. Still, there was one occasion at least when the Cambodian people in the collectives sincerely expressed their feeling for the *Angkar*. That was during the three-day holiday of Bun Pak or the Party's Festival, when Pol Pot proclaimed 29 and 30 September, and 1 October 1977, as national holidays to commemorate the seventeenth anniversary of the founding of the Revolutionary Party. The people ate to their hearts' content then; they even had meat! The same was true of the three-day celebration at the time of the anniversary of the 17 April victory, or sometimes in January to honor the creation of the revolutionary army. But these feasts were far from being celebrated regularly throughout the country.

If the "little people" only feasted well at best three times a year, the Khmer Rouge, civil and military, could "carouse" (*thvœ: bon*) more or less as they pleased, in secret. They did this not at any appointed time, for fear of attack or of their site being bombed, but so as not to run the danger of unnecessary risks. They would announce a celebration among the cadres for the next day so that the "enemies" would unmask. In fact, the partying would not take place that day, but some days later, in order to fool everyone!

Under the Heng Samrin government, the Cambodian Vietnamese collaborators simply replaced the *Angkar* by *pak*, meaning the "Party."

2—THE TACTICS OF THE *ANGKAR*

There must be few governments on earth that more aptly fit the saying, "the ends justify the means." The Khmer Rouge leadership was driven by the belief that they had been endowed with a grand and eschatological mission that authorized them to use all means possible, free from human laws and customs, to fulfill it. Thus their utopia unleashed violence and death. Dazzled by visions of heaven on earth, these leaders were absolutely blind and insensitive to human suffering. In radically denying the world around them, they were unable to tell reality from the chimerical, like all psychotics.

Among the many psychological methods—that is, apart from violence and terror that dominated the Khmer Rouge universe— we have already cited seducing, informing, and intimidating. We also spoke of secrecy, propaganda, and, more often, lies, and the methodical manipulation of the weakest strata of Khmer society— ignorant peasants from outlying areas, and even non-Indianized, animistic ethnic minorities, and lastly, on a massive scale, teenagers and sometimes even children. Owing to the cowardliness and corruption of the Lon Nol regime, these tactics allowed the Khmer Rouge to gain power by manipulating public opinion, both national and international. But, guerrilla tactics, kept intact in revolutionary society after victory, produced catastrophic effects.

Among Khmer Rouge crimes, the most unforgivable, for me, are those committed against children. On the one hand, a large number of children, and even babies, were savagely killed in front of their parents, or sent to prisons along with them. Alas, the political propaganda portraits drawn by the Heng Samrin regime and displayed at strategic places throughout the country, those that graphically depicted Khmer Rouge transgressions against children and babies, faithfully represented eyewitness accounts. All of these paintings gradually disappeared after the return of Norodom Sihanouk in November 1991. But, worse still, if that were possible, was the manipulation of young children, especially boys. These children were turned into robots, programmed to blindly carry out the *Angkar*'s mad orders. Torn from their families at an early age, and not as yet imbibed with traditional values, they became heartless monsters, able to commit the most heinous crimes. They were made to believe that their victims had, at some time, been their parents' torturers. As we stressed earlier, often their parents had not necessarily been wiped out by the "capitalists," "feudalists," or "imperialists," but might still be alive in another part of Cambodia.

Khmer Rouge radical Communism borrowed from its European and Asian models a love of secrecy to such an extent that their so-called administration and government were completely shrouded in mystery. What country under the sun has ever had a supreme leader that only a few foreign experts were able to identify and who was completely unknown to his own people? All of the *Angkar*'s strategic and tactical decisions were steeped in darkness, and leaders' principal means of action was surprise. This obsession with secrecy—akin to the tactics of a mafia—was traditional in Mao's China; it was also a leaf out of Lenin's teachings, further refined by Stalin.

A revealing interview between Nuon Chea, the second most influential Khmer Rouge leader, and a delegation from the Danish Marxist-Leninist party in July 1978, contains the following exchange, beginning with their question posed to Nuon Chea:

Why is illegal work fundamental or essential?
In this post liberation period, clandestine work is essential. We no longer use the term "legal" or "illegal"; we use instead the terms "secret" and "open." Secret work is of essence in all that we are undertaking. For example, the elections of comrades to positions of leadership are secret. The places where our leaders live are secret. We keep the hours and places of meetings secret, etc. . . . On the one hand, it is a question of general principle, and on the other, a way to defend ourselves from the dangers of the enemy infiltrating our ranks.

As long as the class struggle or imperialism exists, our secret work will remain fundamental. It is only thanks to it that we are the masters of our fate and that we shall be victorious over the enemy who is incapable of knowing who is who.[14]

It is remarkable to see how cynically Nuon Chea speaks. It is a cynicism that we find in many a slogan. Propping up this notion of secrecy was the careful screening of rare bits of information from the Ministry of Culture and Information broadcast on DK radio on behalf of the leadership, in which, as exemplified by the slogans, the lie had become government policy. Thanks to this tactic, the people had the feeling that the whole country had entered a black hole from which no one would ever return.

Thus, the decision to evacuate Phnom Penh and *all* the cities and towns, after victory, was taken by the Central Committee at a secret Party meeting in February 1975. The same meeting decided to abolish money, markets, and private property; expel all Vietnamese civilians and military; and execute high-ranking Republican civil and military leaders.[15] In October 1978, Pol Pot himself told the same visiting delegation from the Danish Marxist-Leninist Party that "during the civil war [1970–75], the CIA and the KGB had built up a network of agents and spies, supplied with equipment and secret arsenals . . . But the counterrevolutionary plans were destroyed at one blow by the evacuation of the agents also to the countryside, where they did not have the same opportunity to organise a countercoup."[16] In other words, it was by this most cynical political opportunism, if not total disregard for most basic human rights, and sheer barbarity, that almost four million people (or about 40 percent of the entire population) were forced on the roads throughout the country. The revolutionaries constituted too small a minority to control the towns. By this tactic not only did everyone have to blindly obey the *Angkar*'s orders, but the hunt for "enemies of the revolution" could be more easily pursued and even inexorably intensified, despite the end of the civil war.

This order was paramount and overshadowed all other subsequent decisions. What did this mean for almost half of the population, those who inhabited towns and cities, or those who had sought refuge there? All town dwellers saw themselves completely stripped of their belongings as ownership was collectivized without compensation at one fell swoop. At the same time, many families were broken up and everyone was uprooted from his own, familiar environment. All civil liberties were abolished. Access to modern medical care was brutally stopped and hospital patients were thrown out onto the streets. Finally, all heads of administrative services and all Republican Army officers were rounded up in the following days, always under false pretexts or for imaginary missions (such as welcoming Norodom Sihanouk, head of the new revolutionary state till early 1976), and executed en masse.

In the months and years that followed, all purges reflected dissension within the Pol Pot-ist hierarchy but had little effect on the fundamental decisions taken on D-Day, the day of "liberation," and were *never* questioned, at least at the level of ordinary people's dismal daily lives. During all these years, the streets of the capital and provincial towns echoed only with the sounds of the feet (or mopeds) of *Angkar* civilians and military, as well as the thousands of experts and advisors from the People's Republic of China or North Korea. It is possible that almost all the Khmer Rouge cadres who were not in agreement with this delirious and inhumane revolutionary line (and there must surely have been many) were victims of purges that were carried out all through this bloody regime, intensifying towards its final months. Others succeeded in finding refuge in Vietnam or Thailand.

SECRECY

The imperative for secrecy revealed that the new masters of the country were weak in number and unpopular. If the slogan that follows came from the days of civil war, it was surely retained after victory, since economic development and the struggle against opponents were considered the two principal battlefronts of the regime:

127

លាក់ការណ៍ជាកត្តាជ័យជំនះ

léak ka: chie kata: chey chumnèah

Secrecy is a key to victory.

This tactic shows that the Khmer Rouge operated like a group of underground terrorists or mafia. They were incapable, at the moment of unexpected victory on 17 April 1975, to take the reins of responsible government—as was the fate of many a victorious guerrilla movement throughout the world.

Likewise, many people, especially the "17 April," attempted to hide their real identity in the old society.

128 C

លាក់ការណ៍បានខ្ពស់រស់បានយូរ

ak ka: ba:n khpuh ruh ba:n yu:

High secrecy, long survival

This very general counter-slogan could also be used by the *Angkar* to describe its own tactics.

DECEIT

129

បងប្អូនត្រូវតែចេញពីភ្នំពេញមួយរយៈពេច
(ខ្លាចពួកអាមេរិកមកទម្លាក់គ្រាប់បែក)

bâ:ng pâ'o:n trou taè chénh pi: phnom pénh muey ro:yéak to:ch

(khla:ch puek a:mérik mo:k tumléak kroapbaèk)

> Brothers! Leave Phnom Penh for a short while
> (for we fear that the Americans might come back and bomb us).

Although this famous injunction rang out on the very day Phnom Penh was taken, throwing the whole country into the utter frenzy of total revolution, it not only typified the regime's first days but was also symptomatic of the tactic that would always be connected to the *Angkar*—deception. No Phnom Penh inhabitants would ever forget this insane order. We must also not forget that on 17 or 18 April 1975 this order had become symbolic of all evacuations, since identical commands had been issued for *all* the towns, big and small, as they fell under the control of the revolutionaries. In this respect, the town of Kratie was the model, as it had been entirely emptied of its citizens in the mid-1970s already. Everywhere, it was specified that this "short period" was only "three days," signifying that this order had come down from the *Angkar*'s higher echelons.

As we see, the pretext put forward was that the inhabitants had to take shelter in the countryside because of the supposed menace of "imperialist American bombings." In addition, it was claimed that there was not enough food to feed this enormous population of two to three million people in the capital. The Khmer Rouge pretended that, in the countryside, they had stocks of rice—which, once more, turned out to be a lie.

In fact, the Khmer Rouge were persuaded that there were hidden arms caches in the towns, and that, after they first collected all the ammunition, they could flush out from hiding all potential combatants. In truth, the guerrillas were only a tiny minority in the country, and, although very determined and dedicated, they could not control all the people in the towns—even less the inhabitants of Phnom Penh. In sum, this evacuation was not only a lie, but also a bluff!

130
សង្គ្រាមអាកាសតីអាមេរិកាំង
ទម្លាក់គ្រាប់បែកទាំងថ្ងៃទាំងយប់
sângkriem a:kah keu: a:mérikang
tumléak kroap baèk téang thngay téang jup
Air warfare, that is Americans bombing both day and night.

This truth was repeated to children, particularly in the Battambang region, while in fact much of Western Cambodia was spared from American bombings. The Vietminh origin of such a saying is obvious.

***

The new government was a minority one, and thus, hardly able to win over the majority of cadres, much less the population, to the cause of total revolution. The revolutionaries first tried persuasion and seduction, then menace, and finally terror. In the beginning, they began rounding up civil servants and the professional classes, all called "intellectuals." Then gradually, as repression descended, wider and wider social groups became "intellectuals," that is neither farmers nor industrial workers. "Intellectuals" thus came to mean people who did not work with their hands or who had reached some level of college education and who were therefore denounced as parasites.

131
បងប្អូនដែលជាសាស្ត្រាចារ្យ និស្សិត បញ្ញវន្ត
សូមទៅបង្ហាញមុខចំពោះអង្គការ !
bâ:ng pâ'o:n daèl chie sastra:cha: nisèt panhavoan,
so:m tou bângha:nh mukh châmpuh ângka:
Brothers who are teachers, students, and intellectuals,
go and report to the *Angkar*!

People soon learnt quickly the weight of this request, and remained in hiding as long as they could without being informed on. Yet, during the regime's first days, some naive people were lured by the seductive song of sirens, and ended up in the jaws of a wolf.

REEDUCATION

132
អង្គការស៊ើយកទៅរៀនសូត្រ /ទៅប្រជុំ /កសាងខ្លួន
ângka: snae jo:k tou rien so:t / tou prâ:chum / kâ:sa:ng khluen
The *Angkar* cordially requests you to report for a study session/ a meeting/ a reconstruction of the self!

In his grand speech of 27 September 1977, Pol Pot stressed such indispensable mental exercises, the basis of Khmer Rouge ideological training as it was in Mao's China:

> Comrades that are still young . . . make a real effort to reconstruct yourselves . . . Comrades who have served the revolution for a long time [must] reconstruct themselves constantly. No one can carry out his tasks well unless he is loyal to the revolution, which is the most sublime duty of all.[17]

In fact, Pol Pot repeated again that he could not tolerate anything but faultless obedience to himself—the incarnation of *Angkar*—on the part of the young, who were easy targets as well as seasoned militants. They could not but meet endless difficulties in their struggle for survival in the incessant revolutionary turmoil. Rather than rebel against an inane leadership, these were invited to internalize, so to speak, the errors of the regime, passing on the guilt to themselves, and to perform self-criticism, instead of turning against a totalitarian power.

In actual fact, such a suggestion made people quake with fear, up and down the revolutionary hierarchy. Those well-known expressions became a symbol of the terror that encompassed the regime. The words used were a literal translation of the Maoist idea of *xuexi*, "study session."[18] In Mao's China, everyone knew what that meant: people had to appear before their judges and they were going to receive bad treatment. In Khmer Rouge society, the invitation was perfectly ambiguous: it could mean, say, for a high ranking cadre, that he was being called to Phnom Penh to follow a training session or attend an official meeting. But, it could also be a euphemism for being sent to S-21, the main torture-interrogation center for cadres. The invitee was left in total ignorance, and hence defenseless. It was the same for the lesser-ranking cadres or citizens: it could very well be a question of political training or a meeting; but, if he did not return, it became obvious (though belatedly) that the expression used was no more than a figure of speech for a prison from which he would most likely not be released. Few escaped from Khmer Rouge jails. This is why, for the majority of people *rien so:t* or *kâsang khluen* meant nothing more than death or immediate execution. One also needs to note that *rien so:t* literally means "memorize," "learn by heart," or "learn assiduously," "study with concentration," which is revealing about Khmer Rouge pedagogical requirements.

Those arrested—generally people were apprehended after nightfall—were first interrogated locally, then brought to the district prison, along with biographical records, put in irons, interrogated again more thoroughly, and/or tortured. Most were executed or died of starvation or disease. As far as reeducation was concerned, there was little "thought reform," unlike in China. As is the tradition in Cambodia to this day, forced confessions of "crimes" were the absolute proof of guilt. No indoctrination was carried out in the prisons themselves. Those arrested were automatically guilty (the omniscient *Angkar* had ordered the arrests) and were not thought capable of reform. Above all, prisoners had to confess their treason and conspiracies and denounce their networks of accomplices before, in most cases, being slaughtered.[19] Not even in the work camps for returnees at Dey Kraham in Kompong Cham province or at Boeung Trabek in Phnom Penh, was reeducation the order of the day. Even there, about two-thirds of those so-called "intellectuals" who returned from abroad to serve the revolutionary regime disappeared after being called elsewhere by the *Angkar*.[20]

Sometimes, however, the innocent were spared, released from prison, and sent to another people's commune, after an unspecified stay in a work camp, or a summary indoctrination at nightly meetings. *Rien so:t* or *kâsang khluen* did not therefore necessarily mean death, as a great many Cambodians thought, but surely it often did convey the idea of torture and suffering over many months.

So, the Khmer poet Chuon Meng, in his មើលផែនដីខ្មែរ (= *moe:l phaèn dey khmaè*), *Let us look at the world of the Khmer*s, wrote of "going for a study session":[21]

ពាក្យឮរៀនសូត្រ
ពូជូចស្ទួតបូត គួរត្រែកត្រអាល
តែមិនអប់រំ បន្លួរក្បាល (១)
ភាពពិតពួកពាល ជាកប្រាស់សម្លាប់

[Verse] 53 - The word "study session"
When we hear these words, full of sweetness and honesty,
we are filled with joy; still, it is not a question of education,
but of brainwashing[1]—in truth, a gang of criminals
who are cheating us and put us to death.

133
អង្គការអញ្ជើញមិត្តមកគ្រាន់តែចង់ដឹងថា
តើមិត្តស្មោះត្រង់ ឬមិនស្មោះត្រង់ប៉ុណ្ណោះ
ângka: enhchœ:nh mit mo:k kroan taè châng dœng tha:
taoe mit smâhtrâng reu: min smâhtrâng ponâh
Comrades, the *Angkar* only requests your presence
in order to know if you are loyal or not.

This invitation was also, of course, heavy with consequences, but it was less critical than the preceding one.

134
អង្គការតាមដានប្រវត្តិរូប
ângka: ta:m da:n prâ:voattèru:p
The *Angkar* follows up the track of the autobiography.

The *pravoatterup*, ប្រវត្តិរូប, was an essential instrument for population control. Although it was common in all Communist countries to write your own personal history, it became an essential tool in "thought reform" in Mao's China. The Khmer Rouge further radicalized the practice, making it more repressive and absurd. This word thus conveys the idea of "biography," "personal history," "confession," and "avowal," at the same time. For the cadres, this exercise was paramount, and in each new posting, they were called upon to make a new *pravoatterup*, using their own true name, not the *nom de guerre* they used in everyday life. The bureaucracy and red tape at S-21 were nothing but the tip of the iceberg. In all the country's administrations and jails, pages upon pages, notebooks after notebooks of the personal histories of either cadres or people regarded as potentially deviant were amassed. These were copied or transcribed by an army of clerks and then circulated from commune to commune, or followed the captive after his arrest.

Every citizen who was not a simple peasant, had to, at one time or another, write his autobiography, and then rewrite it again, so that if he had lied, he would expose and convict himself. Hence, he had to have a very good memory if he belonged, or had been very close, to those categories of people meant for extermination, so that if he did hide something about himself, he would have to do it logically and consistently. The interrogators, who probably followed training courses throughout the country, were called upon to use torture to obtain meticulous and documented information.

The true nature of their work was intellectual and bureaucratic: they were to collect and compare confessions, not first and foremost to deal blows and torture. They had, at all cost, to foil conspiracies or trace those who, in the future, might plot against the regime. This work demanded a professionalism—long and fastidious research into a hotchpotch of documents where the true and the false were inextricably entwined: the falsehood was meant to mislead the interrogator and the lie extracted under torture was simply a way to avoid further suffering. But there were also a great many candid truths, as the Khmers are often naturally prone to be "full of kindness and docility" (ស្មោះបូត, *slo:bo:t*), as the expression goes.

Usually these confessions did not lead, as in *1984* or Mao's China, to real thought reform, to an "I love Big Brother" or "I love the *Angkar*"; the individual, most often a "17 April," was found unredeemable in the eyes of the Khmer Rouge. For captives in the prisons, these confessions led to complete self-abasement and to self-betrayal before death: to confess, in the midst of atrocious suffering, that one was a traitor in the pay of a foreign power and to name names.

In provincial prisons, rare were the prisoners who wrote their own confessions themselves; usually, clerks were assigned this task, during interrogations always accompanied by threats, and more often, torture. At times, however, after a multiplicity of checks in villages and collectives, an innocent was washed of all suspicion that weighed on him, and his life was spared.

To make the accused speak more easily—and this was part and parcel of psychological torture—the *Angkar* pretended to already know all his misdeeds. In fact, the security system lacked the sophistication of its Soviet or Maoist models: the Khmer Rouge used so many uneducated people that they were incapable of collecting and comparing properly all the information collected. A boast like this was nothing more than a bluff:

135
អង្គការដឹងប្រវត្តិរូបមិតួអស់ហើយ !
ângka: dœng prâ:voattéru:p mit âh haey
Comrades, the *Angkar* already knows your entire biography.

We shall cite an example of this duplicity. In the archives at S-21 is a copybook of minutes of meetings which bears the initials of Duch, begun in the middle of 1976. It is entitled, *Statistics of the secret police*, with the enigmatic initials *NB*, *noyobay*, or "politics"; *ST*, *sotearum* or "mentality"; *ChT*, *chattang*, which means something like "docility in the face of orders." It is a collection of directives (with endless classification, false distinctions, repetitions, a slew of sophisms—in an almost pure totalitarian language) given by Duch to his interrogators. It was recommended that they remain especially vague in this duel of life and death, for, if the accused believed that he had a chance of living, he would talk more.

136
អង្គការដឹងហើយ តែអង្គការសួរនេះ ចង់ដឹងជំហរបងប្អូនទេ ស្មោះត្រង់នឹងអង្គការឬអត់
ângka: dœng haey, taè ângka: sue nih,
châng dœng chumho: bâ:ng pâ'o:n té smâh trâng neung ângka: reu: ât
The *Angkar* already knows; but, if the *Angkar* asks you questions,
it is because it is anxious to know if each and everyone of you,
brothers and sisters, is loyal or not to the *Angkar*.

The same tactic is implied as in the preceding slogan. The Khmer Rouge asked questions, pretending that they already knew the answers. This was not completely inaccurate, since each accused was brought to his interrogator with documentation about him that had been given either forcefully or willingly.

Let us also note that it was taken for granted that individual Asians could not but be a part of a family or a clan. Investigators could not imagine the divergent political sides taken among family members, or that anyone acted from his own individual free will. This may explain why the Khmer Rouge executed entire families, including very young children.

INTERROGATIONS

137
អង្គការមិនសួរដដែលៗទេ
ângka: min sue dâ:daèl dâ:daèl té
The *Angkar* never repeats the same question twice.

138
អង្គការមិនចូលចិត្តនិយាយច្រើនទេ
ângka: min cho:l chèt niyey chraen té
The *Angkar* is economical with its words.

As in the former expression, this declaration takes on an ominous meaning in the mouth of the *Angkar*-torturer.

During the interrogation nothing was to be withheld. Slogan 106 comes to mind (ឃើងត្រូវស្មោះត្រង់ចំពោះអង្គការ, Be sincere with the *Angkar*!) when we imagine an interrogator hurling at their victim:

139
រឿងអ្វីៗមិនបាត់លាក់នឹងអង្គការទេ
reueng avey avey min bach léak neung ângka: té
Absolutely do not hide anything from the *Angkar*.

This slogan gives an example of how informing was encouraged:

140
រឿងសំងាត់ត្រូវរាយការណ៍ដល់ថ្នាក់លើ
reueng sâmngat trou rieyka: dâl thnak lœ:
Discreetly report all secrets to the echelon up above.

141
អង្គការសួរអ្វីត្រូវឆ្លើយសោះត្រង់ចំពោះអង្គការ

ângka: sue avey trou chhlaey smâhtrâng châmpuh ângka:
When the *Angkar* questions you, answer loyally.

142
សួរភ្លាមឆ្លើយភ្លែត / សួរភ្លាមឆ្លើយភ្លាម !

sue phliem chhlaey phlè:t / sue phliem chhlaey phliem
Quick question, quick answer!
As soon as the question is asked, answer instantly!

Below is another version of the same injunction, which reduced the accused to a simple answering machine when brought before the *Angkar*.

143
សួរអ្វីឆ្លើយហ្នឹង មិនត្រូវបង្វែងដានជាដាច់ខាត!

sue avey, chhlaey neung min trou
bângvaèng da:n chie dach kha:t
Give a direct answer! Stop evading the issue!

These last two commands were furnished by C.S.O. (born in 1946), a former prisoner at the district prison of Phnom Srok in 1976, in the north of Battambang province, now called Bantey Meanchey. They were inscribed on the walls of the straw hut used by interrogators. They must have been very common, as, for instance, they were also heard by an adolescent watching cattle in Ba Phnom district, Prey Veng province, when close to the interrogation hut of the district prison.

Yet another variant was:

144
អង្គការសួរអ្វីត្រូវឆ្លើយហ្នឹង, មិនត្រូវក្បត់អង្គការ !

ângka: sue avey trou chlaey neung min trou kbât ângka:

> When the *Angkar* asks you a question, answer it precisely!
> Do not betray the *Angkar*!

This peremptory injunction could, and did, lead, most of the time, to questions the accused were incapable of answering. To cite two examples from the questions Mœung Sonn was asked in Srae Cham district prison, Prey Nup: "Where did you hide the grenades?" "Who is In Tam's representative in the commune?"[22]

145
បើមិនចង់ត្រូវកំផ្លៀងសួរមេចឆ្លើយអញ្ចឹង
bae min châng trou komphlieng sue méch chhlaey enchœng.
If you do not want to be slapped, please answer the questions!

This type of ultimatum is proof that torture was widespread in Khmer Rouge prisons.

146
ឯងចេះតែរកលេសនេះលេសនោះ
aèng chèh taè ro:k léh nih léh nuh
You are always looking for one excuse or another!

This handy slogan above all reveals the *Angkar*'s distrust, since it suspected each and every one of trying to hide his past or of protecting his loved ones. In actual fact, each and every one was precisely trying to do that, at the risk of his own life. This peremptory remark was widely used.

In Cambodian, *aeng*, is the familiar "you," but the Khmer Rouge usually used the revolutionary term *bong* "brother," or *samamit* or *mit* "comrade." *Aeng* thus became a word of contempt in the mouths of the Khmer Rouge, taking on the meaning of "vile," "loathsome," or "despicable."

CIA AND KGB AGENTS

In the later period of the regime, after the purges of those tied to the former Republican government, and confronted by the growing disorder caused by the aberrant decisions taken in Phnom Penh, the *Angkar*, instead of correcting their policies, stubbornly persisted in carrying them to radical limits in an insane leap into the abyss. With mounting failures and setbacks, the Standing Committee of the CPK, instead of sensing any responsibility, saw themselves, in their collective paranoia, as being surrounded by a horde of enemies from without (especially the Vietnamese whose villages they savagely attacked in border regions) and from within (supposedly "in the pay of both the CIA and KGB")!

Again, trying to win the population over with honeyed words, the *Angkar* proclaimed:

147
ចំណែកពួកភ្នាក់ងារសេអ៊ីអាកាហ្សេបេ បក្សមិនយកទាសពៃរ៍អ្វីទេ
châmnaèk à phnéak ngie sé i: a: - ka: gé bé, pak min jo:kto:h pey avey té
As to the agents of the CIA and KGB,
the Party will never harm them.

This was a particularly deceitful statement, since the *Angkar* was driven by the very need to mercilessly track down so-called agents of foreign secret services and exterminate them after torturing them and making them confess their "heinous crimes" and "give up" their "accomplices"—if there were any in the country. That made little difference! Sharing the same collective psychosis as the Chinese during the Cultural Revolution—who saw everywhere a spy in foreign pay—the Khmer Rouge suspected many an innocent citizen of treason. The KGB was oddly linked to the CIA, in the Khmer Rouge's phantasmagoria, because of their visceral hatred of their former allies, the Vietnamese revolutionaries. We know that the Soviet Union was the principle ally of the Hanoi regime.

One witness, a former Khmer Rouge officer from 1970 to 1979, told me of the arrest of a high-ranking official in the North (*phumpea*) region, Ta Khuon, known as Thoch (ทหฺยุร, ผุธ), Koy Thuon, secretary of state for trade, in January 1977. He was accused of being a "Soviet CIA" agent and his confession has been preserved.[23] We here have to ask ourselves if, in Khmer Rouge parlance, "CIA" might not often simply mean "spy" and should really read "Soviet spy" or pro-Vietnamese.

In a similar situation in the People's Republic of China, at the time of Mao's death in September 1976, the powers that be feared more surprise attacks from Moscow than from Washington. For instance, the medical team in charge of embalming the Great Helmsman was not even allowed to ask expert advice of Soviet specialists in Moscow.[24]

148
សូមកុំអោយធ្វើតាមមិត្តទាំងអស់នេះ
ដែលធ្លាប់ធ្វើការអោយសេអ៊ីអាកាហ្កេបេ
so:m kom aoy thvœ: ta:m mit téang âh nih
daèl thloap thvœ: ka: aoy sé i: a: ka: gé bé
If you please, do not follow the example of all those comrades
who would work for the CIA and KGB.

THE PROLETARIAT

Among the treacherous tactics used by *Angkar*, we named secrecy and blatant lying. We now come to their most perfidious manipulations: the extensive use of the most defenseless people among the poorest and least educated strata of Cambodian society. These came from the "proletarian" class, according to Marxist criteria. They were the poor farmers from the periphery and also the non-Indianized ethnic minorities, all the more malleable if they were young. Those were the cherished groups who were summarily brainwashed into becoming the ideal cadres of the revolution.

149

អង្គការចាត់តាំងអ្នកក្រស្រទាប់បាតអោយធ្វើប្រធានទើបច្បាស់លាស់

ângka: chattang néak krâ: srâtoapba:t aoy thvœ: prâ:thientœ:p chbah loah

The *Angkar* promotes the lowliest of the low
to positions of leadership, and that is a perfectly clear directive.

According to numerous eyewitnesses of purges of local leaders, there were three successive waves of local leaders in most places. The *niredeys*, from the Southeast and Ta Mok region, came always and everywhere last; each wave more repressive than the previous one, for each succeeding wave brought to power cadres who were not only poor and illiterate, but most often ruthless as well.

CHILDREN

The following five slogans tell of how the Khmer Rouge manipulated children to denounce and spy on adults.

150

កូនជាកូនរបស់អង្គការ
កូនត្រូវតែរាយការណ៍ពីសកម្មភាពរបស់ម៉ែឪ !

ko:n chie ko:n râbâh ângka:
ko:n trou taè rieyka: pi: sakamephiep râbâh maè ou

Young ones, you are the sons and daughters of the *Angkar*.
Report everything to us who are your parents.

151

បើចង់ដឹងអោយសួរចាស់បើចង់ច្បាស់ត្រូវសួរក្មេង

bae châng dœng aoy sue chah; bae châng chbah trou sue kméng

If you wish to know how things happen, ask adults;
if you wish to see them in a clear light, ask children.

The Angkar and Its Tactics

According to N. N. from Kompong Trabek in the province of Prey Veng, this bit of Khmer Rouge wisdom allowed the authorities to uncover former Republican soldiers who were hiding among the people. As in most Cambodian provinces, the Republican army was destroyed in three stages: first, the high-ranking officers, in the days and weeks following 17 April 1975; then, petty officers and soldiers, who were gradually arrested and sent to prison or work camps where they usually died; finally, their wives and children in the later period of the regime. They were denounced by their own children, or by other close young relatives and neighbors, thanks to the recommendation in this slogan.

152
ប្អូនៗជាស្នងរបស់អង្គការដែលអង្គការត្រូវការជាចាំបាច់
pâ'o:n pâ'o:n chie snâ:ng ro:bâh ângka: daèl ângka: trou ka: chie cham bach
All younger brothers and sisters are the successors of the *Angkar*, and those who the *Angkar* will necessarily need.

153
គេលុញដីពុម្ព នៅពេលវានៅទន់
ké lunh dey e:t nou pél vie nou tun
Clay is molded while it is soft.

This traditional saying was selected by Khieu Samphan to signify that only young children could be selected by the Party to become the docile servants of the *Angkar*.

Another Khmer Rouge aphorism, modeled on Mao's "blank page," nicely expresses the *Angkar*'s admiration for the newly born—the ideal material for experimentation and manipulation:

154
មានតែកូនក្មេងទើបនឹងកើតទេ ទើបស្អាតស្អំ
mien taè ko:n kméng tœ:p neung kaet té tœ:p sa'a:t sâ'â:m
Only a newborn is free from stain.

Is it not possible to find a faint echo from the Gospel when Jesus describes the innocence of young children, something the little Saloth Sar might have learned at the Catholic Brothers' *École Miche* during the 1930s?

Statements of the privileged role the regime saw for the disadvantaged strata of the population and young children are rarely found in slogans or the numerous official speeches. But, in production and security, the *Angkar* admitted that "our youth plays the most important role in carrying out revolutionary tasks." And, in that "epic" speech of Pol Pot on 27 September 1977, he turned his attention to the young:

> Those, among our comrades, who are young, must make a great effort to re-educate themselves. They must never allow themselves to lose sight of this goal. You have to be, and remain, faithful to the revolution. People age quickly. Being young, you are at the most receptive age, and capable to assimilate what the revolution stands for, better than anyone else.[25]

Here Pol Pot spoke like the experienced schoolteacher that he was—and there were many of those in the revolutionary movement.

3—WATCHWORDS FOR SOLDIERS AND CIVILIANS

This collection of *Angkar*'s words does not attempt to list the various orders and exhortations to guerrilla fighters since the beginning of the civil war in 1968 and 1969, when Pol Pot, Ieng Sary, and Son Sen launched their attack against Sihanouk's Cambodian army in Ratanakiri. Rather, the goal here is to gather slogans the leadership meant to drill into the general population. Now it turns out that in this society dominated by violence and with appalling living conditions, the example of the soldiers' struggle and life in the maquis was continually held up for the civilian population to emulate. We have the feeling that for the leaders, daily life in the countryside had to be very closely modeled on the terrible experiences of guerrilla combatants during the civil war, as though in a fit of vengeance on the rest of the population who fled before the fighting!

Father François Ponchaud, in his pioneering *Cambodia: Year Zero*, listed twelve commandments of *Angkar* to be recited by the guerrilla fighters every morning:

1—You shall love, honour and serve the people of the labouring and peasant classes.
2—You shall serve the people wherever you go, with all the heart and with all the mind.
3—You shall respect the people without injury to their interests, without touching their goods or plantations, forbidding yourself to steal so much as one pepper, and taking care never to utter a single offensive word against them.
4—You shall beg the people's pardon if you have committed some error respecting them. If you have injured the interests of the people, to the people shall you make reparation.
5—You shall observe the rules of the people, when speaking, sleeping, walking, standing or seated, in amusement or in laughter.
6—You shall do nothing improper respecting women.
7—In food and drink, you shall take nothing but revolutionary products.
8—You shall never gamble in any way.
9—You shall not touch the people's money. You shall never put out your hand to touch so much as one tin of rice or pill of medicine belonging to the collective goods of the State or the ministries.
10—You shall behave with great meekness towards the labourers and the peasants, and the entire population. Towards the en-

emy, however, the American imperialists and their lackeys, you shall ceaselessly seethe with hatred.

11—You shall continually join in People's production and love your work.

12—Against any foe and against every obstacle you shall struggle with determination and courage, ready to make every sacrifice including your life for the people, the labourers and peasants, for the Revolution and for the *Angkar,* without hesitation and without respite.[26]

These commands are apparently modeled on the advice to Vietminh soldiers, the Khmer Rouge's former mentors. We must note how the revolutionary soldiers were originally meant to be paragons of virtue defending the downtrodden and how in actual fact some could later become monsters of unspeakable cruelty. Among many renunciations we can note these valorous fighters were required to prepare to endure all sacrifices—including the sacrifice of their lives—to construct the revolution and bolster the absolute power of the *Angkar*. The guerrillas, and later the *yothea*, were never meant to "steal" anything from the poor peasantry. However, the threat of violence forced the peasants to give them their full (if reluctant) support: not only did they have to give them food, but also their adolescent sons (and sometimes daughters), their most precious possessions.

Rule no. 6 was the most often quoted in Democratic Kampuchea days—the chastity imposed on soldiers. Sexual repression was generally ruthless, with delayed or arranged marriages and long separations from spouses. The consequences were dire within the Cambodian culture and mores: collective rape followed by the cruel massacre of the victim was not an exception. A number of soldiers, on the other hand, were taken to prison, tortured, and put to death for having had an affair with a clandestine sweetheart.

The following exhortations were found in collective farms as a model for conduct in civilian life, especially in work, and were borrowed from the days of the civil war from 1970 to 1975. We should remember that the Khmer Rouge army was composed of three levels, as it is specified in the 1976 constitution in Article 19 which deals with the "Kampuchean Revolutionary Army: regular, regional and guerrilla." First, there was the local militia (what the constitution refers to as "regional" troops) found in each people's commune, usually called *chhlop*, who supervised daily work and reported the least fact and movement that might look suspicious. Every region—*phumpea*—also had its own assortment of regular soldiers (*yothea*), usually housed in barracks away from the local people. A large number were stationed in and around Phnom Penh: the *oudor* of Tonle Sap at Pochentong; the *niredeys* of Pochentong at Chhbar Ampeou; the *bophea*—before the Sao Phim purge in 1978—along the river in the east.[27]

The army, it seemed, watched over the country's vast, prison network, hence, over the torture-interrogations and the massive killing of people coldly planned from Phnom Penh, or over special sections of the armed forces under the center's control, especially security. For the people, it was the *yothea*, the ordinary soldier, who carried out arrests. Working closely with civilian officials, these two categories of soldiers were possibly in charge of internal security, that is, the systematic arrest of suspected individuals. There seems to have been no distinct security organization like the KGB or the FBI, save the group around Duch, who kept an eye on all high- and middle-ranking cadres. Every soldier then was a security agent, as were civilian leaders. Reeducation camps for returnee intellectuals, like that of Boeung Trabek and Dey Kraham, were directly under Ieng Sary of the Foreign Ministry's authority, while Tuol Sleng, or S-21 was directly under the supervision of the Security Commission of the Standing Committee.

Finally, there was a third kind of special forces, highly trained and very fanatical, who routinely destroyed everything that came in their path, much like a human pulverizing machine. They were an elite corps, a shock force, often made up of some thirty soldiers.

They were especially feared; they were stationed in border areas from where all the population had been relocated. Most were very young; some among these killers came from the Northeast ethnic minorities, and from the remote regions of Cambodia least influenced by Indianization and Buddhism. This may very well explain why they could so easily be manipulated and showed little, if any, pity.[28]

155

ប្រជាជនដូចយោធា កន្លីដូចគ្នាឱ្យតែខុស

prâchiechun kâ: do:ch yo:thie
kâ: khley do:ch knie aoy tèa khoh

The people and soldiers—same treatment:
if someone makes a mistake, his neck will be shortened.

We must note here that if the life of every citizen is continuously threatened, it is the same for the military who can be arrested and processed through the prison system at any time, be it for the most futile reason, like "illicit" love.

156

ប្ដេជ្ញារួបរួមសាម្គី ស្មាទល់នឹងស្មា រវាងកុមារ
យុវជន សេនាជន និងយុទ្ធជនឱ្យបានស្អិតរមួត
ប្រៀបបានបបូរមាត់លើ និងបបូរមាត់ក្រោម !

pdachnha: ruepruem sa:meki: sma: tul neung sma: ro:vieng koma:
yuvéakchun séna:chun ning yuthachun aoy ba:n sâ'èt romuet
priep ba:n bâbo: moat lœ: ning bâbo: moat kraom

Show solidarity, shoulder to shoulder, between children,
on the one hand, and between militia and soldiers, on the other.
Be as close as the upper lip is to the lower!

Let us note the absence of adults in this solidarity chain: no wonder, since the Khmer Rouge army welcomed child soldiers. Note also, once again, the centrality of the armed forces in this revolutionary society.

Here is the type of metaphor common to all avatars of Far Eastern Communism, from the time of the Long March:

157

ផ្សារភ្ជាប់សាច់ឈាមរបស់អ្នកជាមួយនឹងសាច់
ឈាមរបស់ប្រជាជន ដែលប្រៀបបាននឹងបបូរ
មាត់និងធ្មេញ ហើយប្រៀបដូចជាទឹកនិងត្រីដែរ

psa:pchoap sach chhiem robâh néak chiemuoy neung sach
chhiem robâh prâchiechun daèl priep ba:n tou neung bâbo:
moat ning thminh haey kâ: priep do:chie trey nou knong teuk daè

Fuse your body and soul to the people's and you will be
one with them, as the lips are to the teeth, as fish are to water.

158

វាយសំរុកដាច់ខាត មិនត្រូវចុះញ៉មខ្មាំងដាច់ខាត
ហើយត្រូវស្រលាញ់គោរពសមូហភាព !

viey sâmrok dach kha:t min trou chohnhâ:m khmang dach kha:t
haey trou srâ:lanh ko:rup samo:haphiep.

Go on the attack and do not flinch in front of the enemy,
for you must love and respect the collective!

In the civil context, the "enemy" is only a name the Khmer Rouge gave to daily difficulties in the work routine, because, as we shall see later, as in the works of Mao, the vocabulary of war was used in work. Much like the first years of the Soviet revolution, the Communism of Democratic Kampuchea was a war communism.

159

ខ្លាចខ្មាំង ស្លាប់ឱ្យហើយទៅ !

khla:ch khmang slap aoy haey tou

If you fear the enemy, you might as well die straightaway!

Let us read this as: if you fear work, senseless to remain alive! You are unproductive and therefore useless to the revolution!

160
យុទ្ធមិត្តយើងនៅសមរភូមិមុខ
កំពុងប្រយុទ្ធយ៉ាងសន្ធោសន្ធៅ

yuthemit yœ:ng nou samo:rophu:m mukh

kâmpung prâyut ya:ng sântho:sânthou

Our soldiers at the front line fight with burning fervor.

In civilian life, it was a matter of *kâng chalat*, or "front-line mobile youth brigades," cited always as an example to less vigorous and/or less fanaticized adults.

161
ឈាមក្រាលផែនដីយកភ្នំធ្វើផ្ទះយកថ្មធ្វើខ្នើយ !

chhiem kra:l phaèndey

yo:k phnum thvœ: phtéah jo:k thmâ: thvœ: khnəəy

[Even if] your blood spills on the earth, make the hills your home, rocks your pillow!

These mobile brigades most often had to clear outermost zones under appalling living conditions. If a young worker injured himself, he had to doctor himself with what he could find on the spot and was not allowed to return to the commune. We should point out that "the hills" referred to forested areas generally inhabited by ethnic minorities.

162
បេះដូងគ្មានមនោសញ្ចេតនា
គ្មានមេត្តាអនុគ្រោះ ទើបមានជំហរមោះមុតក្នុងការប្រយុទ្ធ

bèhdo:ng kmien mono: sanhchétana: kmien

méta: anukruh tœ:p mien chumho: muhmut knongka: prâ:yut

> If our hearts are nourished neither by feelings nor compassion,
> then we can hold an unyielding position in our struggle.[29]

This watchword stands in opposition to Indian and Buddhist culture. Khmer Rouge ideology strove to put an end to almost two thousand years of Cambodian history.

***

While the following recommendation dates back to the civil war, from 1970 to 1975, it later became a warning to fighters who might fall into the hands of the Vietnamese. It is truly revealing of how the Khmer Rouge eliminated their enemies. If they were taken prisoner, the Khmer Rouge, in never dying loyalty to the *Angkar*, had to remain as silent as the tomb, even under the worst of tortures. What an indirect confession this bit of advice! Widely used Khmer Rouge methods of execution are herewith evoked—hanging by the neck, or disemboweling the victim alive as he hung crucified on a tree. This made it easier to receive his liver and bile, so that these could be used with utmost potency as, according to traditional medicine, they had to be taken from live human beings.

163

ទោះបីខ្មាំងធ្វើទារុណកម្មយ៉ាងណា ឬត្រូវព្យូរក
ឬវះពោះនៅក៏ដោយ ក៏មិនត្រូវសារភាពចំពោះខ្មាំងដែរ

tuh bey khmang thvœ: tierunakam ya:ng na: reu: trou pyue kâ: reu: vèah pueh chhau kâ: daoy kâ: min trou sa:rophiep châmpueh khmang daè!

Even if the enemy tortures you, hangs you by the neck, or splits your belly open, you must never confess anything!

Put into practice by the ordinary citizen who had to submit to moral, then physical, pressures to confess all to the *Angkar*, this advice could thus be turned against torturers, for some prisoners had the almost inhuman courage to withstand torture and not betray their beloved ones.

164
នៅតែម្នាក់ឯងក៏នៅតែតស៊ូ ក៏អាចធ្វើបដិវត្តន៍បានដែរ !
nou taè mnéak aèng kâ:nou taè tâ:su: kâ: a:ch thvœ: padévoat ba:n daè!

**Even if you are alone, struggle on,
for you are capable of waging revolution!**

If, for example, in civilian life, the head of the collective sent someone to gather rattan, wood, or medicinal plants in the forest, he had to carry out this task with great enthusiasm. This situation, however, was rare, for everyone usually had to work in groups of at least three to lessen the temptation for plotting.

165
ចូរមើលគំរូវិរភាពរបស់យុទ្ធមិត្ត យុទ្ធជន យុទ្ធនារីសមរភូមិមុខ ដែលហូបតែបុសឈើរលីស្សៅៈ រើយសាច់ស្គាំងស្គមសកអាចយក ជ័យជំនះលើខ្មាំងបានដែរ មិត្តដឹងទេ?
cho: mœ:l kumru: viréak phiep robâh yuthemit yuthechun yuthenieri: samâ:rophu:m mukh daèl ho:p taè reuh chhœ: voar sâh haœy sach slang sko:m sâ: kâ: a:ch yo:k cheychumnèah lœ: khmang ba:n daè mit dœng té

**Consider well the example of our fighters and front-line
combatants who only ate roots of trees and vines,
their flesh becoming lean and pale;
but that did not stop them from vanquishing the enemy—
did you not know that, comrade?**[30]

Even though these words go a little beyond the framework of slogans, it is interesting to note this vigorous encouragement to imitate revolutionary fighters, for with these very words local officials embroidered speeches. These men were illustrious examples for the cruel under-nourishment of a people weighed down by endless work—the people's "liberators"! Hence, despite food shortages and, worse, famine, people had to go on toiling with the same fervor on collective farms and on huge public works projects.

166

បដិវត្តន៍ជាសង្គ្រាមប្រជាជន
មានតែការបំផុសប្រជាជនទេទើបអាចធ្វើសង្គ្រាមបាន

padévoat chie sangkriem prâ:chiechun
mien taè ka: bomphoh prâ;chiechun té te:p ach thvœ: sangkriem ba:n

**Revolution is the people's war;
to be able to wage war, we need the people's uprising.**

This slogan is as near as one can get to the Leninist notion of war communism. Even after the violent seizure of state power, revolutionaries must carry on the fight. When there is no more external enemy, the Revolutionary Organization (the *Angkar*) turns on its own people, who have become internal enemies. The fighting will have no end until every citizen is exterminated—in theory at least, for such is the logic of the system.

Sun Hao (left) and Pol Pot

Chapter IV

THE HUNT FOR "ENEMIES OF THE PEOPLE"

"The Cambodians do not trust anyone, they see enemies everywhere, and are convinced that they are in the right,"[1] remarked a diplomat in Bangkok on 29 December 1977, after a visit to Democratic Kampuchea.

Together with the struggle for production, the hunt for enemies of every stripe, from abroad and at home, played a pivotal role in the revolutionary society born in violence. This chapter descends into the Khmer Rouge inferno. The sinister slogans make clear the coldly calculated plans for mass extermination by the anonymous *Angkar*. All governmental action, national and local, and all economic activity carried out by the state were subordinated to the pressing necessity to "crush all plots and conspiracies."[2] Cadres were reminded about Lenin's aphorism, "Revolution is not a gala dinner party":

បដិវត្តន៍ចក្រពត្តិមិនមែនអញ្ជើញភ្ញៀវទៅពិសាបាយទេ
មិនមែនសរសេរអត្ថបទទេ មិនមែនបាំក់ផ្កាទេ
មិនមែនត្រូវអប់រំទេ ទន់ទេ មិនត្រូវព្រះដើយកន្តើយ
សុភាពរាបសាទេ មិនត្រូវខ្លាចខ្លាំងទេ
បដិវត្តន៍គឺជាកំហឹងវណ្ណៈមួយ វាយរំលំវណ្ណៈមួយ ។

padévoat chakrapoat min mè:n enhchœ:ng phnhieu tou pisa bay té

min mè:n sâ:sé atébot té min mè:n pak phka: té

min mè:n trou âprum té tun té min trou pronge:y kontaey

> so:phiep riepsa té min trou khlach khmang té
> kœ: chie komhœng vannak muey viey rumlum vannak muey

> Revolution's victory over imperialism is not about inviting guests to a dinner party,
> not about writing a text, not about embroidering flowers,
> not about having the right education, not about being soft,
> not about turning a blind eye and being indifferent,
> not about being well-mannered and polite,
> not about fearing the enemy;
> the revolution is about seething with anger against one class,
> about striking and destroying that class!

Firstly, we will examine slogans alluding to clearly defined enemies in all Communist regimes such as "feudalists" and "capitalists," as well as foreign enemies, such as "imperialists" and "hegemonists." Secondly, we will examine watchwords concerning Cambodians who were not adapting well to the new revolutionary society and expressing opposition to it. Finally, we will look at slogans describing hidden enemies, even those inside Party ranks. In its mission of political cleansing, this totalitarian government viewed citizens not as human beings, but as members of pre-ordained categories. It mattered little if these classifications did not correspond to reality, and numerous were the unfortunate Cambodians who were indeed unclassifiable. This began the process of dehumanization.

The logic of tracking down the enemy was essentially the mechanical implementation of all the lessons learned first in Moscow (via Paris), then in Beijing (via Hanoi). This logic was exemplified in Mao's two great campaigns: the Great Leap Forward and the Cultural Revolution. During the short-lived Democratic Kampuchea regime, these two mass movements were carried out simultaneously and with lightening speed. *The Little Red Book*, moreover, contains very many sayings about the hunt for enemies. The Khmer

Rouge followed suit, distinguishing types of enemies in the struggle for power. The enemies from abroad included the Americans and others seen as backing the Khmer Republicans, and the Vietnamese, who played the same role that the Japanese did for the Maoists in China. The "enemies from within," to begin with, were the Republicans, who played the same role as the Kuomintang in China.

Thousands of Chinese advisors and experts, plus those from North Korea, were everywhere present in Democratic Kampuchea, and they barely escaped capture by the Vietnamese army in the early days of 1979. These advisors were first of all technicians assigned to factories, transport, utilities, water projects, and the military, and numerous doctors and health workers. All weapons were Chinese made, and China built a major air base, complete with its underground control center in the middle of the country, at Phum Krang Lieou, near Kompong Chhnang. The Khmer Rouge army played a central role in the repression; therefore, it is highly probable that the Chinese were aware of what was really happening in the country. Sun Chao, People's Republic of China's ambassador and dean of the diplomatic corps, was the focal point at official meetings in Phnom Penh. For instance, at one mass gathering organized to mourn the disappearance of the Great Helmsman on 18 September 1976, he declared:

> Comrade Chairman Mao Tse-tung . . . , for the first time in the history of the development of Marxism, penetratingly observed that in the period of socialist revolution, classes and class struggle still exist even after the socialist transformation of the ownership of the means of production has for the most part been completed. He also drew the scientific conclusion that there are bourgeois elements within the Communist Party. He developed the great theory of continuing the Revolution under the dictatorship of the proletariat and laid down the Party's basic line for the entire historical period of socialism. He elaborated the great theory of per-

manent revolution under proletarian dictatorship . . . Comrade Chairman Mao initiated and personally directed the great proletarian Cultural Revolution and defeated the counterrevolutionary revisionist line of Liu Shao-chi, Lin Piao and Deng Tsiao-ping . . . In the past half-century and more, in the protracted struggle against the class enemies at home and abroad, both inside and outside the Party, he continued to defend and develop Marxism-Leninism.[3]

"Comrade" Sun Chao described all the elements for the Pol Pot repression, thereby rendering any "revisionism" or step backward impossible: permanent revolution was thus guaranteed to reign supreme. Many of the diatribes in official Khmer Rouge documents are little more than paraphrases of Mao's sayings. Yet, there is a major difference between Mao's China and Pol Pot's Cambodia. The history of the People's Republic of China since 1949 has swung like a pendulum between periods of revolutionary fervor, accompanied by waves of repression and economic crises, and periods of return to reality and more moderate policies fostering economic growth. Mao's entourage managed to contain him, and thus, stop him from foundering the ship of state on the rocks. However, nothing like this transpired in Democratic Kampuchea; nothing could contain Pol Pot's absolutism. Any and all opposition was nipped in the bud. The *Angkar* pushed the country into the abyss, with mass executions, the collapse of living standards, and famine, followed by years of foreign occupation.

After seizing power, new categories of "enemies" appeared whose profiles were singularly vague: those who, in the future, could potentially turn into opponents, thus becoming what could be termed "tomorrow's enemies." Mao had launched the Cultural Revolution precisely to rid China of "future enemies." It was necessary to nip in the bud all potential for rebellion or revisionism. Mao stated clearly in "On Khrushchev's Phoney Communism and Its Historical Lessons for the World" (9 May 1964) the specter that haunted him:

> While our cadre were to shut their eyes to all this and in many cases fail even to differentiate between the enemy and ourselves, but were to collaborate with the enemy and were corrupted, divided, and demoralised by him, if our cadres were thus pulled out or the enemy were able to sneak in, and if many of our workers, peasants, and intellectuals were left defenceless against both the hard and soft tactics of the enemy, it would not take long before, perhaps only several years or a decade, or several decades at most, before a counter revolutionary restoration on a national scale inevitably occurred . . .[4]

During its reign of terror, misery, and death, the regime reaped rebellions and power struggles between leading factions, yet owing to the repressive nature of the regime, opposition could but only be masked. Only the tightly knit group around Pol Pot were above suspicion, the most loyal among the loyalists (Nuon Chea, Son Sen, Ieng Sary, Ta Mok, Kae Pauk, Khieu Samphan, Khieu Ponnary, and Khieu Thirith, these last two, sisters, and wives, respectively, of Pol Pot and Ieng Sary, were the main characters responsible for the Cambodian holocaust). Pol Pot became more and more paranoid and saw conspiracies everywhere. Most of the other Khmers were potentially *khmang*, "enemies"; they had to obey and suffer degradation, or be finally "destroyed," *komtech*! Reeducation was never really an option.

If it is evident that the Khmer Rouge received much encouragement to embrace the Great Helmsman's doctrine, less is known about their relations with Kim Il-sung's Korea. North Koreans also provided technical assistance to the Kampuchean revolution. However, following the moment of revelation of the *Angkar*'s identity at the end of September 1977, Pol Pot was received as a brother by Kim Il-sung, after his triumphant reception in Beijing. Radio Kampuchea broadcast a congratulatory message, but the following passage was omitted when aired on Radio Pyongyang:

> The heroic people of Kampuchea have destroyed, in a short time, a group of counter revolutionary spies, who had carried out subversive activities, in the revolutionary ranks for a long time, at the instigation of foreign imperialists; they thus demonstrated strength in political and ideological identity of purpose and national cohesion with complete support for the Party's Central Committee.[5]

Here it is evident that Pyongyang was privy to the leadership's secrets, as what was happening in prisons like S-21, now Tuol Sleng, was top secret. If the Workers' Party of Korea officially applauded the purges in the CPK, only to withdraw its applause later, does that imply that North Korea encouraged them other than verbally? Was it a mark of embarrassment or an admission of complicity in Khmer Rouge crimes?

One of the main tasks of all leaders, at every level, was to uncover all opponents, to break all ties of family solidarity, and to quash all attempts at rebellion. This highly political "mission" meant sorting the wheat from the chaff. It was the subject of numerous debates at the Party summits and the object of very precise orders from *Angkar*. In addition, it could be argued that, with its hosts of interrogators and jailers and its mountains of paperwork, it was the sole branch of government that operated efficiently. Yet, this bureaucracy did not abate the paranoia of Pol Pot and his group, who saw themselves increasingly encircled by more and more mysterious enemies.

At the time of the second anniversary of the Khmer Rouge's victory, Khieu Samphan, the so-called nominal head of the state, explained to the international media and to a select Phnom Penh audience, the logic of the system he and his friends had put in place:

> In the field of defending Democratic Kampuchea, protecting our Kampuchean Revolutionary fruits, we were able to do so completely, exercising mastery and without complications or worries,

as our union workers, cooperative peasants and various bases allowed no enemy to infiltrate our territory or our territorial waters or to sabotage our Kampuchean Revolution whether from outside or from within . . .

Immediately after liberation, when we suffered untold difficulties, as we had just emerged from the devastating U.S. imperialists' war, the enemy failed to cause us any serious trouble. Today, the enemy cannot do us any harm. This is our firm belief, stemming from concrete, practical evidence. However, we must carry on the task of defending our Democratic Kampuchea, protecting our worker-peasant administration, and preserving the fruits of our Kampuchean Revolution, by resolutely suppressing all categories of enemies, preventing them from committing aggression, interference or subversion against us. We must wipe out the enemy in our capacity as masters of the situation, following the domestic, foreign, and military policies of our revolutionary Organisation (Angkar Padevoat). Everything must be done neatly and thoroughly.[6]

Khieu Samphan claimed, on this second anniversary of 17 April 1975, that he possessed "concrete evidence" that the "enemies of the revolution" had not been handled with kid gloves, and that the people were literally down on their knees. In fact, already there were around one million dead—that is, one out of every eight Cambodians[7]—and the country was a web of prisons and centers of torture and execution. Another million Cambodians were going to perish in atrocious circumstances, mostly in secret and without any funeral rites. Despite this evidence, today Khieu Samphan claims that he had no inkling such mass extermination was being carried out!

Pol Pot himself eventually explained that "enemies" were outcasts, stripped of Cambodian citizenship; therefore, they had to be wiped out like germs, for they were endangering the very survival of the revolution:

> There is also another handful of reactionary elements who continue to carry out activities against us and attempt to subvert our Kampuchean Revolution. These elements are not numerous, constituting only one or two percent of our people. Some of them operate covertly while others are openly conducting adverse activities. These counterrevolutionary elements which betray and try to sabotage the Revolution are not to be considered as belonging to our people. They are to be regarded as enemies of Democratic Kampuchea, of the Kampuchean Revolution and the Kampuchean people. We must deal with them the same way we would with any enemy, that is, by separating, educating and training elements that can be won over to the people's side, neutralising [*apyeakret*] any reluctant elements so that they will not undermine the Revolution, and isolating and eradicating [*kamchat*] who represent only the smallest possible number of the elements who are cruel and who determinedly oppose the Revolution and the people and collaborate with foreign enemies to fight against their own nation, their own people and their own Revolution.[8]

Note the formidable mental process of totalitarian thought that transfers to its victim the "cruelty" of the torturer. The Kampuchean Communist Party secretary cum prime minister develops the entire rationale of mass exterminations in this short extract from his famous speech in which he came out from anonymity. However, in truth, what happened was the inverse: there was hardly any reeducation under Pol Pot; most of those "separations," that is arrests, were done in such a way that no hope of resistance or escape was possible. The justification was that they had been deprived of their citizenship and no longer belonged to humankind. The figure of 1–2 percent of the population is revealing, for it almost certainly corresponds to the proportion of the population held for a short period (of one week to three months) in the chains of the district prisons throughout the regime before being exterminated. The following slogans clearly indicate how the categories of "enemies" were selected.

1—ENEMIES IN GENERAL

The evacuation of Phnom Penh and every Cambodian town was a deliberate tactic to scatter in the wild, after they had been first disarmed, all those that were perceived as the enemies of the revolution. This policy was indeed most successful. A proof that it was a deliberate part of *Angkar* strategy can be seen in the following watchword:

168
យើងបណ្ដេញប្រជាជនអោយអស់ និងខ្មាំងអោយអស់
yœ:ng bondénh prâ:chiechun aoy âh ning khmang aoy âh
Let us chase away all the people, hence absolutely all enemies!

169
ដៃម្ខាងបង្កើនផល ដៃម្ខាងវាយខ្មាំង
day mkha:ng bângkaen phâl, day mkha:ng viey khmang
One hand for production, the other for striking the enemy

No other slogan sums up so strikingly and succinctly the Khmer Rouge's strategic policy during the almost four years that they held power. It was widely quoted, and more often than not, to soldiers. It unleashed an unbridled repression, an imperious demand, imposed on all the people, save the Khmer Rouge themselves, to work like convict labor. Cambodian money (never distributed) bore such symbolic scenes. On the ten riel bill, on one side we find a harvesting scene; on the other, guerrillas fire a mortar. On the fifty-riel bill, on one side women plant rice; on the other, they shoot a bazooka.

170
ដៃម្ខាងកាន់ចប ដៃម្ខាងកាន់អាវុធ
day mkha:ng kan châ:p, day mkha:ng kan a:vuth
One hand grasps a hoe, the other, a rifle.

A variation on the same theme and better adapted to rural Cambodia, the hoe, being the universal peasant's implement, is used to turn over and harrow the earth, to dig channels for irrigation, and maintain small dikes.

A radio editorial used the same imagery:

> Implementing the slogan holding hoe in one hand and rifle in the other, male and female combatants and cadres of our revolutionary army have heightened the spirit of revolutionary vigilance, defended, with great effectiveness the state power of workers and peasants, the Kampuchean Revolutionary *Angkar*, territorial integrity, national sovereignty, and our Democratic Kampuchea. The general situation of our country is good.[10]

Similarly, in a radio commentary entitled "Our Revolutionary Army's Resolute Respect for the *Angkar*'s Discipline," one could hear that "the combatants [are] also able to clearly distinguish friends from enemies," a clear indication that the army was in charge of repression at home. They were held up as a model in the communes. "With weapons in one hand, strive to defend the country: with hoes in the other hand, help build the country to make it prosper rapidly," read an editorial to the victorious soldiers on Neak Luong, on 25 December 1977.[11]

171 C

ដៃម្ខាងកាន់ចបដៃម្ខាងកាន់អាវុធ ធ្វើអីក៏មិនប្រាកដ ឈរមើល

day mkha:ng kan châ:p day mkhang kan avuth thvœ: avey kâ min pra:kât chho: mœ:l

"One hand grasps a hoe, the other, a rifle"
and we are ditched there, not knowing exactly what to do!

How can anyone get anything done, holding a rifle in one hand and a hoe in the other?

172
ចាក់ខេងចាក់ខាង !
chak khéng chak kha:ng
Stab one side, then stab the other side!

This watchword, used in the Central and Northern region, around Kompong Thom, meant that every citizen/combatant always had to strike out against foreign and domestic enemies. Simultaneously, and with the same fervor, they had to perpetually achieve production goals. It also indicates that every revolutionary was always on alert, ready to report to authorities any and all suspects, including the misconduct of close comrades.

173
ត្រូវសុភាពរាបសារដាច់ខាតចំពោះប្រជាជន
តែត្រូវមានកំហឹងនាបនេះជានិច្ចចំពោះខ្មាំង
trou sophiepriepsa dach khat chompuh prâ:chiechun
taè trou mien trou mien komhœng chhap chèh chie nich chompuh
khmang
You should show a modest bearing towards the people,
but you must burn with anger at the enemy.

2—CLEARLY DEFINED CATEGORIES OF ENEMIES

THE OLD FAVORED CLASSES

174
ប្តេជ្ញាកំទេចពួកសក្តិភូមិ មូលធន នាយទុនកំប្រាដរ័ឱ្យអស់ !
pdachnha: kâmtèch puek sakdéphu:m mu:lethun nieytun komprado:r
aoy âh!
Go at it! Destroy all feudalists, capitalists, and compradors!

Such watchwords simply repeated the usual Communist slogans, especially Maoist. However, they did not reflect the reality of Cambodian society, for most peasants owned their own land, and true capitalists were small in number. Moreover, many had fled abroad before 1975. As to the Portuguese word comprador, the local agent of foreign companies in colonial days, it is doubtful that many Khmers knew what the word meant.

175
ស្លាប់ដើម្បីផលប្រយោជន៍ប្រជាជនមានទំងន់ជាងភ្នំព្រះសុមេរុទៅទៀត
ស្លាប់ដើម្បីពួកមូលធននសក្តិភូមិ និងពួកប្រតិកិរិយា
មានទំងន់មិនបានស្លាបក្ងានផង

slap daembey phâl proyaoy prochiechun mien tumngun chieng phnom préah somaè tou tiet

slap dambey puek mulethun sakkedéphum ning puek protékéria mien tumngun men ban lap kangan phâ:ng

Dying for the sake of the people has even more weight than Sacred Mount Himalaya;
dying for the capitalists, feudalists, and reactionaries does not weigh more than a goose's feather.

Sacrificing one's life for the people's revolution is as great as Mount Meru, but dying for the old favored classes is worthless. Note the erudition of the author of that slogan with its learned reference to Mount Meru, where Indra's Palace is located. Indra is the most celebrated god of the Rig-Veda, a collection of ancient Hindu poems.

176
អង្គការវាយសំរុកចាប់ខ្ទេច អត់ទុកពួកចក្រពត្តិ
សក្តិភូមិឈ្លានពាន, មិតងដឹងដឹងទេ?

ângka: viey sâmrok chap khtèch âttuk puek chakrâpoat sakdéphu:m chhlien pien mit aèng dœng té?

The Hunt for "Enemies of the People"

> The *Angkar* launches violent attacks
> and stops in their tracks all imperialists
> and feudalists who put our state in danger—
> didn't you know, comrade?

177
ពួកសក្ដិភូមិនាយទុនគឺជាឈ្លើងសង្គម
puek sakdéphu:m nieytun keu: chie chhlœ:ng sângkum
Feudalists and capitalists are the bloodsuckers of the nation.

178
សមមិត្តត្រូវដុតភ្លើងកំហឹងឱ្យឆេះក្តៅងជានិច្ចចំពោះពួក
សក្ដិភូមិ នាយទុន និងឆ្កែបំរើវា !
samamit trou dot phlœ:ng kâmhœng aoy chhèh kdau ngum chie nich,
châmpueh puek sakdéphu:m nieytun, ning chhkaè bâmrae vie
Comrades, let your anger burn brightly
against feudalists and capitalists,
and all running dogs at their beck and call!

Those in the service of "the exploiting classes" were very loosely defined. This call for denunciation thus could strike a wide range of the population.

179
អង្គការវាយតែរបបទេ(របបចាស់)តែបើបុគ្គល
ណាៗអោបរបបវាយទៅត្រូវទាំងបុគ្គលនោះទៀត
ângka: viey taè robâ:p té (robâ:p chah) taè bae bokul
na: aop robâ:p viey tou trou téang bokul nuh tiet
The *Angkar* only attacks the [old] regime;
yet if anyone espouses its cause, both shall be struck down.

Repression not only fell upon human beings, but also on people who had been classified as sub-human—outdated pieces of machinery thrown on the dust heap.

180
វាយកំចាត់កំចាយអាខ្មាំងចក្រពត្តិ !
viey kâmchat kâmcha:y a: khmang chakrâpoat
Let's violently attack and scatter the accursed imperialist enemy!

It should not be forgotten that the "imperialists," in the eyes of the Khmer Rouge, were not only American soldiers, who were not really on the ground (except for some military advisors), but also Vietnamese revolutionaries on the ground from 1972–73. After 31 December 1977, officially the date of the diplomatic breaking off between Phnom Penh and Hanoi, the Khmer Rouge began referring more and more to them as "hegemonists."

181
ប្តេជ្ញាវាយកំទេចខ្មាំងបំផុសបំផុលតម្លើរនិយម គំនិតនិយម
ការិយាល័យនិយម សំភារនិយម បុគ្គលនិយម និងបក្សពួកនិយម !
pdachnha: viey kâmtèch khmang bâmphoh bâmphol kumpi:niyum kumnitniyum ka:riya:layniyum sâmphieréakniyum bokulniyum ning pakpuekniyum!
Let us swear to attack and destroy the enemy
who forces us to believe in dogmatism, idealism, bureaucracy, materialism, individualism, and factionalism!

This refers to some of the traditional "enemies" of Democratic Kampuchea. The Khmer Rouge revolution abolished all administrative posts and executed most civil servants of the Republican government. They believed all administration was parasitic, since only agricultural labor, or work in factories, had any social value. Yet, few governments were more bureaucratic than theirs, in the worst sense of the term. Mountains of paperwork were generated by the regime's prison network and possibly hundreds of thousands of "autobiographies" were written by the general population, especially by the "17 April people," to be filed by the local cadres.

It was not very Marxist on the part of the atheistic Khmer Rouge to reject "materialism." In fact, for them, "materialism," carried the meaning of love for riches and consumer goods of a capitalist society, or "consumerist materialism." They zealously exalted the contempt for riches, like all religions. And "individualism" was condemned in a society where every human had been reduced to a simple member of a category.

All persons linked to old governments (Sihanouk or Republican) represented the exploiting classes.

182
មនុស្សសង្គមចាស់តំរាំងចិតមានកម្មសិទ្ធិ
ក្រាស់ភ្លួរព្រៃលើខ្នងគេ

monuh sângkum chah kumréang chaèt mien kamsit
krah pchue sraè lœ: khnâ:ng ké

People from the old regime are antiquated; they seek to amass any amount of riches and plough on the back of others.

THE CLERGY AND BUDDHISTS

The notion that religion is the opium of the people, and that the clergy exploit the people's credulity, to live off them, should not surprise us. What was new was the radical twist given to the literal implementation of this Marxist concept.

A sweeping repression fell on Buddhism. First, the most revered monks were wiped out, except for a few individuals who were able to take refuge in the forest. The monks were defrocked and put to work like everybody else. Pagodas were closed to worship. The monks, who refused to blend into the new civic order, were thrown into prison, where most were liquidated. The number of clergy who survived almost four years of Khmer Rouge rule, was very small, indeed.

Firstly, it should be remembered that during the Republican government and the civil war, 1970–75, many pagodas had already suffered varying degrees of damage, owing to the American and "Lon Nol-ian" bombings, because guerrilla fighters often took cover there. After 17 April, practically all religious objects and statues of the Buddha were destroyed. Very rarely were the people able to save and bury them. However, most religious buildings (pagodas, schools, dormitories, refectories, and meeting halls) were put to other uses. As strategically placed sites, pagodas often served for offices for the new administration or headquarters for the army, or security services. Buildings were used as granaries and as pigsties. However, most were turned into prisons, or *munty santebal*, i.e. "offices of internal security."

This offered a double advantage. The first was practical: since the pagodas had many doors, they often had few windows. Once the wooden doors were closed, no one could observe what was really happening inside them. Village smiths installed networks of bars and rings (*khnohs*) to shackle prisoners. Turnover in prisoners was fast paced: day and night, they were led into interrogation and torture chambers, executed, and buried. Today, a number of pagodas are surrounded by charnel houses, and it is not yet clear how many unfortunate people are buried in these mass graves.[12] The second advantage was symbolic: the Khmer Rouge, in their profanation frenzy, were without doubt happy to turn these places of serenity, tradition, and culture, into temples of hate, horror, and death.

183 C
វិហារវត្តជាឃ្លាំងគ្រាប់រំសេវ

vihie voat chie khléang kroap rumsév

Pagodas are warehouses filled with ammunition and explosives.

Such was the case at Wat Sangkae in the town of Battambang. The revolutionaries set it on fire before they escaped in early 1979 and the pagoda burned for three days, amid numerous explosions at the onset of the fire.

***

The Khmer Rouge were at first satisfied to proclaim the old Marxist slogan:

184
សាសនាគឺជាអាភៀន
sasna: keu: chie a:phien
Religion is the opiate [of the people].

185
លោកសង្ឃជាជនបញ្ញើក្អែក
lo:ksâng chie chun bânhae kâ'aèk
Monks are parasites.

Then the slogans took on a more earthy and metaphoric cast, particular to Cambodian language:

186
លោកសង្ឃជាព្រូនសង្គម
lo:ksâng chie pru:n sângkum
Monks are tapeworms gnawing out the bowels of society.

187
កំទេចព្រះ១អង្គចំណេញស៊ីម៉ង់ត៍១បាវ
kâmtèch préah muey âng châmnénh si:mâng muey ba:v
If you destroy a statue of the Buddha,
you will be rewarded with a sack of cement.

This counsel might seem absurd, since the poured cement had already served its purpose. In fact, the Khmer Rouge meant that the fragments of concrete could be used to build walls or new constructions, or simply to backfill.

***

In order to better understand the following two slogans, which forbid all symbolic representation of the Buddha, one should be aware that, during the 1950s and certainly the 1960s, the standard of living was progressively improving in Cambodia and people were overtaken by a frantic desire to build new pagodas throughout the country. Often, they did so in haste, with little aesthetic concern, and unfortunately, on sites of earlier pagodas. The latter were from an epoch when all pagoda pillars, pediments, and decorations were built from timber. They are now lost to us forever. Concrete became widely used, especially to economize on decorations (eaves, ramps, ornamental frontages, etc.), as well as for statues of Buddha, which were then painted. The aesthetic value of this craft was rather unexceptional, and the Khmer Rouge could easily pretend that these poor Buddhas were nothing but cement.

188
ថ្វាយបង្គំព្រះដូចថ្វាយបង្គំស៊ីម៉ង់ត៍

thva:y bângkum préah do:ch thva:y bângkum si:mâng

[If] you prostrate yourself before the Buddha,
you are only groveling before cement.

189
ព្រះកើតមកពីជាងកំបោរបាយអ

préah kaet mo:k pi: chieng kâmbao ba:y â:

Buddhas were born from a mason's trowel.

190
សំពះលោកសង្ឃដូចសំពះកូនអ្នកស្រុក

sâmpéah lo:k sâng do:ch sâmpéah ko:n néak srok

Joining hands to greet monks
is like joining hands to greet the country children.

All reverent gestures for Buddha and monks were thereby rendered grotesque and empty of meaning, for, in traditional Khmer society, elders were venerated and honored, not children.

191
ធ្វើបុណ្យហ៊ូរហៀរក្នុងវត្តដូចវេរភត្តឱ្យឆ្កែ

thvœ: bon ho:hie knong voat do:ch véphoat aoy chhkaè

Celebrating festively in a pagoda, with abundant food,
was like making an offering to a dog.

Here, the Khmer Rouge are referring to pre-revolutionary society, and the adage is in the past tense. In fact, the only Buddhist services of any sort held in Pol Pot's Cambodia were those celebrated by Norodom Sihanouk and his family at the Silver Pagoda, and, it seems, by Nuon Chea's mother, who had special dispensation to pray in a pagoda in the province of Battambang.[13]

192
ចូរសមមិត្តជ្រាប: ជំនឿព្រះ អារក្សអ្នកតា
ជាកំអែលសង្គមចាស់

cho: samamit chriep: chumneue préah a:réak néak ta: chie kâm"aèl sângkum chah

Comrades, listen well: the belief in spirits and genii
are only effects of the old regime.

As good Marxists, the Khmer Rouge ridiculed all superstitions, beliefs, and most personal convictions that were in contradiction—or rather in competition—with the dogmas of the god-*Angkar*. However, quite a number of *lok kru*, or witch doctors, in the wilds of Cambodia survived the iconoclastic rampage of the regime, with Khmer Rouge leaders among their most "loyal" patients![14]

193
ខ្លាចខ្មោច ខ្លាចត្រីអាំង
khla:ch khmaoch khla:ch trey ang
Fearing ghosts is like fearing grilled fish.

This witticism was ever present in the mouths of local collective leaders, especially during night speeches. In fact, numerous were Cambodians who hardly wanted to work after dusk; not only were they exhausted after a long day's work, but they, like many Khmers today, were often superstitious and truly believed in ghosts.

In addition, the general population feared digging up the remains of those executed in some corner of the forest, or even mass graves, or even worse, replanting rice among cadavers, as the inhabitants of Russey Krang were forced to do by their torturers. It was in the district of Mong Russey, at a place called *munty kuk 32*, i.e., "Prison 32," where thousands from Phnom Penh were deported, and then, much later, in the last year of the regime, other deportees arrived from the Eastern zone. During the rainy season of 1978, the dead bodies were so numerous in the rice paddies that the replanting took place among the corpses, in an area of a couple hectares; the harvest that year was plentiful![15]

194
ខ្លាចខ្មាំង ខ្លាចគល់ឈើ
khla:ch khmang khla:ch kul chhœ:
You are afraid of enemies, you are afraid of tree stumps.

195
អង្គការគ្មានព្រះ គ្មានខ្មោចលង គ្មានអបិយជំនឿ
ângka: kmien préah kmien khmaoch lo:ng kmien apeychumneue
For the *Angkar*, there is no god, no ghosts,
no [religious] beliefs, no supernatural.

196

អង្គការជាអ្នកស្រោចស្រង់ជីវិតសមមិត្ត
មិនមែនព្រះអ្នកតាអីទេ

ângka: chie néak sraoch srâng chi:vit samamit
min mè:n préah néak ta: ey té

It was the *Angkar* who saved your life, neither God nor genii.

In Pol Pot's Cambodia, only the *Angkar* was God!

THE VIETNAMESE

The Vietnamese were one easily identifiable new category of enemy, old comrades and brothers in revolution, later compared to "imperialists," and above all, "hegemonists."[16] For the Pol Pot-ists, the real enemies were the Vietnamese, the enemies from without, the hereditary enemy. Propaganda portrayed and encouraged broadly traditional stereotypes and racial prejudice, for the Khmer Rouge believed that the famous Vietnamese "march to the south" was a unique phenomenon in the history of humanity.

We must not forget that the Vietnamese community numbering some 550,000 people before the civil war had been halved by pogroms and emigration during the Khmer Republic (1970–75). If Marek Sliwinsky has found that about one-third of the community died under Democratic Kampuchea, we do not know how many transgressed *Angkar*'s orders to return (or go) to Vietnam; but they must have been very few and most of them consorts of Khmers.[17] All the Vietnamese returnees one can interview now claim their entire families were all too happy to leave the country at the time. However, some Khmer Krom, to their great regret, went over the border in the southern provinces to escape discrimination in Vietnam, only later to be branded as potential Vietnamese spies, as, for instance, in Tramkak district in Takeo, and imprisoned.

197

ត្រូវកំទេចអោយអស់អាខ្មាំងយួនលេបទឹកដី !

trou kâmtèch aoy âh a: khmang yuen lép teuk dey

We must crush the Vietnamese enemies who devour our country!

The various ethnic minorities living on Vietnam's central plateaus also accused the Vietnamese of "eating up their lands," which has indeed been the case, particularly since the Communist victory of April 1975.[18]

198

កំចាត់ដាច់ខាតយួនឈ្លានពានវៀតមីលេបទឹកដី
ឱ្យវិនាសអន្តរធានពីទឹកដីកម្ពុជារៀងរហូត

Kom chat dachkat Yuen chhlienpien viet ti: léb teuk dey
aoy vinieh andorothien pi teuk dey Kampuchie rieng roho:t

Crush to bits the Vietnamese aggressors who invade and devour our territory.
They will destroy and ruin the Kampuchean territory
piece by piece till the end.

199

វាយយួនត្រូវវាយវាឱ្យបាក់ឆ្អឹងខ្នង !

viey yuen trou viey vie aoy bak chh'œng khnâ:ng

Smash the Viets! Smash them until you break their backs!

This watchword was disseminated during the last year of the Khmer Rouge's regime, at the time of the publication of the famous *Black Book*, written by Pol Pot in French in September 1978. There he put to paper decades-old grief against "the Vietnamese big brother," as well as all the "crimes" Vietnam committed against the Chams, then the Khmers.[19] After being their allies during the years of struggle for independence, the Khmer Rouge revolutionaries, then in the maquis, broke completely with their fellow Communists, beginning in 1972–73, following the line traced in

Beijing. Prince Sihanouk's trip to the maquis in March 1973 was probably the very last collaborative action organized by the three revolutionary movements. It was but the last leg of a long march toward break off and hatred, begun undoubtedly after the stay of Saloth Sar and other Khmer Rouge leaders in Beijing, at the end of 1965 and the beginning of 1966. Until 1977, Hanoi thought that it could impose a compromise on Cambodian revolutionaries, that is, to a large extent control their revolution. But the atmosphere only darkened and relations became more and more tense.

From the very first weeks of the Pol Pot regime, the Vietnamese were expelled—even those who had lived in the country for generations. Other town dwellers tried, often successfully, like some of the Sino-Khmers, to pass themselves off as Vietnamese and flee from this hated regime. They were mercilessly driven back at the border by the Vietnamese and turned over to their torturers. They were numerous in the province of Kampot and finished their life in the town's prison, at the beginning of the Khmer Rouge regime.

Hanoi made various attempts at reconciliation in order to solve the various border problems. Then the Khmer Rouge troops attacked villages inside Vietnam more and more frequently. They tried to take soldiers prisoner, better still officers; they were brought to S-21 in Phnom Penh where they were interrogated and tortured in order to uncover "plots" which Hanoi was hatching against Cambodia. Meanwhile, as the number of Cambodian refugees fleeing Pol Pot's bloody regime swelled in Vietnam, and as the months and years passed, the Vietnamese drew up invasion plans and put them into effect during Christmas 1978.

Since their defeat, the Khmer Rouge leadership has been attempting to make Cambodians forget their crimes. They have been trying to make them believe that it was the "American imperialists" on one hand, and those "Vietnamese traitors" on the other, who carried out the slaughters in the country during the years they held power. Once again, for the Khmer Rouge, the victim became the torturer, and the torturer became the victim!

200
វាយកំចាត់កំចាយអាខ្មាំងយួន !
viey kâmchat kâmcha:y a: khmang yuen
Let us violently attack and scatter the Vietnamese vermin!

This slogan might have very well been screamed as the fanatic, Khmer Rouge commandos attacked Vietnamese villages, in Vietnam proper, especially in the region of Tay Ninh, beginning in August/September 1977. During long months some young Khmers were brainwashed into seeing the Vietnamese as nothing but loathsome monsters. They were being prepared to kill all that came into their path.[20]

201
ប្រយ័ត្នអាខ្មាំងយួនយកក្បាលខ្មែរដាំតែអុងទៀត !
prâ:yat a: khmang yuen jo:k kba:l khmaè dam taè ong tiet
Beware of the enemy from Vietnam
who takes Khmer heads as trophies
and ingredients for the giant pot
in which he boils water for his master's tea!

អុង "*ong*" is a Vietnamese word; it means "gigantic pot," which the Cambodian peasants in the countryside use to boil palm juice to extract sugar. In pre-colonial days, at the time Vietnam controlled Cambodia, those who did not wish to complete work details were arrested and buried to their necks. And a pot was placed on three heads. It is not clear whether this is a traditional tale, a rumor, or a myth. It circulated in the region of Chaudoc, on the border of Takeo. The myth originated in the eighteenth century, and was transmitted from one generation to the next. The slogan comes from the district of Kompong Rau, Svay Rieng province, very close to the border with Vietnam.

***

Paradoxically, for the Khmer Rouge, the Vietnamese could easily become the enemy from within, with their spies and secret supporters who could hide behind any Cambodian face. The accusation emerges thus:

202
ក្បាលយួនខ្លួនខ្មែរ
kba:l yuen khluen khmaè
Vietnamese head, Cambodian body

"Head" obviously carries the meaning of "spirit, mentality, way of thinking" as opposed to physical appearance. In other words, this very widespread accusation is proof that the Khmer Rouge were not after ethnic Vietnamese in their flesh, but Khmers who were accused of collaborating with the traditional enemies and being brainwashed by them.

This very well-known slogan implies that it was all right to kill Cambodians, asserting that they possessed Vietnamese souls! Xenophobia already was a basic element of Khmer Rouge ideology and was directed against all non-Khmers. Its primary victims were Chinese and Sino-Khmers, and all Europeans. In this regard, note should be taken of the stupidity of Khmer Rouge beliefs about racial purity, for the majority of its leaders had some Vietnamese or Chinese ancestry. If it was true that mixed marriages of Cambodians and Vietnamese had always been less well viewed than those between Chinese and Khmers, the mingling of people from various ethnic origins nonetheless was common on either side of the border. Cochinchina was and is largely populated by Cambodians. What essentially distinguishes the large delta populations has less to do with physical appearance than with language and customs.

The mass killings the Khmer Rouge carried out, however, hardly fall within the terms of the 1948 International Convention on Genocide, since their crimes were political, not racial. They killed for ideological motives, and certainly not because the victims belonged to a particular race, as was generally true in Communist countries. Rumor had it among Cambodians that, if the authorities committed mass murder, it was for *lebensraum*, to clear the area in order to install millions of Chinese from the People's Republic of China. Though it may be perfectly true that Chinese "experts" were numerous, and that they lived high on the hog, there is no basis for believing that this wild rumor supported a shadow of truth. But it is significant in that it shows the state of panic among Cambodians in the face of the terrifying number of victims.

It is ironical to learn, thanks to David Chandler's biography of Pol Pot, that this very same slogan could be used against Saloth Sar himself.[21] After his return from France in 1953, his ideological journey began with close collaboration with the Vietminh and, at times, he was under their direct protection, for some twenty years until about 1973. Beginning in 1965–66, the time of his first stay in Mao's China (a rite of passage if there be any) until 1973, the Khmer leader gradually freed himself from Vietnamese tutelage, which he resented, and placed himself under the protection of the Chinese Maoists, whose interests he always loyally served because they were the ones who served best his own personal ambitions. Here we find the double game, which was one of the unshakeable elements in relations between Communist countries. Officially, the Party followed a stated policy, but in practice, it did the opposite. This discrepancy was particularly evident in 1972–73 in the Khmer Rouge maquis. From 1972 onward, the break was complete between revolutionaries in the country, and there were armed confrontations between the Vietnamese and Cambodian guerrilla fighters. Officially, however, Samdech Norodom Sihanouk's trip to the liberated zones in March 1973 was organized in complete harmony and cooperation.

We must also recognize that when Saloth Sar went underground in 1963, he joined the Vietminh maquis because he had nowhere else to go. In late 1967, after his protracted Chinese stay, he set up his first Kampuchean base under the protection of his Vietminh friends in Ratanakiri. There he was safely close to the supply line of the Ho Chi Minh trail reaching down from Laos to South Vietnam. He only left that region during the civil war when his old comrades were becoming his enemies. This sharp turn certainly stunned his friends the Khmer *Loeu*, who did not understand how Saloth Sar could turn against the very people who had offered him protection all these years and make them his principal adversaries. They came to the commonsense conclusions that Saloth Sar must have been deceitful all along!

The above slogan makes clear that the criterion for repression was, above all, political and ideological since the selected enemy to annihilate was physically a Khmer who had allegedly betrayed his national identity to embrace that of the "hegemonist" enemy.

Below is a variation on this watchword:

203

ខ្លួនខ្មែរខួរក្បាលយួន

khluen khmaè khue kba:l yuen

Cambodian bodies with Vietnamese brains

3—ENEMIES AMONG THE ORDINARY POPULATION

THOSE WHO DO NOT ADJUST TO COLLECTIVISM

For Khmer Rouge revolutionaries, numerous social groups were liable to be considered superfluous: town dwellers, civil servants, monks, foreigners, and the sick. Excluded were the poor peasants of the periphery, whom the revolutionaries could easily terrorize or flatter with promises of riches and power, especially the young and uneducated. Only one activity found approval in their eyes—"proletarian" labor, that is, work in factories or on the land. Every other activity was considered more or less parasitic, hence a destabilizing element in a new revolutionary order.

204
កញ្ជ្រែងរែងយកតែដើមអង្ករ

kânhchraèng rè:ng yo:k taè daem ângkâ:

The winnowing basket separates the wheat from the chaff.

This traditional saying here is made to mean that the revolution will weed out undesirable elements.

205
សមមិត្តណាមានកុណវិបត្តិច្រើនគឺជាខ្មាំង

samamit na: mien kunvibat chraœn keu: chea khmang

A comrade guilty of many faults is an enemy.

This aphorism shows the utopian view of these revolutionaries who dreamed of purity and perfection.

Among the easily spotted "enemies" were those who adapted with difficulty and did not respect collective ownership:

206
អ្នកណាយក ឬក៏លួចសម្បត្តិរបស់សមូហភាពជាខ្មាំង

néak na: jo:k reu: kâ: luech sâmbat robâh samo:hapieph chie khmang

Those who steal anything from the community are enemies.

This notion of respect for the public good would be admirable in another context, but in Khmer Rouge society *all* property belonged to the state, and such an aphorism could have serious and dramatic implications. For example, starving members of a people's commune had no right to a piece of fruit or a yam or a chicken, nor even a grain of rice in the fields. They could face arrest when, at night, they stole the least bit of food in order to survive. Children could be punished for scavenging for food. As for adults, they could be transported to the nearest district prison. Yet, most people survived by "stealing" food and were not punished—either they evaded surveillance, or some local officials chose to turn a blind eye.

207
អ្នកណាលួចលាក់ដាំបាយហូបឯងជនអ្នកនោះខ្មាំង
néak na: luech léak damba:y ho:p aèkchun néak nuh khmang
Those who boil rice in secret or in private are enemies.

During the first year of the regime and before communal eating was introduced, "new people" were organized into so-called "solidarity groups" of around fifteen families. This was mainly for collective labor and reeducation, but each family prepared food at home. They then had more leisure to complement their rice rations (always lower as time passed) distributed by the *Angkar* by foraging for food in rice paddies or the forest, gathering crabs, frogs, fish, leaves, and herbs according to Khmer ancestral customs. This is why, paradoxically, until the end of 1975 and after five years of civil war, when food was most scarce, there were simply food shortages but no overall famine.

There is some evidence that all this changed at the time of the first harvest in December 1975/January 1976. Whereas during the back-breaking labor of clearing lands, replanting rice, and harvesting, the regime never stopped humming the refrain that everything belonged to the people, in reality 100 percent of the harvest was taken from the laborers. No rice was taken home; instead, it went to collective granaries. Families no longer had the right to cook at home, but had to eat in new collective refectories if they wanted food. Looking for food in the countryside became a "fault," a "crime," but in order to survive, everyone defied this impossible injunction.

THE "17 APRIL PEOPLE"

All the town dwellers, at the moment of the brutal power seizure on 17 April 1975, plus all refugees who had fled revolutionary controlled zones and their collectivist policies in the countryside, became "depositees." Stripped of Cambodian citizenship and legal status, they were called the "17 April people" or "new people." A few slogans refer specifically to them:

208
កន្លែងណាមានពួក១៧មេសា កន្លែងនោះគ្មានការរីកចំរើនទេ
kânlaèng na: mien puek dâb prampi: mésa:
kânlaèng nuh kmien ka: ri:k chomraen té
Where there are "17 April people," no development is possible.

This is a disconcerting assertion, which again throws light on Pol Pot's own declarations. Speaking of towns in general, he averred:

> The enemy is everywhere: in the parliament, the courts, the prisons, the police, and the armed forces. Enemy networks honeycomb the country. The make up of social classes (*samaspheap vanna*) in the towns is very complex and varied.[22]

This citation from the watershed speech of 27 September 1977 contained three ominous truths:

- One, the evacuation of Phnom Penh, and all towns and small market towns in Cambodia, was effected for security reasons. It was the sole means the revolutionaries found to tightly control the general population who were hostile towards them, and to put into place their utopian schemes.

- Two, the Khmer Rouge rejected modern society and all the complexity of its social structure.

- Three, all men, as well as women, children, and the sick from the towns were possibly outcasts in the revolutionary scheme of things. This affirmation contains the germ of logic for the exterminations.

209
អ្នក១៧មេសាជាជនបញ្ញើក្អែក
néak dâb prampi: mésa: chie chun banhaœ kâ'aèk
The "17 April people" are parasitic plants.

The idea of "parasites" or "germs" belongs to a Maoist or Stalinist vocabulary and refers to social, political, or ideological groups that must be closely watched, and eventually eliminated. For the Khmer Rouge, almost half of the population that had been ruralized were irredeemable.

210
ពួកអ្នកថ្មីគ្មានយកអ្វីមក
ក្រៅពីពោះអាចម៍ និងពោះទឹកទេ
puek néak thmey kmien yo:k avey mo:k
krau pi: pueh ach ning pueh teuk té
The new people bring nothing but stomachs full of shit,
and bladders bursting with urine.

This is the sort of declaration the Khmer Rouge made to the old people (*paracheachun chas*) in villages upon the arrival of the wretched from the towns, after the first wave of mass deportation. This slogan equally revealed the atmosphere at the time, awash in mud, sweat, tears, vomit, excrement, and blood! In short, it was the mental and physical environment of a concentration camp universe.[23]

211
ពួក១៧មេសាគឺជាអ្នកចាញ់សង្រ្គាម
puek dâbprampi: mésa: keu: chie néak chanh sângkriem
The "17 April" are the vanquished of war.

We must bear in mind that, during the civil war, from 1970 to 1975, the Khmer Rouge simply executed most of the Republican soldiers they captured or who surrendered. About one-third of the 240,000 people who died at the time were murdered.[24]

212
ពួក១៧មេសាគឺជាអ្នកចាញ់ ជាឈ្លើយសឹក
puek dâbprampi: mésa: keu: chie néaktchanhtchietchlœ:y sœk
The "17 April" are the vanquished and prisoners of war.

Here the Khmer Rouge affirmed that they would consider their compatriots as foreign enemies, defeated in battle. Anthony Reid, in his seminal work *Southeast Asia in the Age of Commerce, 1450–1680: Vol. I, The Lands below the Winds,* explains that it was a centuries-old custom to bring home prisoners of war. And that was precisely what the Khmer Rouge did, since they force-marched large groups of people toward the Northwest and certain forest regions, where their first bases were. Traditionally, in a Southeast Asia not lacking vast, sparsely populated areas, armies did not capture territory but brought home captives as slaves.[25] In imagining a society of the future, the Khmer Rouge only repeated the most ancient and barbaric practices of their ancestors.

In theory, the "17 April people" were clearly identifiable, but in reality they belied this abstract categorization. Mixed among the true town dwellers were refugees from rural zones, including some of the poorest elements of the population. If these "town dwellers," as well as the real members of privileged social groups, had not regained their native villages after evacuation, they were less likely to be denounced and could more easily hide their true identities, escaping classification as "pariah."

However, one more category could only with great difficulty escape the wrath of the new masters of the country: a purely Khmer Rouge creation—the sick.

THE SICK

Another category of citizens especially singled out for the Khmer Rouge's vengefulness was the sick.[26] There is nothing specifically

Maoist in the slogans that follow, except the exaltation of physical labor. In that way the Khmer Rouge diverged from their model. However, it may be admitted, in defense of revolutionaries, that their fellow citizens lacked the work fervor of their Vietnamese and Chinese neighbors. During the regime's first months, when the surveillance machinery had not yet been permanently established throughout the country, many former town dwellers, on a variety of pretexts, exempted themselves from the rude labor in the fields. Hence:

213
ទម្រន់ស្ពឹកទ្រមក់ស្ងួយ
tumrun stuek tro:muek stuy
The slothful are spineless, the sluggish are lazy.

The Khmer Rouge scoffed at the "17 April" whom they accused of laziness and shirking their duties. Once more, a traditional slogan targeted a segment of the population that had fallen into official disfavor.

214
អង្គការចំរាញ់យកតែជនមិនចេះនឿយហត់
ângka: châmranh yo:k taè chun min chèh neuey hât
The *Angkar* only favors those who are indefatigable.

In effect, it was a society that sorted out, selected, and made roundups of suspects. Besides socio-political criteria, selection was based on willingness to work. The above slogan, and others that follow, lend credence to the theory that, when all things are said and done, the "17 April" had been slated from the beginning to be eliminated, but only after the *Angkar* had squeezed the last drop of sweat and blood out of them. In this context, the sick could not be anything other than malingerers, because they could or would not work, and therefore, were sabotaging the revolution. The implications of the following declarations are quite clear.

215
ត្រូវចាំដាច់ខាត ដកចេញមិនខាតមនុស្សខ្ជិលខ្ជាទុកវាធ្វើអ្វី
នាំតែកម្មពៀរត្រូវបញ្ជូនវាទៅឋាននរក

trou cham dach kha:t dâk chènh min kha:t monuh khchi: khchie tukvie thvœ: avey noam taè kampie trou banhchu:n vie tou tha:n noruek

We absolutely must remove [from society] the lazy;
it is useless to keep them, else they will cause trouble.
We have to send them to hell.

216
<u>ឈឺសតិអារម្មណ៍</u>

cheu: saté'a:rom

The sick are victims of their own imagination.

All Cambodians heard these rebukes shouted out at them with violence and unusual harshness every time they had a fever or fell ill. As a general rule, especially if they were "17 April people" who were sick or tired, they were accused of malingering. Worse was when they were suffering from malnutrition and outbreaks of illness, owing to the complete absence of hygiene and modern medicine. Many Cambodians soldiered on and literally worked themselves to death. Usually only the Khmer Rouge cadres, of course, had access to Western medicine.

But the phrase is ambiguous, for in Khmer Rouge parlance សតិអារម្មណ៍ (*saté'arom*) could also mean "ideological frame of mind." In other words, those accused of malingering were behaving so because their minds were infected with the ideology of the old society. Their reeducation had so far failed.

217
ត្រូវបំបាត់អោយអស់ជំងឺសតិអារម្មណ៍ក្រៅសង្គម !

trou bâmbat aoy âh chumngeu: saté'a:rom krau sângkum!

We must wipe out all those who imagine they are ill,
and expel them from our society!

This announcement could signify a death sentence. It could also be quite harmless as a suggestion not to be lazy, not to fall ill.

218

គាត់ហ្នឹងជំងឺសង្គមចាស់ទាល់តែដាក់ថ្នាំលេនីន

koatneung chumngeu: sângkum chah toal taè dak thnam léni:n

If you have the disease of the old society,
take a dose of Lenin as medication.

This assertion might very well be a counter-slogan, if it were said in jest. However, the Khmer Rouge would say it, apparently, without the slightest trace of irony. Moreover, within this collection of slogans on the sick, no one has reported a counter-slogan. The matter was all too serious and painful. If "sick" here is taken in the figurative meaning, we can note the rhyme of the Khmer pronunciation of "quinine," a much-used medicine in Cambodia, with "Lenin."

219

ផ្ដេកផ្សំផ្ដួលរមួលផ្សំក្រេច ឈឺតិចៗ
ថាឈឺខ្លាំង ពួកមិត្តឯងទុកកម៍នចំណេញ ដកចេញក៍មិនខាតដែរ

phdék phsâm phduel ro:muel phsâm krèch chheu: tèch tèch,
tha: chheu: klang puek mit aèng tuk kâ: min châmnènh dâ:k chènh kâ:
min kha:t daè

You take advantage of a fall to pretend to be asleep;
instead of a cramp in the leg,
you pretend you twisted your ankle;
when you are a little ill, you say you are seriously sick.
Comrade, keeping you is no gain, taking you away, no loss!

This traditional expression suggests that the malingerer finds a way of doing the least work possible. It took on a dark meaning for the Khmer Rouge; everyone was forced to go to the rice paddies or work site, even if they were very sick or on the point of dying from starvation. Indeed, some died at work while the Khmer Rouge were accusing them of play-acting.

220
ត្រនញាក់ត្រនញ័រ ត្រនត្រាក់ទ័រត្រនឡាន ត្រនបាយបានត្រនខ្សល់ឱល ត្រនសតិអារម្មណ៍

krunhéak krunhoar krun traktoar krun la:n krun ba:y ba:n
krun khtyâl dil krun saté'a:rom

You shiver with fever, you shake like a tractor, you vibrate like a motor car, you ache for food, you quiver from laziness, you've caught an imaginary disease.[27]

The principal means of ruling over a people is not by force of arms, but through starvation. The sole reward of labor was food twice a day, in communal refectories; anyone who was not at work, including the sick, had their daily food rations reduced.

221
ឈឺបាយបាន

chheu: ba:y ba:n
The sick have a hearty appetite!

This was considered proof they were pretending. In any case, the Khmer Rouge hit upon a cruel, ingenious way to dissuade people from saying that they were ill: they simply reduced their food rations.

222
ឈឺទន្សាយបាយមួយឆ្នាំង

chheu: tunsa:y ba:y muey khlam
The ill are sly as rabbits, and can swallow a whole pot of rice.

In Cambodia, the rabbit has the reputation of slyness and of playing tricks on those who wish to catch it. The slogan is more than unjust because Cambodia teetered between food shortage and famine. The principal cause of sickness was, above all, lack of food. Thus, a sick person on death's doorstep only dreamt of food, the more especially since fish and meat were in very short supply.

223
អ្នកមានជំងឺមិនចាំបាច់ស៊ីទេ ពីព្រោះជំងឺ
វាធ្វើឱ្យបាត់ការស្រេកឃ្លាន ឯការអត់អាហារបណ្តាល
អោយជាសះស្បើយ

néak mien chumngeu: min chambach si: té pi:pruh chumngeu: vie thvœ:
aoy bat ka: srék khlien aè ka: ât a:ha: bânda: aoy chie sah sbaey

The sick do not need to eat, for hunger cuts the appetite.
A good diet will cure you.

There are several words in Khmer for "to eat." The Khmer Rouge wished to simplify the language; they wanted to use only the word ហូប *ho:p*, and not ស៊ី *si:* a more familiar variant. Here, the use of *si:* conveys a hint of irony.

As always in Khmer Rouge doctrine, it starts off with a grain of truth (here, putting the ill on a diet), but applying it to an entire people caused untold sufferings. This directive was applied to the letter in what the Khmer Rouge called "hospitals." These were more often a collection of unsanitary straw huts, or former public buildings, where the bedridden were denied the presence of family and left without food, medication, or the care of competent personnel, in the name of the following directive:

224
មិត្តមិនបាច់ទៅមើលអ្នកជំងឺទេ ពីព្រោះមិត្ត
មិនមែនជាគ្រូពេទ្យ ហើយក៏មិនមែនជាវេជ្ជបណ្ឌិតដែរ
មិនបាច់ទៅមើលអ្នកឈឺទេ មិត្តឯងមិនមែនជាគ្រូពេទ្យទេ

mit min bach tou mœ:l néak chumngeu: té pi:pruh mit
min mè:n chie kru:pèt haœy kâ: min mè:n chie vèchéabândit daè
min bach tou mœ:l néak chheu: té mit aèng min mè:n chie kru:pèt té

> Comrade! It is useless to visit the sick, for you do not belong
> to the medical staff; you are neither nurse nor doctor.

Such an injunction is singularly cruel on many levels. To be refused the moral comfort and support of a loved one was absolutely inhuman. A sick person—and you could only be a very sick person for the *Angkar* to send you to the hospital—could have malaria, beriberi, cholera, or one of the other tropical diseases which had become very widespread, owing to the deplorable lack of sanitary conditions and scarcity of food. Not even a mother or grandmother could visit her child or grandchild. The sick had to agonize alone, with possibly the comforting words of another ill person, equally isolated and uncared for, but who took pity on a neighbor, giving some sugar or a grain of rice carefully hidden away, to suck on before expiring. If a charitable soul was absent, the desperate children would have to lick their putrefying wounds to stay the hunger gnawing at their bowels, and die alone.[28]

The "care" was essentially injections with reused, unsterilized needles of a reddish liquid kept in Coca Cola bottles, or coconut juice—or, traditional medicine in small round balls, which had the shape of "rabbit droppings," as all Cambodians called them. Leaves and plants were collected in the forest by citizens especially assigned to this duty (a very sought-after duty, for it allowed them to eat their fill and work less). The plants were then chopped up, folded, crushed in mortars, and finally shaped into little balls distributed at random to anyone ill, without a medical examination.

No one will ever know how many victims went to these "hospitals." Bodies were never returned to families. People were led to a hospital, the way they were brought to prison, more often than not never to come out alive. Everyone feared going to the hospital; they preferred to remain in their straw huts where at least they benefited from the care of a family member or a neighbor; but they were constrained to go to the hospital when sick.

225 C
ថ្នាំសង្គមកិច្ចដូចអាចម៍ទន្សាយ
thnam sângkum kèch do:ch ach tunsa:y
The medicines from the Ministry of Social Affairs are like rabbit droppings.

226
ធ្វើបដិវត្តន៍មួយចំហៀងខ្លួនក៍ធ្វើបានដែរ
thvœ: padévoat muey châmhieng khluen kâ: thvœ: ba:n daè
You can be part of the revolution even with half of your body.

This saying could have had different interpretations. First, if it was aimed at the very ill or handicapped, it meant that in spite of their physical state, they had to make a superhuman effort to continue working for the *Angkar*, even if that resulted in death through exhaustion.

It also meant that the revolution did not need all the people in order to attain its objectives. It could achieve them with half the social body—the base or old people. And, the revolution could very well do without the other half—the "17 April people"—which had become redundant. The revolution really did not need many people, if they were truly infused with a good revolutionary spirit. That idea was an echo of Mao's thoughts at the time of the Great Leap Forward. In a speech in Moscow in 1957, he is to have said that "he was willing to lose 300 million people—half of China's population. Even if China lost its population, Mao said, the country could suffer no great loss. It could produce more people"![29]

The Khmer Rouge also liked to repeat that they could carry out any action with half the people they used, and boast that they could clap with a single hand! Everything was truly possible for them, and they mocked not only the laws of economics, but also of physics!

4—HIDDEN ENEMIES

In approaching the question of hidden "enemies," we are entering a still murkier zone of Khmer Rouge ideology where it becomes more and more impossible to distinguish between political doctrine and psychosis. In fact, the domestic enemy, who dared not show its face, was simply an opponent of the Pol Pot, ultra-left, Maoist political line. The latter progressively came to believe in the existence of plots from abroad by the great powers' secret services, which for years, if not decades, had worked to sabotage the *Angkar*'s grandiose designs. Hu Nim, a central figure in the Organization, well knew that to appease the torturers at S-21 he had to confess his own crime, which was "to infiltrate the Kampuchean Communist party, the better to destroy it."[30] When we read his forced confession, one wonders if it says more about the paranoia of Pol Pot and the leadership group than about an old militant's treachery, a man who espoused Maoism in his youthful days.

The frightened sycophants surrounding Pol Pot believed everyone in the Party had to put his shoulder to the task of exposing the enemy:

> Our children, youths, workers, peasants, and combatants have also received education in correct and unflinching revolutionary patriotism. They have been taught to draw a clear distinction between the friends and the enemies of their revolution. [applause]
>
> It is absolutely necessary to draw a clear line between us and the enemy . . . First of all, we must determine who we are . . . so that we can detect the enemy which is planted within our revolutionary rank, . . . distinguish clearly the collective system, the revolution of the Party of the proletariat and from the system of private property of anti-proletarian classes, and the CPK from another antinational, counterrevolutionary sham party . . .
>
> This does not mean all of us clearly know the enemy and have

drawn a clear distinction between ourselves and the enemy. Many joined the revolution at first and later switched to the enemy's side against the revolution . . . To know the enemy well is to have a resolute political, ideological, political and organisational stand geared for the fight against the enemy to the end. Knowing the enemy without the determination to fight him to the end is useless . . .

In the past, the enemies, running dogs of all stripes, planted within the cooperatives, sabotaged the three-ton-per-hectare target of our Party and cooperatives. This was possible, because some of our cadres and comrades were not sufficiently vigilant to cleanse them of enemy elements. In other words, the movement whipped up to wipe out the enemy planted within the cooperatives was not vigorous enough. This allowed saboteurs to carry on their activities. The explanation is that the stand of drawing a clear line between the cooperatives and the enemy planted within them, is not firm and resolute.

. . . The enemy shall and will always remain an enemy . . . Only when you have a seething hatred of the enemy, . . . you will remain vigilant in your efforts to weed out and exterminate the enemy planted within the cooperatives, trade unions, and units, and completely succeed in solving the problem of the people's livelihood by making every effort to fulfil the three-ton-per-hectare and six-ton-per-hectare goals ordered by the Party, endeavouring with a constantly burning enthusiasm to carry out all tasks entrusted by the Party.

This editorial always returns to the imperious necessity for each and everyone to be moved by "a boiling hatred against the enemy," who "must be exterminated at all costs."[31] Those quotes contain the rationality that led to the extermination of some two million Cambodians in the three years, eight months, and twenty days of the regime.[32]

THE ENEMY INSIDE THE PARTY

227

បក្សស្អាតគឺបក្សខ្លាំង ចលនាបដិវត្តខ្លាំង

pak sa'a:t keu: pak khlang cholena padévoat khlang

A clean Party means a strong Party
and a strong revolutionary movement.

228

ក្របីលាក់ខ្លួនពួនសម្រួចស្នែង
ដល់ពេលទឹកលិចត្រែងទើបចេញវាល

krobey léak khluen puen somruech snaèng
dâl pél teuk léch traèng tœ:p chénh viel

A buffalo hides to sharpen his horns.
When the water floods, the reeds come out.

In the two sayings of this last slogan the Khmer Rouge uses a poetic form, with an internal rhyme in [*aèng*]. They "imply that enemies burrow within the revolution in order to build up strength to destroy the revolution" from within.[33]

229

ក្នុងការបំផុសចលនាមហាជនអោយខ្លាំងក្លានោះ ត្រូវបំផុសតាមម៉ាត៉ា នយោបាយរបស់បក្សកុំបំផុសតាមអត្តនោម័ត គឺកុំឆ្វេងកុំស្តាំ បើឆ្វេង គឺខ្មាំងបង្កាប់ស៊ីរុងផ្ទៃក្នុង វាដុតអោយខ្លោចថែម បើស្តាំ គឺខ្មាំងបង្កាប់ស៊ីរុងផ្ទៃក្នុង វារោចអោយឆៅ

knong ka: bomphoh châlana mohachun aoy khlang khla nuh trou bomphâh tammiekie no yobay robâh pak kom bâmphohtam atanaomat keu:kom chvéng kom sdam bae chvéng keu: khmang bângkâb si: ru:ng phtey knong vie dot aoy khlaoc thaèm bae sdam keu: khmang bângkâb si rûng phtey knong vie ro:ch aoy chhau

If you want to make our entire people understand most clearly,
they must be made to follow the political leadership of the Party.

> Don't follow your own personal opinion; don't be leftist or rightist. If you are a leftist, you are a hidden enemy eating from inside, burning and smoldering; if you are a rightist, you are a hidden enemy eating from inside, taking out [food from the fire] while it is still raw.

This series of recommendations given to cadres uses rhetoric common to Communist regimes, particularly to the Maoists. However, here the apparent balance between extremes of moderation and radicalism in revolution was purely rhetorical. *Angkar* orders and watchwords from the Standing Committee repeatedly required local cadres to implement ever more radical Maoist policies, surpassing the worst excesses of both the Great Leap Forward and the Cultural Revolution, at least as far as education was concerned. This kind of discourse was heard during nightly meetings in the collectives.

The most common tactic used by the Khmer Rouge to catch the hidden enemy was, metaphorically, this old method of catching fish in Cambodia:

230
ចង់និយាយអី និយាយ ចង់ធ្វើអី ធ្វើ ប៉ុន្តែត្រូវយកកំពិសស្ទូចបង្កង
châng niyey ey niyey chong tvœ: ey tvœ: pontaè trou yo:k kompeuh stu:ch bongkong
You want to speak, speak; you want to work, work;
but you must use a shrimp to catch a prawn.

In other words, "enemies" could be ensnared and unmasked with sweet words that flattered their prejudices. One could use something that looked small and harmless to trick them. However, most people were not fooled by the bait. They recognized the trick and remained silent and apparently submissive.

THE ENEMY THAT WEARS A MASK

231
ខ្មាំងចេញមុខ ខ្មាំងលាក់មុខ

khmang chénh mukh, khmang léak mukh

There are enemies who bare their faces to all;
there are enemies who wear masks.

Few slogans, if any, strongly evoke the mentality of the Khmer Rouge leadership. Those that follow disclose its collective psychosis. They show the universe of what resembles a sect in the throes of delirium manipulated by a guru rather than a modern country with a two-thousand-year history.

232
ចូរសមមិត្តប្រយ័ត្ន ចំពោះអ្នកនៅជិតយើង
គេអាចជាខ្មាំងបង្កប់ !

cho: samamit prâ:yat châmpuh néak nou chit yœ:ng
ké a:ch chie khmang bângkâp

Beware of the people at your side; they could be secret agents!

This type of counsel is characteristic of internal orders to the Khmer Rouge *nomenklatura* and remind us of the People's Republic of China in the heyday of the Cultural Revolution.

233
សំលៀកបំពាក់បិទបាំងរាងកាយបាន
តែមិនអាចបិទបាំងពូជអំបូរបានទេ

sâmliek bompéak bet bang rieng kay ba:n
taè min ach bet bang puch ombo: ba:n té

Clothes can hide the body, but they can't hide the origin.

234

ត្រូវតែកំចាត់ចោលនូវខ្មាំងរូបភាព
និងអរូបភាព ខ្មាំងសតិអារម្មណ៍ !

trou taè kâmchat chaol nou khmang ru:phiep
ning aru:phiep khmang saté'a:râm

You must destroy the visible enemy,
and the hidden one, too—the enemy in the mind!

Khmer Rouge militants and all of the people had the mission to hunt down the enemy even in their very own hearts and souls. The task was an arduous one since this amounted to a philosophical task, for the "enemy" could wear the face of an angel, and one must distinguish truth from lies, the sincere supporter of the revolution from a simulator. One had to learn to distinguish truth from falsehood. This infernal quest could not reach a satisfactory conclusion, for which of the accused could swear, under the mortal threat of the interrogator, never to have entertained—in his heart of hearts—the slightest thought of rebellion, or simply doubt, about the revolution? Purifying Cambodian society proved an impossible task.

The quest for ideological purity was common to all Communist regimes and did not stop at the perpetrators: the enemy "has hidden and buried itself inside our flesh and blood," Pol Pot would say.[34] He was here echoing a warning of Ho Chi Minh who claimed that the enemy was within the heart of each and every one.[35]

235

ប្តេជ្ញាកំទេចអោយអស់ខ្មាំងស៊ីរុងផ្ទៃក្នុង
សេអ៊ីអាកាហ្គេបេ (គូមីនតាំង) !

pdachnha: kâmtéch aoy âh khmang si:ru:ng phteyknong
sé i: a: ka: gé bé (kuemintang)

Be prepared to annihilate the CIA and KGB (and Kuomintang),
enemies gnawing at our society from inside.

Numerous, too, are *Angkar* orders which use the imagery of a worm in the apple or of the ship of state rotting from within so that it sinks. They sought ceaselessly to strengthen the *Angkar*'s control over all people's collectives, work units, and hearts and minds, since conversations were spied on even at night.

We see once again that the CIA is linked to the KGB! In some people's communes, there were a number of Chinese, who, in Cambodia, were reputed to have sympathized with the Kuomintang, and thus, were considered counterrevolutionaries.

236
ដាំទឹកឱ្យពុះចាក់ក្នុងប្រហុកទើបឃើញដង្កូវ
dam teuk aoy puh chak knong prâhok tœ:p khœ:nh dângkou
Boil water and pour it over the *prahok*,
only then will you see the worms come out!

The Khmer Rouge adopted this traditional saying and gave it another spin. Metaphorically, pouring boiling water here suggests mental pressure or physical torture of suspected persons to confess their treachery.

237
មិនអនុញ្ញាតឱ្យដង្កូវចូលរុករានក្នុងសាច់ទាល់តែសោះ
min anunha:t aoy dângkou cho:l rukrien knong sach toal taè sâh
Do not ever let the worm wriggle under your skin.

238
មិនអនុញ្ញាតឱ្យដង្កូវចូលស៊ីរុងផ្ទៃក្នុង
min anunha:t aoy dângkou cho:l si: ru:ng phtey knong
Never allow the worm to gnaw at your bowels.

This slogan is also an old adage. It basically meant that every leader had to pay great attention so that people of whom the *Angkar* was unsure could never penetrate the power structure. If it was aimed at the ordinary people, it alerted them not to be swayed by revisionist doctrines. During purges that decimated the Party and the army, especially in 1977 and 1978, victims were always accused of being "worms who gnawed from within the Party."

239
បើចង់វាយសត្រូវឈ្នះ ត្រូវវាយសត្រូវក្នុងខ្លួន
bae châng viey satrou chhnéah trou viey satrou knong khluen
If you wish to destroy the enemy,
you must destroy the enemy within your own person!

The enemy became ever more internalized and drew nearer and nearer to the center of power, as this recommendation put forward during reeducation sessions shows. No ordinary citizen, no cadre, however high his position was, could be spared from lurking suspicion and then repression. The ruthless extermination system established by the *Angkar* inexorably cast doubt about the ideological integrity of everyone, including oneself. That reality can be illustrated by an interview of Laurence Picq, the wife of a Khmer Rouge official who worked with Ieng Sary at the Ministry of Foreign Affairs under DK.[36] Inside the ministry, Ieng Sary enjoined his underlings to denounce all the traitors who were hiding in the various departments. Those who refused to inform on others were threatened with accusations of treachery themselves. Laurence Picq even added, "According to him, we all had an enemy within ourselves. And, in order to struggle against that enemy, we were to ponder over his teachings from morning when we opened our eyes till the night."[37]

240
ត្រូវប្តេជ្ញាកំទេចឱ្យអស់ខ្មាំងស៊ីរូងផ្ទៃក្នុង«ខ្មាំងបង្កប់»

trou pdachnha: kâmtéch aoy âh khmang si:ru:ng phtey knong khmang bângkâ:p!

Be determined to annihilate the enemy who saps from within, the infiltrated enemy.

241
ខ្មាំងអង្គការ ខ្មាំងប្រជាជន ខ្មាំងសតិអារម្មណ៍ ខ្មាំងស៊ីរូងផ្ទៃក្នុង !

khmang ângka:, khmang prâchiechun, khmang saté'a:râm khmang si:ru:ng phtey knong

The enemy of the *Angkar* is the enemy of the people, the enemy by his cast of mind, the enemy gnawing from inside!

As in all Communist and tyrannical regimes, any political opposition, any rebellious thoughts, were not only equated to an opposition to the constitution, but as a betrayal of the people and the nation.

242
រៀនពីបដិវត្ត ដើម្បីវាយបកបដិវត្តវិញ

rien pi: padévoat dambey vieiy bâ:k padévoat vinh

Learn from the revolution to be able in return to fight the revolution.

This slogan is quoted by Ben Kiernan in his *The Pol Pot Regime: Race, Power, and Genocide in Cambodia under the Khmer Rouge, 1975–79.*[38] A note tells us that it was found in a report written by Duch (Kaing Khek Ieuv), director of S-21, the torture-interrogation center in Phnom Penh, which was transformed into a genocide museum named Tuol Sleng by the Vietnamese in 1979. This watchword clearly explains the logic of Duch's mission which consisted precisely in tracking down "enemies" within the state apparatus, who were purported to be using the Party's own tactics of secrecy and underground plotting.

243
បើទុកជាចកសូត្រធម៌ទាំងយប់ទាំងថ្ងៃយ៉ាងណាក៏ដោយ កូនពពែនៅតែមិនទុកចិត្តដែរ

bae tuk chie châchâk so:thoa téang yup téang tngay yang na kâ: daoy
kâ: ko:n popè: nou taè men tuk chet daè

**The wolf can say prayers night and day;
the kid will not trust him.**

One can suppose that this traditional saying was given to cadres at study sessions by Khieu Samphan to warn them against the false pretenses of the "17 April people" or those who claimed they had been won over to defend the revolutionary cause.

244
ចិត្តជាចក្រពត្តិ មាត់ជាអង្គការ

chèt chie chakrâpoat moat chie ângka:

Your heart is imperialist; your mouth only speaks of the *Angkar*!

This paraphrases a well-known Buddhist maxim admonishing against hypocrisy:

ចិត្តជាទេវទត្ត មាត់ជាទេវតា

chèt chie tévotoat moat chie tévoda:

"Your heart is like Devadatt's, your mouth like a *tevada*."

Devadatt was a cruel prince who tortured his parents, the king and queen, during the Buddha's time. The *tevadas* are angels in Buddhist mythology. It is an affirmation that again sees a potential "enemy" in every citizen.[39]

HE WHO COMPLAINS SHALL DIE!

245

តវ៉ាខ្មាំង ប្រឆាំងខ្មោច

tâ:va: khmang prâ:chhang khmaoch

He who protests is an enemy; he who opposes is a corpse!

Sometimes, it is difficult to express briefly in English what is said with such brutality in Khmer language. These are four words that cut with the sharpness of a well-honed blade: *protest, enemy, oppose, corpse!* Everything is told with these four words! The alliteration of *khm* and the assonance of *ang* make the words resonate with terror and must have frozen the blood of those who heard them.

246

បើអ្នកណាឃ្លានខ្លាំង
អង្គការនឹងនាំទៅកន្លែងសំបូរហូបចុក

bae néak na: khlien khlang
angka: ning noam tou kânlaèng sâmbo: ho:p chok

**If someone is very hungry,
the *Angkar* will take him where he will be stuffed with food.**[40]

Like the Nazis, the Khmer Rouge wished to make the best use of the corpses of their victims—the "17 April people" or their "enemies." They considered that human remains constituted the best possible fertilizer and were therefore associated with plentiful food. This threat means that every citizen complaining of hunger could be expediently reduced to fertilizer.

Corpses were put at the foot of fruit trees, even those of people who died in the collectives without being violently murdered, since customary incineration and funeral rites had been abolished. The victims of mass executions could be thrown into the rice fields, when they were not put in shallow pits.

It could be that the ashes of those who had been incinerated with straw in open pits, as at Ta Kriem, Banan district, Battambang province, were then spread in the rice fields.[41] Worse still, it appears that in Preykabas district, Takeo province, the *Angkar* forced its local population to exhume cadavers to tear away the flesh from the bones to scatter it into the rice fields.[42]

247
បើមិនជួយច្រុកជួយចែវ កុំយកជើងរាទឹក

bae min chuey cho:k chuey chaèv, kom jo:k chœ:ng rie teuk

If you don't want to help others to make the small boat move on,
don't block its progress with your leg.

The Khmer Rouge gave a new meaning to this traditional saying: any individual who does not contribute to the advance of revolution must be eliminated.

***

Now we come to a crafty trick—the invitation to self-denunciation. Whereas this could give reason to hope that there would be forgiveness for the repentant, it is in fact heavy with menace for those who talk. In this Machiavellian and violent society, the accusers always artfully balanced to their advantage the promise of rewards and the implicit threat of terror.

248
អង្គការមិនចាប់កំហុសសមមិត្តទេ
អោយតែសមមិត្តរាយការណ៏នូវបណ្ដាញខ្មែរយះខ្មាំង

ângka: min chap kâmhoh samamit té
aoy taè samamit rieyka: nou bânda:nh khsaè royéak khmang

Your past faults mean little to the *Angkar*, comrades,
so long as you reveal all enemy networks.

Khmer Rouge leaders often had recourse to this watchword during meetings and tried to persuade the people to be willing to disclose everything they knew about the regime's "enemies." If anyone volunteered such information, they had to be wary for the Khmer Rouge would sooner or later put him under arrest. In truth, they were convinced that if people had any information, it was a sure sign that they were accomplices of dangerous individuals.

It also happened that if informers were not immediately arrested, they would surely be within two or three months, in order for them to continue naming names to the *Angkar*. To make them feel at ease, they might even be given some responsibility in people's communes or even enlisted in the army. Yet, since they had talked, they were considered dangerous, and sooner or later, would mysteriously disappear. And, no doubt, they would be taken to the district prison, where, under threats and torture, they had to give over more "enemy" names, real or imaginary.[43]

249
បើមិត្តហ៊ាននិយាយ មិត្តត្រូវទទួលខុសត្រូវដោយខ្លួនឯង
bae mit hien niyiey mit trou to:tuel khohtrou daoy kʰluen aèng
If you dare say anything, comrade,
you must take full responsibility for your own words.

5—THE THREAT OF PRISON

250
ខ្សែទន់ទើបចងចំណងល្អ
khsaè tun tœ:p châ:ng chomnâ:ng lâ'â:
A flexible string can make a good knot.

This recommendation was given to cadres to make it clear to them that, when they arrested an enemy, they had better take any available string or cloth (often a *krâma*) to tie his hands tightly behind his back.

251
សមមិត្តណាក្បត់ទឹសដៅអង្គការកាត់ទោស ខ្លួនឯងជាទមួន់ ហើយដាក់ច្រវាក់ខ្នោះឃ្នាងខ្លួនឯង

samamit na: kbât teuh dau ângka: kat to:h khluen aèng chie tumngun haœy dak chrâvak khnâh khnieng khluen aèng

Comrade, if you betray the *Angkar*, you have severely condemned yourself and put on shackles and irons.

It should be pointed out that the Khmer word ខ្នោះ [*knoh*] means sliding iron rings on a long iron bar, the length depending on the number of detainees. The number of rings varied as well. They were attached to the ankles, thereby preventing the one chained from even standing up and were, therefore, the sole means the revolutionaries used to make escape impossible.

It is very surprising that the Khmer Rouge uttered such threats, for the leg irons for Cambodians were traditionally associated with prisons. And the revolutionaries were very careful to keep the existence of these sinister institutions a secret—officially, at least. It was nevertheless an open secret, since everyone knew that there were such terrible places of internment and torture from whence few came back alive, or so it seemed. It was necessary however that the threat of prison was well known, so that it could dissuade action against the government. Here again we run up against another contradiction of the regime: prisons had to be a well-kept secret, but everyone knew about them; yet, they projected an aura of mystery and thus, in the mind's eye, became the more horrific.

252
សមមិត្តណាបំពានច្បាប់អង្គការ ត្រូវដាក់គុកខ្លួនឯង

samamit na: bâmpien chbab ângka: trou dak kuk khluen aèng

He who breaks the *Angkar's* laws condemns himself to prison.

253

សមមិត្តណាបើល្មើសនិងច្បាប់អង្គការ
ទោះទៅទីណាត្រូវដាក់គុកពី២០ ទៅ៣០ឆ្នាំ

samamit na: bae lmœ:h ning chbab ângka:
tueh tou ti: na: trou dak kuk pi: mophey tou sa:msèp chhnam

Every comrade who breaks the *Angkar*'s laws
shall be put behind bars for twenty or thirty years.

254

ផ្ទះថ្មីគឺជាគុក

phtéah thmâ: keu: chie kuk

Permanent structure buildings are prisons.

This declaration is revealing. It shows, firstly, that most Khmer Rouge came from regions of the periphery where concrete buildings were virtually unknown. Secondly, buildings such as villas, Chinese shop houses, pagodas, or schools, and administrative buildings of every description, were used as semi-permanent detention centers. Under the Khmer Rouge, when *Angkar* refers to ផ្ទះថ្មី *(phtéah thmâ)*, it often meant a prison.

255

សូវចាប់មនុស្សច្រឡំ កុំអោយតែលែងច្រឡំ

sou chap monuh chrâlâm kom aoy taè lè:ng chrâlâm

You can arrest someone by mistake;
never release him by mistake.

This inhuman assertion flies in the face of justice and throws to the winds the liberal tradition of *habeas corpus*. It turns on its head a fundamental precept of justice that it is better to release a guilty man than to condemn an innocent one. In affirming this, the Khmer Rouge did nothing more than copy and endorse a basic rule of the Vietminh penal system: "better arrest an innocent person than leave a guilty one free" or "it is less dangerous to keep someone in prison for too long than to release him too soon."[44] After all, it matters little if an innocent is slaughtered, since it is for a good cause! As in all revolutionary Communist regimes, the end justifies the means. In the Khmer Rouge's mindset, this was proof of the spirit of sacrifice, as though the man had given his life for his country. They found great merit in dying for one's country, even if it was by mistake!

In the name of such a principle, in any number of detention centers throughout the country, tens of thousands, or perhaps hundreds of thousands of completely innocent victims, were massacred. The *Angkar*, despite long and thorough investigations, found no proof of guilt for the majority of those detained. They were solely judged on the basis of the whims of their interrogators/torturers. The suspicions that dwelt in the minds of their executioners were proof enough. When in doubt, execute!

256
សម្លាប់ច្រឡំអ្នកដែលគ្មានទោសកំហុសម្នាក់
ជាជាងទុកឱ្យសល់ខ្មាំងសត្រូវម្នាក់ !
sâmlap chrâlâm néak daèl kmien to:h kâmhoh mnéak
chie chieng tuk aoy sâl khmang satrou mnéak
Better to kill an innocent by mistake
than spare an enemy by mistake!

The following slogan repeats the same idea:

257
សុខចិត្តចាប់ខុស១០ មិនអោយលែងខុស១ !
sokh chèt chap khoh dâb min aoy lè:ng khoh muey
Better to arrest ten innocent people by mistake
than free a single guilty party!

258
ទុកមិនចំណេញ ដកចេញក៏មិនខាត
tuk min châmnénh, dâ:k chénh kâ: min kha:t
No gain in keeping, no loss in weeding out[45]

This slogan was among the most well-known countrywide during the days of Khmer Rouge rule, and, without doubt, owing to its rigid logic, is the one cited by the students of Khmer Rouge ideology. True, it contains in its terseness the germ of a political program, a plan for mass murders by the *Angkar*. The metaphor of the second verb *dah* suggests the clearing of a field, to uproot all poisonous weeds, before sowing the good seed. The new society thus had to begin again from scratch. All the survivors of those days said as much. And it is with such watchwords that the Khmer Rouge could be accused of possessing the cold-blooded will to organize and plan from the center of government the extermination of a whole stratum of Cambodian society.

Father François Ponchaud, in his well-known book *Cambodia Year Zero,* mentioned "the well-known quip" (I presume heard over the radio, or reported by witnesses who fled the country) "we need but two million young people to create the new Kampuchea."[46] The facts seem to point out that such could well have been the *Angkar*'s intention. Nevertheless, no one ever reported this assertion to me, and it has now disappeared from the American version of François Ponchaud's book.[47]

259
ស្លាប់ជាការធម្មតារបស់អ្នកតស៊ូ
slap chie ka: tomeda robâh néak tâ:su:
To die is banal for the one who fights heroically.

Life had little value for the Khmer Rouge leadership—especially as they were jeopardizing the life of others to satisfy the leadership's own thirst for power. Since the above warlike rhetoric applied also to economic production, everyone was to be a warrior in this heroic battle, and no one's life was to be spared.

6—THE WHEEL OF HISTORY

260
បើជំទាស់នឹងផែនការបក្ស ខុសដៃយកដៃ
ខុសជើងយកជើង

bae chumtoah ning phaènka: pak khoh day yo:k day
khoh chœ:ng yo:k chœ:ng

Whoever opposes the Party's policies
and does wrong with his arm, his arm shall be taken.
Whoever does wrong with his leg, his leg shall be taken.

Here we have, side by side, a Khmer Rouge command and a traditional saying. The saying means that in the traditional chain of command, when the lower level commits an error, the superior will punish him accordingly.

261
កង់ប្រវត្តិសាស្ត្រវិលទៅមុខជានិច្ច បើអ្នកណាជំទាស់
ប៉ះដៃកិនដៃប៉ះជើងកិនជើង

kâng prâvoatèsah vil tou mukh chienich bae néak na: chumtoah
pah day, kèn day pah chœ:ng kèn chœ:ng

As the wheel of history inexorably turns, if you are in its path
and if it touches your arm, it will crush it;
if it catches your leg, it will roll over that, too.

In this slogan Communist doctrine and the ancient Hindu mythology meet. Marx and his disciples were convinced that they alone had found the true meaning of the history of mankind: the glorious (if not bloody) march towards a Communist society. Nothing, then, could stop the inevitable progression of history. Since all the revolutionaries who fought for the proletarian revolution were engaged in a good cause, all means for attaining it were good.

Mao Zedong evoked the same image in his *Little Red Book*:

> This is an objective law, independent of man's will. However much the reactionaries try to hold back the wheel of history, sooner or later revolution will take place and will inevitably triumph. Communism is at once a system . . . the most complete, progressive, revolutionary, rational in human history . . . The Communist ideological and social system alone is full of youth and vitality, sweeping the world with the momentum of an avalanche and the force of a thunderbolt.[48]

Mao and Pol Pot built for eternity, "for a period of one hundred, one thousand, or ten thousand years."[49] Nuon Chea, president of the Assembly of the People's Representatives, during a mass meeting on 16 January 1977 in Phnom Penh commemorating the ninth anniversary of the Revolutionary Army of Democratic Kampuchea, said:

> We liberated our country on 17 April 1975 . . . We did that for the defence of Democratic Kampuchea, for the Cambodian workers and peasants in cooperatives, for the next decade, the next century, the next millennium, the next ten thousand years, and forever.[50]

Two other almost identical slogans are:

262
កង់ប្រវត្តិសាស្ត្រវិលទៅមុខជានិច្ច បើអ្នកណាជំទាស់
លុកដែរដាច់ដែលុកជើងដាច់ជើង

kâng prâvoatésah vil tou mukh chie nich bae néak na chumtoah
lu:k day dach day lu:k chœung dach chœ:ng

As the wheel of history inexorably turns, if you are in its path
and if you stick out your arm, your arm shall be cut;
if you stick out your leg, your leg shall be cut.

263
កង់ប្រវត្តិសាស្ត្រវិលជានិច្ច
អ្នកណាដើរមិនទាន់កង់ប្រវត្តិសាស្ត្រកិន

kâng prâvoatèsah vil chienich
néak na: dae min toan kâng prâvoatèsah kèn

The wheel of history is inexorably turning:
he who cannot keep pace with it shall be crushed.

Or even more abruptly:

264
ដើរមិនទាន់គេកង់បដិវត្តន៍កិន

dae min toan ké kâng padévoat kèn

He who does not move forward fast enough
will be crushed by the wheel of history.

Lastly, here is a more Khmer metaphor:

265
ទោះជាមាន់មិនរងាវក៏ដោយ ក៏ព្រះអាទិត្យរះដែរ

tuh chie moan min ro:ngieu kâ: daoy kâ: préak atet réah daè

Even if the cock does not sing, the sun will still rise.

Khieu Samphan, Hu Nim, and Vorn Vet

Ieng Sary

Chapter V

LABOR

Article 12 of Democratic Kampuchea's constitution proclaimed that all Khmers "had the right to work" and that "there is no unemployment in Democratic Kampuchea."[1] Witnesses are unanimous that the country had become a giant public works project. Before, as was usual in the regions where a one-crop economy of rice prevailed, Cambodian peasants worked hard only about half of the year. This included plowing, sowing, and replanting—a backbreaking task often performed by women. This was followed, five months later, by harvesting the single crop of rice during the dry season. Under the Khmer Rouge, this age-old rhythm was shattered; the country became an immense work site, closer to the *laogais* of Mao's China, or an extension of Chinese prisons, instruments of "reform through work." The Khmer people were sentenced there for life, since, according to the *Angkar*'s dreams, the regime would know no end.

Without exception, Cambodians who lived under the Khmer Rouge remembered, aside from the ever present reign of terror and food shortages, only one thing: you had to work, work, and work forever! Very many slogans (some already cited in earlier chapters) dealt with that imperative. The Khmer Rouge were convinced that leisure and holidays—of great value in Cambodian tradition— were so essentially reprehensible that they had to be abolished! Thanks to a tenfold increase in the average citizen's productivity, Cambodia was suddenly going to make a great leap forward into the twentieth century. Moreover, work was understood as nothing more than manual labor, by a perverse twist of fundamentalist Maoism. All other human activities were considered parasitic, save for the duties of leadership and repression, of course, reserved for Party cadres and the army.

There were no such things as rest periods, for outside the time of rice planting, inhabitants had to labor relentlessly to complete, by hand, grandiose irrigation projects. On the other hand, the regime's leaders sought unstintingly to dramatically increase rice production by resettling people in remote border zones, in dense or sparse forest areas, to clear and prepare for so-called "strategic crops" (like maize, cassava, etc.). In these faraway zones, the task fell to shock troops of young people; in areas closer to the vast Tonle Sap lake in the central plains, the work was done by the general population. The goal was, here, there, and everywhere, the same: to dramatically increase rice yields. The great hardships inflicted on the Cambodian people are well known. The results were pathetic. People were displaced in the most incoherent ways: for example, many town dwellers from Kompong Som had been resettled in the jungles of Koh Kong, while many fields at the base of Mount Bokor, in Kampot province, had been abandoned.

Still, in the sacrosanct principle of self sufficiency, a watchword guiding the revolutionary country to "rely solely on its own resources," and in the ideal of "independence and national sovereignty"[2] taught by Mao, Cambodia, bled white after five long years of civil war, always had to export more rice to the People's Republic of China, bartering it for all manufactured goods. Hence, it imported from the "Asian Communist metropolis" the instruments necessary for rice growing and weapons necessary for keeping the people in place. The more the Khmers worked, the more their executioners possessed the instruments for the people's enslavement: the Cambodians were forced to forge their own chains. In a number of speeches directed at the general population, it became apparent that the fruits of their labor were for export. "In less than two years, Cambodia has not only solved the food problem, but has also saved a quantity of farm products which can be used for national economic building."[3] So announced the omnipresent Sun Hao, the People's Republic of China's ambassador and doyen of the diplomatic corps, at a reception given by Ieng Sary, minister of foreign affairs, commemorating the second anniversary of 17 April 1975 and proclaiming it the "victory and birth of Democratic Kampuchea." The ambassador knew of what he spoke, since his country received thousands of tons of rice, arriving in full trainloads from the port of Kompong Som for shipment to China.[4]

As in Mao's China (recall his famous saying, "work is struggle"[5]), Khmer Rouge rhetoric equated work with war. Cambodia's rice fields in the central plains were "rear bases"; the newly cleared zones grew crops deemed "strategic," like yams; these were designated "first" or "front line" areas. It is interesting to observe that, after seizing power in Phnom Penh, the Khmer Rouge only continued using the same policies they applied during years of guerrilla warfare in the maquis, "developing their war-time life style," as His Excellency Sun Hao remarked approvingly.[6]

1—WORK HARD

GENERAL DIRECTIVES

The general idea was that, in the context of the Super Great Leap Forward, if someone did not work for the revolution, his life was worthless.

266
រស់នៅត្រូវធ្វើការ !
ruh nou trou thvœ:ka:
While alive, you must work!

267

ត្រូវរស់នៅឱ្យរឹងដូចក្ដារបន្ទះ
ហើយឱ្យទន់ដូចចង្វាយនំបញ្ចុក

trou rueh nou aoy reung do:ch kda: bântèah
haey aoy tun do:ch chângva:y num bânhchok

**In order to live, become hard like plywood
and soft like vermicelli.**

In a revolutionary society, you had to be, above all, courageous, but also supple, knowing how to adapt to all difficult circumstances. The threat of death for sluggards is here implicit.

268

អ្នកដែលមិនបញ្ចេញពលកម្មដេកស្រួល ត្រូវឱ្យបង្កបង្កើតផល

néak daèl min bânhchénh pulakam dék sruel trou aoy bângkâ:
bângkaetphâl

**Those who have never labored but slept comfortably,
those must be made to produce fruit.**

This watchword makes it clear that the townspeople, who in the eyes of the Khmer Rouge were nothing but idle parasites, must be set to hard work in the fields and contribute to massive agricultural production.

269

មិនត្រូវជិះជាន់កំលាំង ពលកម្មគេទេ
មិត្តត្រូវចេងងឯករាជ្យម្ចាស់ការ !

min trou chih choan kâmlang pulekam ké té
mit trou chèh aèkriech mchah ka:

**Do not exploit the work of others, comrades,
but rely on your own strength!**

270

ចិតតែការងាររបស់អ្នកទៅ កុំរវល់នឹងការងារអ្នកដទៃ

Ket taè ka:gnie roboh néak tou kom rovul neng ka:ngie néak dâ: tey

Always think of your own job;
don't interfere with other people's jobs!

This was a capital command. Every worker should attend to his own business and leave other people alone. This enabled the *Angkar* to totally atomize the society and made it easier for the leadership to wield its absolute authority.

271

ចាបដល់ពេលអរុណរះ ចាបតែងតែហើរទៅរកស្រែចំការ
គឺមិនដែលស្រែចំការហើរមករកចាបទេ

cha:p dâl pél arunréah cha:p taèng taè hae tou rok sraè chomka:
keu men daèl sraè chomka: hae mok rok chap té

At dawn, birds fly towards the fields;
never do fields fly towards the birds.

This traditional saying means, in the context of Democratic Kampuchea, that everyone had to get up before dawn in order to get ready to do farm labor before the first glimpse of the rising sun.

272

គ្មានថ្ងៃអាទិត្យទេ មានតែថ្ងៃចន្ទ

kmien tgnay a:tit té mien taè tngay chan

There are no Sundays; there are only Mondays.

Monday being the first day of the week, this means every single day of the week is a working day with the Khmer Rouge.

***

Any number of slogans strongly incited the general population to follow the lead of model workers, not malingerers. We find here a traditional saying that becomes quite ominous in the context of life under Democratic Kampuchea:

273
បានស្រួលប្រឹង ដល់តឹងប្រះ

ba:n sruel prœng dâl tœng prah

When everything is easy to obtain, you apply yourself;
when everything is difficult, you give up.

This very same idea could equally be expressed by another traditional saw:

274
ធូរប្រឹង តឹងប្រះ

thu: prœng tœng prah

When things are easy, you tire yourself;
when things are difficult, you shun work.

Village militia gladly used earthy metaphors:

275
រស់នៅត្រូវធ្វើការផង ត្រូវសន្សំសំចៃផងជាមួយបងៗ
ពុកម៉ែមីងមា កុំចាំតែស៊ី ដូចមាន់ដូចទា
ត្រូវបំពេញការងារដែលបក្សប្រគល់ជូន

ruhnou trou thvœ:ka: phâ:ng trou sânsâm sâmchay phâ:ng chie muey
bâ:ngbâ:ng pukmaè mingmie kom cham taè si: do:ch moan do:ch tie
trou bâmpénh ka:ngie daèl pak prâkul chu:n

Since you are alive, you have to work and save, along with your
brothers and sisters, fathers and mothers, uncles and aunts, and
not wait to be fed, like chickens and ducks.
You have to accomplish the goal the Party assigned you.

It is tempting to state that members of farm collectives were accused of waiting for their daily pittance like farmyard animals awaiting their daily ration of grain; indeed, the Khmer Rouge treated them like beasts of burden.

276
ធ្វើការដៃមួយ ទទួលបបរដៃពីរ
thvœː ka: day muey, totuel bâːbâː day piː
You work with one hand, but you receive *bâbâ* with two hands.

The Khmer Rouge again accused the people of lacking determination in work, but of eagerly rushing forward for their meager ration of watery rice soup. These were the words of collective canteen cooks.

***

Another danger for workers was to be tarred with the enemy's brush:

277
ត្រូវមានគោលជំហរនឹងនរ
កុំផ្តេកផ្តួលតាមខ្សែញ្ញាក់របស់ខ្មាំង
trou mien koːl chumhoː neungnoː
kom phdéck phduel taːm khsaè nhéak robâh khmang
Your stand must be resolute and not allow the enemy
to lead you by the nose.

This was another way of saying, one more time, that those who did not work enthusiastically, falling behind the pace of their neighbors on the work site, leaving others to pull their load, were playing into the hands of the revolution's enemies. They became their accomplices, hence traitors, it was asserted, without any thought to the physical condition of "slackers."

Another threat was night work:

278
បើធ្វើថ្ងៃមិនគ្រប់ ធ្វើយប់បន្ថែម
bae thvœ: thngay min krup thvœ: yup bânthaèm
If you do not complete your task during the day,
you will complete it by night.

Depending on the season, night work, under moonlight, was frequent, for example, at the time of replanting paddy or the harvest, or when the *Angkar* had decided to accelerate the work pace on irrigation projects. Night work was so common that, very often, the undernourished workers were incapable of fulfilling their impossible quotas. In such cases, an extra ration of food, usually yams, was given out late in the night.

279
ប្រែក្លាយជនបទអោយទៅជាទីក្រុង
praè kla:y chunbât aoy tou chie ti: krong
Let's turn the countryside into a town.

We know that one of the most surprising characteristics of Khmer Rouge society was the will to destroy towns and all their evils. The move was suggested by Mao, with the shipping of millions of individuals to people's communes during the Cultural Revolution, and was completely realized by Pol Pot. Paradoxically, the Khmer Rouge pretended that towns would be built in the countryside. But it appears that the Khmer Rouge only built huts, cabins, and other miserable dwellings—not one public building, not one school, not one new factory. Besides some model peasant houses on stilts, all in a row and all the same, the only buildings of any importance were prisons, which have almost all been completely destroyed at this writing. Khmer Rouge architecture was penitentiary architecture!

On the other hand, the very harsh working conditions in the countryside not only resembled those in collective farms in Communist countries, but also the Soviet Gulag. They were often worse than the disgraceful workers' conditions in the early decades of the Industrial Revolution in Europe. In actual fact, the Khmer Rouge had *de facto* abolished the traditional Khmer peasant way of life, and while many commentators speak of "a peasant revolution" under Democratic Kampuchea, in fact the complete subservience to the *Angkar* and the very rigid work discipline were akin to the nineteenth-century industrial world, not the free, leisurely world of the Cambodian countryside.

At the same time, the revolutionaries brought the countryside to the towns. Thus, in Phnom Penh, emptied of all its inhabitants like the ancient ruins at Angkor, sprawling, creeping tropical vegetation invaded the streets. The Khmer Rouge planted some coconut and banana trees there, as well as in provincial towns. Finally, each ministry or administrative office, each factory, had more or less to look after its own needs for food and to grow its own vegetable gardens. Vegetation inexorably took possession of the deserted towns.

280

ត្រូវចេះឯករាជ្យម្ចាស់ការ !

trou chèh aèkriech mchah ka:

You must know how to be your own masters!

It is useful to consider here the Maoist slogan calling on everyone, as a symbol of the entire country, to learn to be self-reliant, a notion we noted before. It was the refrain for all, sung at work. It implied that everyone had to be highly motivated to carry out designated tasks docilely, without recourse to lengthy explanations. This method of exhortation aimed at making every worker internalize *Angkar*'s orders until they became second nature, thereby diminishing the need for continuous surveillance.

281
កុំធ្វើការលំៗ សើៗយើងជាម្ចាស់ការ !
kom tvœ:ka: lum lum sae sae, yœ:ng chie mchah ka:
Do not work carelessly and half-heartedly:
now you are in charge!

One more refrain was that everyone had to toil without interruption because the exploiting classes had been destroyed. Everyone, therefore, could benefit from the fruits of his own labor.

Another watchword affirms the same goal—never relax your fervor at work:

282
ខ្វះស្មារតីទទួលខុសត្រូវបដិវត្តន៍
khvah sma:rodey totuel khohtrou padévoat
You lack a responsible revolutionary attitude.

283
ត្រូវចេះលើកស្ទួយវិស័យសេដ្ឋកិច្ចឱ្យបានសំបូររុងរឿង
trou chèh lœ:k stuey visay séthekèch aoy ba:n sâmbo: rung reueng
Raise national production for our country
to become fabulously prosperous.

We find here the idea of the Great Leap Forward, justifying all and any sacrifice, since the radiant future was available to be seized. We have difficulty imagining, however, how a people, as undernourished as the Cambodians were, and forced to labor very long hours in the rice fields and on collective work projects day in and day out, could have attained such a goal.

***

To conclude this section, let us note this exhortation, very typical of Pol Pot-ism: To leap into the radiant socialist society of the future, the technician of the modern world must model himself on the man from the forest, like the Jarai, for instance. In late 1967, Pol Pot (then known as "Ta Puk," or "the Venerable Father") lived among the Jarais and the Tampuons, from whom he recruited his faithful bodyguards.

284

ពួកបច្ចេកទេសត្រូវជន្លៀសចូលព្រៃកសាងជីវភាពពីបាតដៃទទេ

puek pachékatèh trou chunlieh cho:l prey kâ:sa:ng chi:vaphiep pi: ba:t day to:té

Technicians,
enter the forest to learn how to work with your bare hands!

285

ត្រូវយកការងារធ្វើគ្រូ តែកុំធ្វើគ្រូការងារអោយសោះ

trou jo:k kangie tvœ: kru: taè kom tvœ: kru: kagnie aoy sâh

Work must be your teacher,
but don't be at all the teacher of work.

This general saying echoes the Maoist slogan that you learn by practicing and working. The Khmer Rouge further radicalized the dictum by implying that not the least initiative was expected from the people at work: each and every person was to be a mere cog in the gigantic machine set in motion by the *Angkar*.

286

កុមារឈានមុខឧទ្ទេចតែខ្លួន
ក្រមុំពេញពោះភារកិច្ចមម៉ាញឹក

koma: chhien mukh to:ch taè khluen
krâ:muen pénh pueh phieréakèch mo:mienheuk

Children sent to the front lines are still young,
but they are bursting with energy to do their duty
and do not stop to take a breath.

As in the People's Republic of China, work groups were organized on a military model: front line shock troops, or *kong chalat*, were sent to the "front line" of production, and composed, as we have seen, of young people and the hardiest of single men. Adolescents would join their ranks to back them up and eventually take their place. They were presented as models of devotion to the revolutionary cause. And it was the best imaginable schooling for them. For example, Khieu Samphan, the president of the Supreme Presidium, explained, in a long speech on 15 April 1977 marking the second anniversary of the victory, that farm work was their "natural sciences" classroom:

> Is there any schooling in our country? Of course, there is. But our education is mainly carried out within the framework of our workers' unions at various factories, within the framework of our peasants' cooperatives and within the framework of each unit of our Revolutionary Army.
>
> . . . Our children do not play with toy cars, toy boats and toy guns, which were formerly imported at considerable cost. Our children are happy with driving sparrows away from the crops, tending cattle, buffaloes, collecting natural fertiliser and helping to build dams and embankments and dig reservoirs and ditches. Our children have made great progress. They are well-disciplined, alert, skilful, brave, but not arrogant or vicious. They love work and production. They love the cattle, buffaloes, fields, orchards, rice field embankments, irrigation ditches, the villages, the nation, and the people. They respect the people and stay close to them. They are well trained in manual labour and farm chores.
>
> That is why we praise our children [applause].[7]

THE WARRIOR LABORER

287
ការដ្ឋានជាសមរភូមិក្តៅ
ka:rotha:n chie samo:rophu:m kdau
Every work site is a fiery battlefield.

We should stress that the warrior metaphor was not only used for labor. The Khmer Rouge leadership also imagined they were ruling the country as if they were conducting guerrilla warfare from *Angkar* headquarters in Phnom Penh. Violence lay at the heart of each and every single move of the Khmer Rouge's so-called government, running a kind of war economy. As we have already noted in the foregoing chapter, the authorities never ceased repeating:

> With a rifle in one hand, we will remain vigilant to fulfill the task of defending the country, the Revolutionary *Angkar* and the people; with the other hand we will fulfill the task of building the country.[8]

288
សមរភូមិកសិកម្ម ឧស្សាហកម្ម សិប្បកម្ម ប្តេជ្ញាវាយសំរុកសំរេច
ផែនការ១០០ភាគរយ និងលើសថែមទៀត
samo:rophu:m kasékam usa:hakam sepakam pdachnha: viey samrok somrach phaènka: muey roy phiekroy neng aoy leuh thaèm tiet
In the battlefield of agriculture, industry, and handicrafts, let us be determined to struggle to fulfill 100 percent of the plan and even go beyond it.

289
សមរភូមិសង្គមកិច្ចសុខាភិបាល សិក្សាយោធសនាអប់រំ
ប្តេជ្ញាវាយសំរុកសំរេចផែនការ១០០ភាគរយ និងលើសថែមទៀត
samo:rophu:m sangkumakec sokha:phiba:l seksa: kho:sna:operum pdachnha: viey samrok somrach phaènka: muey roy phiekroy neng aoy leuh thaèm tiet

In the battlefield of social affairs, health, study, and propaganda,
let us be determined to struggle
to fulfill 100 percent of the plan and even go beyond it.

290
ប្រែកំហឹងឈឺចាប់មកប្រយុទ្ធនឹងការងារ
praè kâmhœng chheu: chap mo:k prâ:yut neung ka:ngie
Transform your anger [against the enemy]
into enthusiasm to launch an attack on work.

You had to show, in attacking work, that you fought with the same ardor and same furor you did on the battlefield. As in Mao's China, work teams took names from the military lexicon. The language used in work had a military ring to it; you did not work, but "went on the attack along the front line in the battle for production." This type of advice was quite common in official speeches. In this example at the beginning of 1977, the Party encourages the people to work with more enthusiasm:

> Inspired by the spirit of battle, a glorious sense of revolutionary sacrifice and heroism, principles of collectivism, independence, frugality and creativity, our people (trade unionists, peasants in cooperatives, combatants, and our revolutionary army cadre) have joined efforts to rebuild our fatherland, gradually increasing rice production and other crops. They have turned their anger into energy and their pain into fervor for the reconstruction and defence of our motherland.[9]

We must also remember that it was Sihanouk who introduced this kind of large, collective, Mao-like work project, in the mid 1960s. But it was mostly a matter of staging grand operettas of high-ranking leaders working alongside joyous common folk, in front of the camera's eye, for the needs of government propaganda. However, after they left, the peasants were left to finish the work themselves. Yet, they are scenes of some earthly paradise compared to the Pol Pot-ian hell, where everything was real!

This watchword repeats the idea of the previous slogan:

291
ប្រែកំហឹងឈឺចាប់អោយមកជាការអនុវត្តជាក់ស្ដែង

praè kâmhœng chheu: chap aoy mo:k chieka: anuvoat chéak sdaèng

Transform your anger [against the enemy] and your suffering into zeal with which you work.

292
វាយសំរុកបុកកំទេច !

viey sâmrok bok kâmtéch!

Strike through [the enemy's lines],
smash, reduce everything to dust![10]

The roots of these four biting verbs described the brutal tactics of revolutionary soldiers. Then, after the seizure of power, they symbolized institutionalized violence. Later, after the coming to power, this watchword was directed toward the general population: the people were called upon to sweep away all obstacles in the realization of gigantic work projects. The regime had succeeded in raising a modern army of slaves.

This injunction was heard during work:

293
បេជ្ញាវាយសម្រុកបុកទំលាយ !

pdachnha: viey sâmrok bok tumliey

Let's swear that we are going on the attack.
Let's break through [enemy lines]!

Like the preceding slogan, this order was used both on the battlefield and on collective work sites.

294

ធ្វើការផងហើយប្រយុទ្ធផងអោយក្តៅកុកដូចភ្លើងឆល់

thvœ:ka: phâ:ng haey prâyut phâng aoy kdau kokuk do:ch phlœ:ng kul

**Work is a fight:
you blaze like fire and reduce tree stumps to ashes.**

As the people were incited to obey the *Angkar* blindly and without question, the slogans for work must have been legion. Here are some examples:

295

សូមសមមិត្តប្រយុទ្ធ កុំសំចៃកំលាំង !

so:m samamit prâyut kom sâmchay kâmlang

Comrades, fight on tirelessly!

296

ស្នើសមមិត្តសស្រាក់សស្រាំ សកម្មការងារ

snae samamit sâ: srak sâ: sram sakam ka·ngie

**We ask you, comrade,
to buckle down to work with boundless energy.**

The necessity to work for the *Angkar* became more urgent:

297

ប្តេជ្ញាពលីជីវិតបំពេញពលកម្មជូនអង្គការ !

pdachnha: péakli: chi:vit bâmpénh pulekam chu:n ângka:

Pledge to sacrifice your life to accomplish the *Angkar*'s work!

298

មូរជើងខោឱ្យត្រឹង វ័តក្បិនឱ្យណែន
សម្រុកមែនទែន បង្កបង្កើនផល

mu: chœ:ng khao aoy tœng rit kbèn aoy naèn
sâmrok aoy mè:n tè:n bângkâ: bângkaœn phâl

**Roll up your trousers, tie up your *sampot*
to launch a fierce attack for production!**

This was heard at Kamping Puey in Battambang province to incite the new people, in 1975, to work with enthusiasm in the rice fields.

Revolutionary enthusiasm was to increase the work rhythm tenfold:

299

ប្ដេជ្ញាកសាង និងការពារប្រទេសជាតិមាតុភូមិ បំពាក់
បំប៉នពង្រឹកពង្រឹងគោលជំហរបដិវត្តន៍ខ្ពស់ !

pdachnha: kâ:sa:ng ning ka:pie prâtéchiet mietophu:m bâmpéak
bâmpâ:n pungri:k pungreung ko:lchumho: padévoat khpuh

Let's pledge to build and protect the sovereignty of our motherland! Let's work hard, and reinforce our revolutionary advances!

This was one of the many exhortations to work proclaimed with clenched fists waving in the air, a characteristic of Khmer Rouge voluntarism, seeking, by all possible means, to pressure the people to work with utmost enthusiasm and energy.

300

ចូរសមមិត្តប្រយុទ្ធលុះដល់តំណក់ឈាមចុងក្រោយ !

cho: samamit prâyut luh dâl dâmnâk chhiem chong kraoy

Dear comrade, let's fight until our last drop of blood!

Young fanatic Khmer Rouge soldiers displayed in battle blind fearlessness in the face of death. The *Angkar* demanded the same resoluteness before superhuman tasks from workers in the people's communes.

301

វាយសម្រុកបង្កបង្កើនផលឡើងតាមថ្ងៃ !

viey sâmrok bângkâ: bângkaœn phâl laœng ta:m thgnay

Go on the attack in production and accelerate your work pace,
just as the sun rises toward its zenith!

This slogan points to the infernal rhythm of daily work, especially during the dry and hot season, when the sun gave off rays of suffocating tropical heat. It admonished the workers to step up the pace of work.

Finally, here are general orders for civilians and the military concerning the work of farming, irrigating, and the clearing of land.

302

មុខសញ្ញា និងទិសដៅកងចលាត័÷
សមរភូមិមុខលើកទំនប់ ជីកប្រឡាយ
លើកភ្លឺស្រែ គាស់គល់ឈើ

mukh sanha: ning teuh dau kâ:ng chalat:
samo:rephu:m mukh lœ:k tumnup chi:k prâla:y
lœ:k phleu: sraè koah kul chhœ:

The role and program of shock groups are:
on the front line battlefield, construct dams, dig canals,
build small dikes around rice fields, tear the bark from trees.

If, in theory, regular troops also had to engage in production duties, they certainly did not work at the same pace as civilians. They were too much absorbed in the control and repression of the general population. Survivors have hardly ever told of soldiers doing hard manual labor, but they did say they did a lot of reveling in secret. They certainly spent most of their time obeying the second, and not the first, order in the watchword below—that is, they were definitely more involved in repression than in production!

303

សំរាប់កងទ័ព ការចែកមុខសញ្ញាមានដូចតទៅ
១-ដៃម្ខាងកាន់អាវុធ ដៃម្ខាងបង្កបង្កើនផល
២-ត្រូវផ្តល់សង្គមចាស់ ប្រែក្លាយសង្គមថ្មីបដិវត្តន៍
៣-ត្រូវរៀនសូត្រពីប្រជាជន តែមិនត្រូវដើរក្រោយប្រជាជន !

sâmrap kângtoap ka: chaèk mukh sanha: mien do:ch tâ:tou
day mkha:ng kan a:vuth day mkha:ng bângkâ: bângkaen phâl

trou phduel sângkum chah praè krâlah yo:k sângkum thmey padévoat
trou rienso:t pi: prâchiechun taè mint trou daœ kraoy prâchiechun
For soldiers, the orders are as follows:
1 - A rifle in one hand, and production with the other.
2 - Overthrow the old society
and create the new revolutionary one!
3 - Learn from the people, but do not tail them!

All the ambiguities of Pol Pot-ism are contained in this apparently contradictory order. In fact, according to revolutionary Marxist ideology, the Party is nothing more than the spokesman of the proletariat. And besides this, the *Angkar* repeated constantly that the poorest strata of society were models to be followed in everything. At the same time, specifically with regard to the agricultural activities to which almost all the population were assigned, the Khmer Rouge leaders, in their directives on daily labor, took no account of traditional customs and wisdom of the Cambodian peasantry. The third directive meant that on collective work projects and in the fields, workers should not slavishly imitate past peasant customs. For example, if villagers planted rice seedlings in a certain way, the Khmer Rouge overseers made them do it in a completely opposite way, to break ancestral habits.

It was the same for ethnic minorities living in the country's hinterlands, although they were favored by the regime: dry rice growing on the hills was abandoned in favor of wet rice cultivation. Here, especially, we see why the regime was hardly popular among those segments of the population they were supposed to serve.

2—WORK HARD, IN THE RICE PADDIES ESPECIALLY

RICE IS THE SOURCE OF ALL WEALTH

As is well known, rice production played a central role in the Pol Pot-ists' politico-economic system. In a country without money where "to eat," ញាំបាយ *(nham bay)*, literally means "to eat rice," it is not surprising that rice was the means of exchange, not only for trade within the country, more or less secretly (at least at the beginning of the regime), but also as a means of obtaining foreign exchange for purchases abroad. Thus, "*The Party's Four Year Plan to Build Socialism in All Sectors, 1977–80*," drawn up by the *Angkar* in July/August 1978, foresaw:

> To produce rice for food, in order to raise the people's standard of living, and in order to export so as to obtain capital for the imported goods we need.
>
> Thus the paddy and milled rice are our capital base. Besides rice, we have other industrial products. These products are only complementary. For every 100,000 tons of milled rice, we would get $20 million; if we had 500,000 tons, we'd get $100 million . . . We must increase our rice production so that we obtain necessary capital.
>
> . . . From 1977, the ration of the people will average 13 *thang* or 312 kilograms of paddy per person per annum, throughout the country.[11]

These figures, probably like all Khmer Rouge statistics, exist only on paper and have nothing to do with reality. It is also very likely that people's rations were not copious, save for the regime's civilian and military upper cadres, as well as members of technical services, along with the Montagnards of the periphery. These very figures were taken up, a few months later, by Nuon Chea, president of the permanent committee of the People's Representatives, and interim prime minister (sort of alter ego to Pol Pot) who announced on 16 January 1977, during a mass meeting in Phnom Penh celebrating the ninth anniversary of the Kampuchean Revolutionary Army, that

> each Cambodian receives 312 kilograms of rice to eat per year. This is a very large quantity of rice ... In other words, our people have enough to eat. We have set aside two bushels of paddy per person in 1977. At the same time, we have a surplus of more than 150,000 tonnes for export. This signifies that we have totally achieved the 1976 plan.[12]

Pol Pot himself said as much during an interview by the militant Marxist Jan Myrdal for Swedish television, on 24 August 1978, that every inhabitant was the recipient of 312 kilograms of rice per year, and, "what is more, there is a surplus for export."[13]

The year was keyed to the tempo of rice production: harvest and clearing of new fields during the dry season, as well as irrigation projects of Pharaonic proportions; and tillage, burning, sowing, and replanting during the wet season. The work day was keyed to the same tempo. A gong woke everybody before dawn; everyone quickly formed into groups and set off for work on an empty stomach until the middle of the day. The first of two daily meals was then eaten either in the paddy fields or work site, or in the people's commune's canteen, if distance allowed. The rest period was very short, and work began again, ending at dusk, the time of the second meal. The needs of work very often required night work, except during the rounds of nightly meetings, during which the leaders waxed long on the same things over and over again, to which no one really listened, for they fell asleep from sheer exhaustion. But, sleeping was dangerous, a sign that you were a counter-revolutionary. The eight-hour day in 1975 stretched to ten, then twelve, then fourteen hours, according to the "demands of work"! Days of rest were rare—theoretically every ten days—and were above all devoted to propaganda meetings, as *Angkar* directives recommended, or to the few Party celebrations.

304

បុគ្គលខ្ញុំកើតចេញពីជ្រលងនង្គ័លសុទ្ធសាធ

bokul khnhom kaet chènh pi: chrolo:ng néangkoal sotsa:t

I was born straight from the plough's furrow in a rice paddy.

Here we have an old Khmer proverb which bears the stamp of Hindu influence on Cambodian culture. It recalls the myth of Sita, the wife of Rama, in the Ramayana, who was born from a furrow in a rice paddy. As was often done, some commentators, like Malcolm Caldwell,[15] would have pointed to such slogans as proof that the Khmer Rouge revolution was an authentic peasant one, not a classical Communist one. It does not seem that this is an exact description. The rhetoric, perhaps, is rural, but the doctrine is that of pseudo-intellectuals educated in Paris and in Asian Communist centers such as Beijing, Pyongyang, and Hanoi, and not at all in the Cambodian rice paddies as the Khmer Rouge leader liked to pretend. The Khmer peasants themselves understood nothing of this senseless, mad revolution.

305

ធ្វើស្រែនឹងទឹកធ្វើសឹកនឹងបាយ

thvœ: sraè neung teuk thvœ: sœk neung ba:y

With water you can grow rice, with rice, you can make war.

This slogan is a traditional Khmer saw that we take note of here because it was very often repeated at the time. It took on a singular importance in a political and social system entirely based on armed struggle and the central role of the *yothea*, or soldier, in Khmer Rouge society.

306

ដាំ! ដាំ! មិនអោយសល់ដីមួយចំអាម !

dam! dam! min aoy sâl dey muey châm'a:m!

Sow! Sow! Do not leave the least bit of soil alone,
not even a hand's width!

On the other hand, the Khmer Rouge strove to teach their fellow countrymen good habits of agronomy, like the Chinese, who even in Cambodia were traditionally good market gardeners. Especially they fought against wasteful farming, but to little effect because they were using the most absurd strategies.

307

បង្កបង្កើនផលលើកស្ទួយជីវភាពប្រជាជន

bângkâ: bângkaen phâl lœ:k stuey chi:vephiep prâchiechun

Sow and grow in order to raise the people's living standards.

The Khmer Rouge strongly encouraged the production of vegetables, since every cell within the social organization had to cultivate its own garden, including every ministry in Phnom Penh, every factory, every Internal Security Center, and every prison. Khmer Rouge soldiers even observed habits learned during the civil war and planted yams and other vegetables in forest clearings or in pockets of fertile land, in case of need. This proved to be very useful during the retreat to the Cardamoms in 1979. This policy was due to problems of management, transport, and communication, and of course the abolition of markets; but more often it was also due to the *Angkar,* which wanted everyone "to work with his own hands so that he would be molded into the New Man," according to Mao's directives.

***

Khmer Rouge political economy could well be summed up in the following slogan:

308
អោយតែមានស្រូវគឺមានអ្វីៗទាំងអស់
aoy taè mien srou keu: mien avey avey téang âh
He who has rice possesses absolutely everything.

Another one, terser in form, simply says:

309
មានស្រូវ មានអ្វីទាំងអស់
mien srou mean avey téang âh
He who has rice possesses all.

This slogan constituted a favorite Khmer Rouge watchword. This economic theory was, in a way, a justification for the revolutionaries to literally "harness" the "17 April people," according to many eyewitnesses in a number of places, to ploughs that they pulled in the fields. Was this the result of a lack of beasts of burden or an exercise in bullying?

On the other hand, the revolutionary leaders were not completely in the wrong when they expressed their anger at the people who disdained sweet corn, the production of which was also being developed at that time.

310
អង្គរ៤បាវដូរបានឡានមួយ
ângkâ: buen ba:v do: ba:n la:n muey
Four sacks of rice can be swapped for a motorcar.

This is an assertion heard in O'Taki commune, near Battambang, which was typical of Khmer Rouge economic strategy. Mass production of paddy was supposed to enable revolutionary Cambodia to buy from the international market all sorts of commodities, with rice serving as a hard currency. One can fully measure, in this sally, the total lack of economic realism of the Khmer Rouge. They thus express their contempt for the materialism and greed that, they claimed, characterized the new people forced to labor in the rice fields.

311 C
បាយមួយគ្រាប់ជាប់កន្ទុយផ្កែដេញដណ្ដើមគ្នាលិទ

ba:y muey kroap choap kântuy chkaè dénh dândaem knie lith
A grain of rice on the tail of a dog, we run after it and we fight to lick it.

This is a traditional proverb that urged the young not to waste anything and spare as much as possible. Older people considered this saying as a prediction of the Buddha to the effect that, one day, food would be in short supply in the country. This is what happened under Pol Pot and the people would discreetly take up again this piece of folk wisdom.

YIELDS MUST BE MULTIPLIED BY THREE

312
ត្រូវធ្វើឱ្យបាន១ហិកតាពាយតោន !

trou thvœ: aoy ba:n muey hèkta: bey taon
Produce three tons per hectare!

Or simply:

១ហិកតាពាយតោន !

muey hèkta: bey taon
One hectare, three tons!

Of course it was a question of three tons of rice. It puts in a nutshell the Khmer Rouge's economic strategy. It was a feature of the Great Leap Forward that the country had to realize all at once. According to David Chandler, the Pol Pot-ists did nothing more than repeat (without, once more, acknowledging from whom they borrowed it) a slogan used by Vice Premier Hua Guofeng towards the end of 1975.[15] It was an exercise in what Orwell called "doublethink," a very apt description of Communist leaders' reasoning. Pol Pot, we can imagine, was persuaded that this object was fully attained, although he knew full well that it was a lie. On 18 January 1978, during the official visit of "Comrade" Teng Yingchao, member of the Chinese Communist Party's Central Committee, and vice president of the National People's Congress, and head of the People's Republic of China delegation to Kampuchea, and in the presence of the ubiquitous "Comrade Ambassador" Sun Hao, he proclaimed: "In national construction, in 1977, we completely achieved the 3-to-6-tons-per-hectare production goal."[16]

As a measure of the complete unreality, if not insanity, of such a watchword, we must point out that Cambodia had one of the lowest crop yields in the world. In fact, most of the soil in the central plains of the country (especially in the provinces of Kandal, Takeo, Kompong Speu, Kompong Chhang, or Kompong Thom) is sand or clay and quite exhausted. For half the year, in the course of the dry and hot season, it is desert-like. Irrigated soil is rare. The average crop yields were only one ton per hectare. To multiply that by three and obtain several harvests, as if by waving a magic wand, you needed fertilizer—most of all compost which the regime desperately tried to produce—and water.

This watchword was thus at the origin of many projects for the conveyance of water and the digging of canals, dikes, and dams; they were collective works, and done by human hands, since bulldozers and lorries were very much in short supply. Moreover, throughout the country, small dikes surrounding rice fields were standardized and rebuilt, so that everywhere were squares of 100 meters, making all fields one hectare. Thanks to this ingenious work of simplification, often defying nature and centuries-old traditions of building small dikes, which took into account water levels, the head of the collective farm's economy (*settakek sahakâ:*) had a complete count of the number of hectares, and on paper, multiplied the number by three. In this way, he believed that he knew how many tons of rice the collective had after harvest, and thus, the tonnage of the rice surplus! It was supposed to be distributed to regions that did not meet quotas, but, in truth, some was exported to China for consumer goods and arms that the regime needed to survive and retain power, while some must have been stored away and wasted.

This demonic slogan, repeated again and again during the years the Khmer Rouge held power, was paradoxically a principal reason for the general famine in the country, of course, varying in degree, from one people's commune to another, from one zone to another. If there were any differences on the matter at the summit of power, no one at the bottom heard them. Why? Very simply because few could attain, let alone approach, such a goal. To say so outright to their superiors was impossible for all local cadres, because the *Angkar Loeu* would have immediately accused them of wanting to sabotage the revolution. They would then risk arrest, imprisonment, torture, and execution.

The only solution was to furnish false crop returns. Yet, as it was necessary to turn over to the *Angkar* a large part of the harvest to feed cadres and export abroad, and build up secret reserves in the forest—an old reflex from the days of guerrilla warfare—the quantity of rice for collective kitchens was pared down. Very quickly the people had almost nothing to eat. As in the Ukraine during the 1930s under Stalin, the Cambodians died from starvation by ukases from the central government!

Thus, the more the Cambodian people grew rice, the less they had to eat. The watchword responsible for this sad state of affairs was heard throughout the country; there was not a single Khmer who had not heard it time and time again. For the Khmer Rouge, it became the leitmotif for the Great Leap Forward, and the glorious and radiant beginning of a new society. It was likewise used metaphorically in other contexts. As such, we find the jailer-interrogators at S-21–Tuol Sleng increasing the number of people interrogated and comparing the information collected from interrogations and torture sessions, in order to increase at the same ratio, the hunt for saboteurs of the Revolution. It seemed that the entire new society acted out this myth of the sudden tripling of production and riches and work rhythm—at least according to the *Angkar*'s dreams. It was swept up and swept away in the current of Khmer Rouge paranoia. A local leader in the region of O'Rangoeu, at Kompong Cham, went so far as to shoot for *muoy hekta prampoeul ton*, "seven tons per hectare"!

Although Khieu Samphan had a doctorate in economics from the University of Paris and acted as first personage of Democratic Kampuchea, the Khmer Rouge leadership certainly understood nothing about economics. They believed that economic problems would be resolved by a stroke of the Politburo's pen, and by never-ending spontaneous chanting of slogans throughout the country!

313

វាយសំរុកបុកកំទេចស្តារសេដ្ឋកិច្ច
មួយហិកតាបីតោនឱ្យបានដាច់ខាត !

viey sâmrok bok kâmtéch sda: séthkèch
muey hèkta: bey taon aoy ba:n dachkha:t

Strike, crush, and win absolutely the production goal
of three tons per hectare!

For Cambodians, including the very poor *mulethans*, inveterate consumers of rice, this draconian rationing was the cause of much suffering, sublimated in these counter-slogans (ពាក្យ បញ្ច្រាស, *pieh banhchuh*). The one most often heard was:

314 C
ត្រូវធ្វើឱ្យបាន១ហិកតាពាតៅ

trou thvœ: aoy ba:n muey hèkta: bey tau

We must produce three bushels per hectare.

Tau in Khmer is a large basket with a capacity of a dozen or so liters, used to weigh grain, which approximately corresponds to one bushel in English. It was absolutely essential that the *Angkar* did not hear you utter this word of sacrilege!

The more audacious came up with a saying that gained widespread popularity:

315 C
ធ្វើស្រែនឹងមេឃស៊ីបាយ ធ្វើស្រែនឹងប្រឡាយស៊ីបបរ
ធ្វើស្រែនឹងទសុពោត

thvœ: sraè neung mékh si: ba:y thvœ: sraè neung prâla:ysi: bâ:bâ:

thvœ: sraè neung to: si: po:t

If we use rain water for the rice field, we shall eat rice;
if we use dikes and canals, we shall eat bâbâ;
if we use drain pipes, we shall eat corn.

In the first hypothesis, traditional methods allowed the Khmer peasant to eat as much rice as possible; the use of Khmer Rouge methods in rice culture (irrigation), ended with him seeing his rice turned to corn, a hardly appetizing thought for the Cambodian palate. It could be worse still, eating nothing but *bâbâ*, a liquid rice soup, which had become the standard fare, and often the only food, during long months of the year, from 1976 onward. For Khmer taste, eating corn is worse than drinking rice soup!

The even more audacious would utter the more coarse:

316 C

ធ្វើស្រែនឹងមេឃស៊ីបាយ
ធ្វើស្រែនឹងប្រឡាយស៊ីបបរ ចូលសហករណ៍ស៊ីអាចម៍

thvœ: sraè neung mékh si: ba:y
thvœ: sraè neung prâla:y si: bâ:bâ: cho:l sahakâ: si: ach

If we use rain water for the rice field, we shall eat rice;
if we use dikes and canals, we shall eat bâbâ;
if we live in the collectives, we shall eat shit!

317 C

ធ្វើបដិវត្តគឺ ហូបបបរវាវជាមួយនឹងត្រកួន
កាលណាយើងឈានដល់សង្គមនិយម យើងហូបតែត្រកួនសុទ្ធ

tvœ: padévoat keu: ho:p bâ:bâ: rieiu chie muey neug trâ:kuen
ka:lna: yœ:g chhien dol sangkumniyum ho:p taè trâ:kuen sot

Doing the revolution means eating clear bâbâ *with water bindweed;*
when we reach Communism, we shall eat only bindweed.

318

យើងធ្វើស្រែប្រាំង និងស្រែវស្សា
ក្នុងមួយឆ្នាំណាបានឱ្យបីដង

yœ:ng thvœ: sraè prang ning sraè vo:sa:
knong muey chhnam na: aoy ba:n bei dâ:ng

If we grow dry season rice and rainy season rice,
we shall have three crops a year.

To understand the arithmetic of the Khmer Rouge, we must understand that in Democratic Kampuchea's utopian vision of agriculture, two crops are to be produced during the drier months of the year, thanks to the massive irrigation projects.

319 C
ពូជស្រូវពពីកយកមកអំពល់ទុក្ខ

pu:ch srou prampi: tœk yo:k mo:k âmpul tukh

*The paddy shoots that grow seventy centimeters
only bring us suffering and grief.*

This protestation refers to a new rice variety imported from China. It mattered little to the population if it gave a high yield, since this meant hard work in ploughing, transplanting, and irrigation to be repeated the same year, with no benefit to the undernourished laborers. Without fail, the *Angkar* would steal from the Cambodians the greatest part of the fruits of their labor.

320
បងប្អូនពុកម៉ែត្រូវខិតខំបង្កបង្កើនផលឱ្យសំបូររុងរឿង

bâ:ng po'o:n puk maè trou khet khâm bângkâ bângkaen phâl aoy sâmbo: rung reueng

*Brothers and sisters, fathers and mothers,
you have all gloriously raised abundant food.*

In such a manner did the Khmer Rouge exhort the general population—the "17 April" and *mulethans*—to participate in collective agricultural endeavors and produce, in joy and happiness, a striking abundance of diverse foodstuffs for the glory of the nation and the *Angkar*. This production was all the more indispensable because it had to pay for the arms coming from People's China. They were paid in various products from Cambodian soil, from which the Chinese liked to prepare their refined cuisine, and some of their traditional medicine.

NATURE MUST BE DEFEATED

321
ប្តេជ្ញាធ្វើស្រែមិនពឹងនឹងមេឃ !
pdachnha: thvœ: sraè min peung neung mékh
Let us be determined to work in the rice fields
whatever the weather!

Traditionally, hard work in the fields did not take place until the rainy season had softened the soil, which had become as hard as brick during the dry season. Then, it was customary that, if the laborer began his work at dawn, he would return to his village when the sun had reached its full strength. If he worked longer hours, it was when large storm clouds sent temperatures tumbling. Besides, beasts of burden—oxen or water buffaloes in the waterlogged fields—worked according to the weather. Irrigation allowed him to depend less on the monsoon rains.

All these traditional habits were swept away under the Khmer Rouge, and the universal order of things was reversed. In the eyes of the people, the *Angkar* took into account neither the monsoon rains nor the seasons, and this could lead to nothing but chaos.

The following directive is a variation on the previous slogan:

322
ធ្វើស្រែកុំពឹងមេឃឱ្យបាន១ហិកតាពាញ់តោន !
thvoe: sraè kom peung mékh aoy ba:n muey hèkta: bey taon
Work in the rice fields without considering the skies, to grow
three tons a hectare.

323
ម្ចាស់ការលើទឹក ម្ចាស់លើធម្មជាតិ
mchah ka: lœ: teuk, mchah lœ: thoamchiet
Let us be master of the water, master of nature.[17]

324
យើងត្រូវម្ចាស់ការលើទឹក ពីព្រោះមេឃសេរីណាស់
yœ:ng trou mchah ka: lœ: teuk pi: pruh mékh sérei nah
Let us be masters of the water, for the skies are very free!

With the Khmer Rouge, "free" has always had a negative connotation. It is synonymous with lawless and anti-revolutionary.

325
ប្រព័ន្ធភ្លឺស្រែកែប្រែទុស្សន:
prâpoan phleu: sraè kaè praè tusanak
The system of dikes in the rice fields means a new worldview.

In only a few years, the Khmer countryside was transformed by the *Angkar*'s big, collective work projects. Small dikes that had incorporated natural water levels, the quirks of the lay of the land, or human whimsy, were in many places realigned and made perfectly rectangular. This rationalization was supposed to increase production. The results were often deplorable, with water tending to accumulate on a side of the field, owing to the faulty distribution of water in the new, rectangular rice paddies. This sort of authoritarian reconstitution of land has left its marks even until today: all these rearrangements, usually conceived with the help of Chinese advisors, were not totally ill planned, for some could be used or modified to develop irrigation. As in industry, Cambodian technicians and engineers were often temporarily employed before they had trained their replacement of proletarian origin, and more often than not, were executed afterward. That was the reason that Chinese and North Korean experts became indispensable to make the economic machinery work. Sometimes, native technicians and experts managed to melt into the general population on collective farms.

The new landscape signified a utilitarian and totalitarian universe.

326 C
លើកដី ដាក់លើដី

lœ:k dey dak lœ: dey

Lift some earth to put it on the earth.

This counter-slogan shows the people's silent anger. They were forced to destroy old small dikes on individual rice fields to trace new rectangular ones surrounding collective rice fields, the area of which had to be a hectare. More generally, they were forced to toil at jobs that were absolutely useless.

327
ធ្វើស្ថានីយ៍ដើម្បីបានទឹក

thvœ: stha:ni: daembey ba:n teuk

Build a dam to have water.

328 C
ស្ថានីយ៍អង្គការមិនដល់ស្ថានីយ៍កេមឃទេ

stha:ni: ângka: min dâl stha:ni: mékh té

Angkar's dams are not equal to the dams in the heavens.

. . . echoed the people, facing the very poor results of many a project.

Irrigation projects were often planned by experts who knew nothing about the country's environment. Even the Khmer Rouge leaders wanted to make a clean sweep of traditional methods, since the *Angkar* wanted to reconstruct society from zero.

329
យើងមិនតោងកន្ទុយប្រជាជនទេ

yœ:ng min taong kântuy prâchiechun té

Do not hang on to the people's tail.

This slogan takes up, under a slightly different form, the third directive from slogan 303, "Learn from the people but do not tail them." This rejection of centuries-old knowledge was equally applied to the relatively privileged minorities in the Northeast of the country. In his 27 September 1978 speech celebrating the eighteenth anniversary of the "founding" of the CPK, Pol Pot noted that "our people of Mondolkiri and Ratanakiri . . . now have dessert, sugar, and decent clothing, like the rest of the population. They have blankets, mosquito nets, and decent housing that meet standards for the rest of the country."[18]

In other words, they were now perfectly assimilated and identical to all other Cambodians. They now wore the ritual black pants and black shirt, whereas in the past they went around scantily clad, a custom that always shocked the Khmers of the plains. The elegant and imaginative style of straw and bamboo huts that varied among the minority groups were now built in accordance with the *Angkar*'s specifications.

330
យើងមិនចាញ់ធម្មជាតិ !
yœ:ng min chanh thoamechiet
Let us not be defeated by nature!

This revealing watchword indicated that the Khmer Rouge saw the world through utopian, rose-colored glasses and were incapable of imagining the least compromise with nature and reality.

The more pragmatic Cambodians mockingly answered:

331 C
កិតតែឈ្លោះនឹងធម្មជាតិមិនកិតស៊ីទេ
kit taè chhluh neung thoamechiet min kit si: té
You are always quarrelling with nature
instead of being concerned about food.

The people were often exasperated at being led by ignorant incompetents and at suffering hunger. Without nonsensical slogans and disdain for tradition, they could have raised food in abundance.

Fifty-riel bank note, front and back

Chapter VI

COLLECTIVISM: THE DISSOLUTION OF THE INDIVIDUAL

The slogans in this last chapter mainly evoke the atmosphere of people's communes or collective farms, where the general population had been settled. The unit at the revolutionary society's base was the *sahakor*, usually translated as "agricultural cooperative" in official documents. The rendering seems very unsatisfactory, for it implies free will, and thus, a choice by "members of the cooperative," which does not correspond to what was actually happening. Nowhere was it with a glad heart that peasants, who all over the world are individualists, gave up their parcel of earth, which had been theirs since time immemorial, no matter how small it was. Nor was it with a happy heart that they handed over agricultural equipment, beasts of burden, and even kitchen utensils for collective ownership. Nor was it with a broad smile that families gave up the right to prepare food at home and instead queue up twice a day at the canteen, since the *Angkar* had taken away all of the paddy they had planted themselves. The *sahakor* were, in truth, "state farms," or "collective units of production," where often handicrafts or tools were also manufactured or repaired.

It would, on the other hand, be false to conclude that the Khmer Rouge wanted to abolish the nuclear family and the individual homestead. It is true that children were largely brought up in the មណ្ឌលកុមារ (*mondolkoma*), or camps for children, teenagers and young people were sent to join "shock groups," and adults were frequently separated from their spouses to go to collective work sites, often far away. Nevertheless, the nuclear family, like the units at the society's base, was maintained in theory. The family was very bruised, though, by separation beginning with the first deportations from towns, then by departures for faraway work projects, and by death. By the last days of the regime, death had so decimated the family that many a Cambodian sought to find either an adoptive mother, or brother, or grandmother, or a companion. A good many children had died; many starving women had amenorrhea; the skeletal population often no longer possessed a trace of libido. If in practice the family was torn apart, this was not the result of deliberate policy. Never did the *Angkar* desire its disappearance, nor encourage divorce; on the contrary, the revolutionaries dreamed of a rapid increase of population, on condition that it had been cleansed of undesirable elements.

Alas, the inhabitants were less and less able to find consolation in the village community. On top of an iron discipline and long and harassing work, the size of what properly has to be called "people's communes" or "collective farms," never stopped growing during the brief time the regime was in power. Pol Pot and his group were probably so hypnotized by the Chinese model that they aspired to blanket the country with vast "people's communes" composed of up to one thousand families. But how was that possible, since the general population never stopped decreasing in number? There was a precedent, however, for the French colonial administration had once created, distinct from the traditional village grouped around its monks and pagoda, a new, larger entity, "the commune," which, contrary to the French model, included (and still does even today) several villages. In colonial days, there was a mayor (*mekhum*) at its head, who was elected by all those who paid the personal tax—that is, almost universal suffrage. The Khmer Rouge adopted the same administrative division which cut across village communities and gradually the "*sahakor phum*" became "*sahakor khum*," that is, collective village farms became "collective communes." Pol Pot gives us some points on the matter:

> Each of these cooperatives constitutes a small collective society, which is a brand new community where all kinds of depraved cultural and social blemishes have been wiped out. This new, sound, equal, harmonious collective society, with all the facilities for livelihood, such as food, health services, culture and education, is being consolidated and developed. [Applause]
> To date, these cooperatives have been expanded in size. Now, an average 50% of the entire countryside's cooperatives are made of 700 to 1,000 households. Thus, in general, most of our cooperatives have already been upgraded to commune-cooperatives (*sahakor khum*). Only a few remain village-cooperatives (*sahakor phum*).[1]

> All remnants of the work system, production techniques, beliefs and individualistic way of life of the old society have been abolished by our co-operative peasants. . . . Since we have a socialist collective system and our masses, capable of distinguishing friend from foe, are armed with a strong revolutionary philosophy—they have drawn a clear dividing line between friend and enemy.[2]

These words clearly bear the stamp of their author, Pol Pot. As we pointed out above, the outspoken aim is to dramatically increase production in the collective system. But, as is clear from the second quotation, the people in the state base unit of production found themselves caught in a stranglehold and the ultimate purpose was for the *Angkar* to exert ultimate control over every individual. Just as the cities were evacuated to allow the CPK to grasp hold of the entire society, here perceived "enemies" could be culled by the security apparatus and the totalitarian state could reign supreme. In the agricultural collectives, it became easy to distinguish friend from foe, an echo of those ominous words.

In the first quotation, we have an idyllic vision of people's communes, light-years beyond the harsh reality of this "murderous utopia," and an example of the inability of the country's leaders to actually see this reality. The slogans that follow will paint an image closer to what the commune's inhabitants really experienced. This chapter first looks at some slogans related to Party celebrations, then marriage and the family, then the new social order of uncompromising equality, then the renunciation of all private property, and lastly, the dissolving of the individual for the sake of the community.

According to unanimous testimonies, the dominant mood of this society was gloom, and this was true for all social strata, including Khmer Rouge soldiers, whose Spartan life was very harsh. Besides occasional feasting—and mainly among the officers, it seems—what was it that really brightened military life? We should recall here that all traditional holidays had been abolished, save for the Buddhist new year in mid-April, because it fell very near to 17 April, the very day of the revolutionaries' victory, the nation's largest yearly celebration. In 1976, 1977, and 1978, all satisfied their hunger during that time: there was even meat in abundance. In some places, the Chams, it is reported, voraciously even devoured pork! Traditional marriage ceremonies were likewise banished from Khmer Rouge society; the calendar of public rejoicing, so very important for the Khmers, was replaced by a revolutionary one.

Celebrations first of all consisted of listening to interminable speeches, sometimes accompanied by "artistic" performances, according to aesthetic criteria established during the Cultural Revolution. How meticulously did the Central Committee plan Party holidays, with their Maoist rites: loud speakers blaring out slogans and revolutionary songs with words extolling violence; inartistic and unemotional dance performances ("dance like the possessed," commented Cambodians); dramas on the life of poor peasants! How could these offer a respite from the vicious cycle of work, criticism/self-criticism, and the hunt for the enemy? The taut, tense atmosphere went from fear to terror, as the months passed and the country inexorably sank into a living hell.

If the *mulethans* had undeniably suffered less than the "17 April people" at the hands of the Khmer Rouge regime, we should not pretend for one moment, as some commentators have, and as the revolutionaries themselves asserted, that they were advantaged during the forty-five months the Khmer Rouge held power. Or must we count among these "privileges" the right to be inducted into the army, or to participate in the administration, or to tyrannize and also rob (through various secret illegal trafficking) fellow Cambodians? Although the *mulethans* had usually not been deported, or seen their families broken up, or had their few belongings confiscated, or suffered, above all, from famine, it is very doubtful that their standard of living improved at all. It is probable that it collapsed, owing to the regime's insane economic policies. Especially, for the Cambodian peasant, public holidays and all social life centered around the pagoda vanished from one day to the next, on 17 April 1975. For the peasants, everything that relieved the daily routine in their universe, and much of what brought them joy and gave a sense to their lives, had been brutally taken away from them.

The leaders in Phnom Penh gradually drew up a revolutionary calendar, much like the French revolutionaries of 1789. In addition to a number of national or local holidays that were politically linked (5 January, was, from 1976, the birthday of the new constitution) or tied to the Party (excuses for speeches to the general population, or discreet carousing among local civilian and military cadres), there were three great holidays. The Buddhist new year holidays, usually beginning on 13 April, the largest celebration for all Cambodians, was abolished and replaced by three days of celebration marking *Angkar*'s victory, around 17 April.

The second holiday in importance was proclaimed by Pol Pot during his famous 27 September 1977 speech, on the occasion of the twenty-sixth anniversary of the seizure of power in Beijing by the Chinese Communist Party. The date deliberately chosen by the Khmer dictator was symbolic, for not only did he announce it to the world, but it gave him the opportunity to relate his party's glorious epic. In previous years, Pol Pot was satisfied with sending lengthy telegrams of congratulations to Beijing. The day of 27 September 1977 witnessed the prime minister's decision to proclaim three days of celebration on the seventeenth anniversary of the Communist Party of Kampuchea (CPK), and to commemorate that event with no more than a small gathering of some twenty-one radical Khmers at the Phnom Penh railway station, which nominated Saloth Sar for the third position on the Party's Central Committee, behind Tou Samouth, secretary general, and Nuon Chea, his assistant.[3] Pol Pot, in his *Black Book*, dates that moment as the Cambodian Communists' emancipation from Vietnamese tutelage, an example of his way of rewriting the Party's history.[4] The 29 and 30 September and 1 October were hence proclaimed major holidays honoring the CPK as well as all the world's great Communist leaders. It is equally interesting to note that the CPK was supposed to have been founded on the very anniversary of the date that Mao seized power in Beijing—a curious coincidence, indeed! Another coincidence, the birth of the Party, strangely fell at the beginning of Pchum Ben, or the Cambodian month of the dead, a time when every Khmer participated in the touching rituals of honoring the dead within pagoda walls throughout the land. The Khmer Rouge did not hesitate to appropriate it to commemorate their heroes who died for the Revolution.

The third holiday was the so-called anniversary of the founding of the Revolutionary Army on 17 January 1968. Thus, every 17 January was the occasion to sing the frenzied and impassioned praises of an army capable of exterminating with great courage enemies from without, and, more and more, traitors from within, and to herald the triumph, even before the Vietnamese, over the greatest "imperialist," "hegemonist," and "capitalist" country in the world: America! The army, as we have already said, was presented as "the dictatorship of the party's finest, noblest, and most efficient weapon of execution." The Party and its military arm became the new god that people had to venerate during that gloomy revolutionary calendar.

As for traditional family holidays like marriages—which were at the same time religious festivals—they were also abolished. Marriage was replaced by austere, collective, civil ceremonies, conducted under the auspices of the local *Angkar*. Substituting itself for traditional, parental authority, the Party chose spouses, more often than not without consulting the interested parties. No one doubts that these occasions were hardly joyful. Forced marriages fell well within the Party's policy of sexual repression that affected all strata of revolutionary society—with the exception, perhaps, of course, of the *Angkar Loeu*, who retained all the feudal privileges of deflowering virgins. This official Puritanism went completely against the country's tradition—at least as far as the stronger sex was concerned.

It took two forms: chastity for young people, and the delay and strict control of marriage. Numerous were the cases of arrest, imprisonment, and execution for simple "adultery" between consenting adults, including partners who were very much in love with each other but from whom the *Angkar* withheld permission to marry.[5] Even spouses separated for months at a time might be hit by the most severe sanctions, if under the cover of night they exercised their conjugal rights when one partner did not have the proper pass. What other society was as repressive in this domain? Cambodians called it *saletha ti pram muey*, "moral rule no. 6." It was the sixth commandment, among the twelve promulgated by the *Angkar* and especially directed toward soldiers.[6] Below we shall see it was tersely distilled into a simple watchword. How many unhappy people found themselves put in irons for "sexual misconduct," especially if the "guilty" parties did not belong to the same "caste," as in the case of any Khmer Rouge who dallied with the "17 April people"? Even an old Party militant who had fought decades for the Revolution, endured all sorts of hardships in the forests, ran all kinds of risks, and sacrificed his entire youth to the *Angkar*, could be thrown in prison, shackled naked in mud, or left in the sun to die of starvation, wallowing in his own excrement, if he had a weakness for a young—moreover a consenting—"17 April woman."[7]

The same rule did not apply to Khmer Rouge leaders who, it seemed, spared themselves nothing. For instance, Ta Thuon, (real name Koy Thuon), secretary for the North region (*phumpea oudor*) and secretary of state for commerce, was arrested in January 1977 for having deflowered seventy virgins during his long, revolutionary career—at least that was the rumor in his own regiment. He married off his "victims" to his soldiers. One had been married, it was said, to another high-ranking military official, a certain Ta Suon. But, Ta Khuon might also have occasionally spent nights with her after the marriage. Her husband reported his conduct to his superiors, and our Don Juan was arrested, and, in a sweep, so were all the officers and non-commissioned officers under his command, some 350 people in all.[8] According to witnesses, such practices were quite common in high places—especially in Phnom Penh. Officially, Ta Thuon (as well as his wife) was arrested for political reasons and duly charged for being in the pay of the CIA. The entire region was then purged.[9] But since these "gentlemen" never went without Western medicine, or luxury motorcars, or abundant supplies of food, or wines from France, why then should they not partake in the pleasures that the rest of the people at their mercy were denied? This was just one more contradiction of the regime and Mao could well have served as their model.

Finally, we should take note of the fact that in the impressive array of tortures inflicted in all prisons throughout the country, sexual ill treatments were practically absent—another Khmer exception to the general rule of the world's horrors. Or was it that witnesses dared not speak of them? Yet, some cases of rape—individual and collective—by soldiers, who executed their victims, have been reported. On the other hand, the mutilation of women's breasts and sexual organs was probably common, at the moment of execution. Too many witnesses equally reported that the fetuses were taken from wombs of pregnant women, dead or alive, by torturers, another horrific reality of this murderous regime.

Let us say in passing that Saloth Sar/Pol Pot took as another wife a young peasant woman thirty years his junior, with whom he had a daughter. His older wife Khieu Ponnary, stricken with mental disorder, is said to have consented to the match.

1—COLLECTIVISM ACCORDING TO POL POT

Pol Pot had made a great discovery which enabled him to catapult his Democratic Kampuchea thirty years ahead of his main models and competitors—Vietnam first, then the People's Republic of China—on the way to the Communist utopia. It was the collectivization of the entire society at one fell swoop. Turning individuals into a colony of ants under the enlightened guidance of the Party, Brother Number One reckoned, would multiply the Cambodian people's ability to produce tenfold.

This watchword from Pol Pot himself put into words this great "discovery":

332
បំផុសចលនាមហាជនបង្កបង្កើនផល
bâmphoh châlna: moha:chun bongkâ: bângkaen phâ:l
Generate a mass movement to multiply production.

With the image of the frail waterdrops that can merge into a mighty ocean, Pol Pot gives a vivid twist to this thought:

333
យើងមិនអាចធ្វើបដិវត្តតែម្នាក់ឯងបានទេ ពីព្រោះបក្ស បដិវត្ត
នឹងប្រជាជនផ្សារភ្ជាប់គ្នាជារាប់។
យើងទាំងអស់គ្នាប្រៀបបីដូចតំណក់ទឹក
ដែលរួមផ្ញុំគ្នាបង្កើតបានទៅជាមហាសមុទ្រ
Yœ:ng min ach thvœ: padévoat taè monéak aéng ba:n té pi: prueh pak padèvoat

> ning prâchiechun phsa:phchoap knie chie dâ: ra:p
> yœ:ng téang âh knie priep bey do:ch dâmnâk tœk
> daèl ruem pdom knie bângkaet ba:n chie moha:samot
> We cannot do the revolution on our own since the Party,
> the revolution, and the people are always welded.
> We are all like droplets that can merge together
> to create a mighty ocean.

Once the individuals had been diluted into the tempestuous seas of the permanent revolution, they were tossed about and lived a life of unspeakable misery.

According to Khieu Samphan, Pol Pot's tactic at any meeting— be it an *ad hoc* committee, the Standing Committee, or even the Central Committee of the Party—was first to listen carefully to the laborious reports of his semiliterate underlings who dressed up their performances. Then, he managed to make the most inarticulate cadres express themselves. Next, he would round up the debate, singling out the ideas that comforted his prejudices. He finally expressed his final decision making everyone believe they had each contributed to its formulation. All were mesmerized by the unctuous way he spoke and by his benign and winning smile. No one would even think to raise objections. The Pythia had uttered the words of wisdom. There was no vote. And each individual, each unit, was to implement that decision dutifully. Central Committee meetings were identical. In actual fact, they were merely reeducation sessions prepared by Brother Number One, assisted by Brother Number Two (Nuon Chea).

Note that in all Communist regimes the strategy of the one-party state is to collectivize not only society and the economy, but the leadership also, so that every political force, every individual personality, is supposed to be at one with their leader. Contrary to democratic societies that believe in differences, disagreements, and a balance of power that checks one another, the Communist regimes tend to become totalitarian states in so far as that principle contains its own contradiction and the group is dominated by an individual who will become the dictator. This is also what happened in the case of Pol Pot, although this was not to be revealed to the face of the world until after the fall of the regime.

This Machiavellian tactic can be summed up by one of Pol Pot's favorite watchwords:

334
សមូហភាពសំរេច បុគ្គលទទួលខុសត្រូវ
samuhaphiep somrach bokul totuel khoh trou
The collectivity decides, the individual is responsible.

By a sleight of hand, Pol Pot could take all decisions by himself (or so his entourage claims), along with Nuon Chea—since he claimed that he had the most proletarian mind and revolutionary spirit. He prided himself (and convinced his associates) that a life sacrificed for the cause of revolution was the very embodiment of the proletariat and therefore the mouthpiece of the poorest peasants. Then he turned to ordinary citizens and, through his state apparatus, coerced them to blindly obey his most aberrant commands. Later, in confronting the disastrous consequences of such orders, he could turn against the people and hold them accountable. They then entered the heinous tribe of "enemies" to be arrested, interrogated, tortured, and annihilated. This dictum contains in a nutshell all the sophistry and criminal frame of mind of the Khmer Rouge leadership. This is the ultimate recipe for a totalitarian state.

335
ពិគ្រោះពិភាក្សា និងរួមមតិសំរេចកិច្ចការ ទាំងអស់របស់បក្ស
ដោយធ្វើទៅតាមលក្ខការណ៍ប្រជាធិបតេយ្យប្រមូលផ្តុំ
pikrueh piphiek sa: ning ruem matè sâmrach kèchka: téang âh robâh pak
daoy thvœ: tou ta:m léakkha: prâchiethipatèy prâmo:lphdom

> Consult and debate,
> then the strict procedure of the Party is to unite all those views
> according to the requirements of democracy
> and gather them all closely together.

For the Khmer Rouge, the method of coming to a decision was a model of democracy, as the Party only verbalized the decision once everyone had expressed an opinion. Thus, the Party was supposed to be merely the voice of the collective mind.

2—REVOLUTIONARY CELEBRATIONS

No need to increase the number of feast days, as we see in the following slogan:

336
ថ្ងៃណាក៏បុណ្យ
thngay na: kâ: bon
Every day is a feast day.

This means that, under *Angkar*, every day was so joyous that it was indeed a holiday. The days set aside for special events or days of rest, had thus become unnecessary! In fact, most often, there were three days of rest a month, or one every ten days; yet, most of these "days off" were spent listening to long speeches by political commissars.

337
សង្គមចាស់គិតតែពីធ្វើបុណ្យ
sângkum chah kit taè thvœ: bon
The old society did nothing but celebrate.

Few Khmer Rouge commentaries on the old society, at least before the beginning of the civil war, might have been so on target. Khmers, like all the peoples of Southeast Asia, liked festivals, dances, and all demonstrations of the fullness of life; and that, precisely, was what the stern, puritan, and frankly sinister revolution killed. The people scoffed at their new masters in secret, saying:

338 C
សង្គមចាស់គិតតែពីធ្វើបុណ្យ
តែគេមានហូបគ្រប់គ្រាន់
sângkum chah kit taè pi: thvœ: bon taè ké mien ho:p krup kroan
The old society thought only of celebrating, but food was sufficient.

339
ភ្លេងសង្គមចាស់ជាភ្លេងខ្មោច
phléng sângkum chah chie phléng khmaoch
Music in the old society was music fit for ghosts.

This epigram seems to indicate that, like all traditional arts, traditional music has become irrelevant to revolutionary society. Still, this was not the case, as in every district or even at times collectives, traditional music was played to create a pleasant atmosphere while waiting for a political oration (it could even be wedding music, with the cheerful xylophones), or to accompany revolutionary songs and dances during Party celebrations.

True, a melancholy and nostalgic tone does prevail in traditional Khmer music. However the Khmer Rouge strove to speed up the beat and introduce marches according to the models from the Chinese Cultural Revolution. They tried to energize the Cambodian people in their frantic race toward Communism.

3—MALE-FEMALE RELATIONS

As for sexual abstinence, we have here a warning which says everything succinctly:

340
សម្ផស្សល្អជាឧបស័គ្គនៃឧន្ទ:ប្រយុទ្ធ
sâmphoah lâ'â: chie upasak ney chhantèak prâyut
Physical beauty hinders the will to struggle.

You gave yourself body and soul to the revolution as if you were entering holy orders, thereby renouncing the pleasures of the world.

Let us recall that when the Khmer Rouge speaks of "struggle," they mean it in two senses—for war and for production. How many hidden dramas were played out in the course of these years of blood baths? Here we might cite the story of an assistant prison warden who fell in love with a female prisoner. One night, they both disappeared. The next day their naked bodies were found embracing each other; they had taken poison from their own hand! The dead man had been summoned to appear before the *Angkar* to answer for his "crime."[10]

341
កុំរំលោភទៅលើសិទ្ធរបស់ប្រជាជន
kom rumlo:ph tou lœ: sit robâh prâchiechun
Do not violate the people's rights.

Depending upon the situation, this counsel, often repeated, especially to Khmer Rouge soldiers, meant that they should not be cruel to, say, children; but it principally meant that young cadres should respect young women.

A similar recommendation is more explicit:

342
កុំរំលោភទៅលើយុវនារី!
kom rumlo:ph tou lœ: yuvéanieri:
Do not defile young girls!

343
មិត្តមិនត្រូវប៉ះពាល់នារីភេទម្ចើយ
mit min trou pahpoal nieri: phét laœy
Comrades, do not touch the female sex.

Everyone knew "moral rule no. 6" (សីលធម៌ទី៦ *Salethoa ti pram muey*): "Thou shalt not commit any indecent act with a woman."

344
យុវជនត្រូវរក្សាគោលជំហរឱ្យរឹងប៉ឹង
ឯខាងនារីត្រូវប្រយ័ត្នកុំឱ្យធូររលុង
yuvéachun trou rèaksa: ko:l chumho: aoy reung bœng
aè kha:ng nieri: trou prâyat kom aoy tho: ro:lung
Young men must retain a strong position,
young girls must never become lax!

345 C
ចូលកងមេម៉ាយភ័យខ្លាចខ្មោចលង
cho:l kâ:ng méma:y phey khla:ch khmaoch lo:ng
*Joining the widows' brigade
is running the risk of being haunted by ghosts.*

This was a mischievous remark by the people implying that when a woman lost her husband, her status changed, and if she was still young, she was put in the youth brigade. As they were working not far from the men, she was put in a position where she could be courted.

As for marriages, they were strictly controlled by the *Angkar*. Before marrying, the Party repeated there were three conditions to be met.

346

១-អាចជ្រើសរើសប្ដីស្រករដោយខ្លួនឯង
២-អង្គការចាត់តាំង
៣-មិនពោរពតាមអង្គការចាត់តាំងទេ
ត្រូវបញ្ជូនទៅរៀនសូត្រមួយរយៈ

1 - a:ch chrœ:h rœ:h ku: srâhkâ: daoy khluen aèng

2 - ângka: chattang

3 - min ko:rup ta:m ângka: chattang té,
trou bânhchu:n tou rien so:t muey royéak

1 - You can choose your spouse yourself.

2 - *Angkar* endorses [your partner].

3 - If you do not obey *Angkar*'s discipline,
you will be sent to a study session for a time.

Again, another example of Orwellian "doublethink." Young people had to accept a partner chosen by the Party and at the same time convince themselves that it was their own personal choice. Likewise, for the authorities, the spouse they chose was by definition the best, and therefore desired by both parties, since the Party was infallible in matters of the heart, as in all matters. On the one hand, the *Angkar* proclaimed *urbi et orbi* that everyone was his own master in the revolutionary society; yet, at the same time, *Angkar* threatened him or her with a dire penalty—reeducation or even death—if he did not accept the Party's choice. However, there were strange twists to this rule and, thanks to the kind-heartedness of some leaders, some could discreetly make their own choices and have them sanctioned by the *Angkar*. Still, let us not forget that in traditional Cambodia it was essentially the parents—the bride's mother in particular—who chose the spouse, usually sanctioned by the approval of the interested parties. In the new Khmer Rouge society, the *Angkar* took over the role of father and mother for every young Cambodian. Thus, it was natural also that it chose who would marry whom, generally without demanding the consent of the future spouses. There is some indication, too, that the choices were carefully discussed among local Party cadres.[11]

All Cambodians will describe to you these imposed, collective marriages. Young men and women, from a few to up to six hundred, would stand in rows facing each other, with men on one side and women on the other, and each had to marry the partner that stood directly in front of him or her, preselected by the *Angkar*. In certain cases, the *Angkar* might accept the choices of interested parties, especially the young men's, but also sometimes the young women's, which traditional Khmers found shocking. Luck at times had a hand in this, and in some arranged marriages the couples learned to love one another and have remained together ever since.

Everyone would stand or sit on the floor, in two rows, facing one another. A local leader from the commune or the district would deliver a speech, saying that from that day onward, the young married couples should stand hand in hand in order to struggle for production, defend the country, fight against enemies of all stripes, etc.—ever the same refrain. After the discourse, each couple rose, approached each other, and shook hands. They repeated after the leader the following words: "I take you by the hand, in order to participate with all our energy in the reconstruction of our country and to achieve the goals of our agricultural production . . ." They could also repeat:

347
ប្តេជ្ញាស្រលាញ់គ្នាដល់ស្លាប់រៀងខ្លួន
pdachnha srâlanh knie dâl slap rieng khluen
Be determined to love each other until death.[12]

When there were many couples, it could happen that in the confusion some could not immediately find a partner. In the case of Khmer Rouge cadres or soldiers, the celebration was more festive and the number of pairs more restricted. They would sing a couple of revolutionary songs. There could also be a band and the couples might dance three or four revolutionary dances, fists held high toward the heavens in the "dance of the possessed." Then they exchanged small gifts—an orange, some tobacco, fruit; the husbands, a *krâma*, or a mat. For the more fortunate, a meal with chicken was shared.

Finally, each couple went off, a rolled mat on the shoulder, looking for a place for a night of honeymooning. That would be the occasion for laughter everywhere in the community, for if the couple had lived in collective dormitories, there was no place for them to be alone and have some privacy. The newlyweds at times sought in vain for a quiet place until the small hours of the morning! Still, they could usually find refuge in one of their parents' homes, which could be some distance away.

When it was possible, the people officially married by the *Angkar* made a very secret traditional ceremony later at home.

***

The two announcements that follow meant that unmarried young women in people's communes had to perform their revolutionary duty and take care of wounded soldiers, often missing an arm or a leg or two. They foreshadow forced marriages to physically disabled, so feared by young women educated in the towns. Some preferred suicide to what they considered a shameful plight.

348
កំបិកំបាក់០៥រង់ចាំនារីឃុំ
kâmbèkâmbak so:npram rung cham nieri: khum
Handicapped soldiers from squad 05
are expecting the young women from the commune.

349
កំបិកំបាក់០៥រងចាំនារីដាច់ខាត
kâmbèkâmbak so:npram rung chamnieri: dach kha:t
Handicapped soldiers from squad 05
are expecting the young women
who are resolved [to serve the revolution].

4—THE COLLECTIVE IS THE NEW FAMILY

It was no wonder if the newlyweds tried to protect their privacy for, in this revolutionary society, the very nature of the nuclear family was transformed.

350
រស់នៅក្នុងមហាគ្រួសារថ្មី
តែមួយហើយគិតតែប្រយោជន៍សមូហភាព
ruh nou knong moha: kruesa: thmey
taè muey haœy kittaè prâyaoch samu:haphiep
Let us all live as one huge new family
and think only of the interest of the collective.

351
លះបង់កម្មសិទ្ធិសួនតួ÷ ឪពុកម្តាយញាតិសន្តាន
lèahbâng kamasit suentue - oupuk mda:y nhietsânda:n
Give up all personal belongings:
renounce your father, your mother, all your family.

Here is one of fundamental commandments of the society created by the Khmer Rouge, although it broke with all the country's traditions. It was addressed, above all, to young soldiers and revolutionaries. The *Angkar* willed that all family ties be more utilitarian and less emotional. It was a matter of producing children. That may explain the cruelty of some young Khmer Rouge toward their own parents. During the education they received away from the household, the adolescent soldiers were taught to no longer call their mothers "mama" (*maè*), but "auntie" (*ming*), like any other woman of that age, the mother being no longer distinguishable from her female peers. The only social relation—and equally, emotional relation—that counted was the vertical relation of filial affection toward—in truth, submission to—the *Angkar*. At the same time, the Khmer Rouge kept other words of kinship ("uncle," "aunt," "brother," etc.) in order that the revolutionary society be seen as "one big family," with the *Angkar* as its head, at once tutor and parent of an entire people that they had infantilized. All affection and love that a son or daughter had for his or her mother and father, and that parents had for their children, had to be transferred to the *Angkar*.

This grand idea of one large, revolutionary family is clearly expressed by the following dictum:

352

ត្រូវពះរេងង់គ្រួសារតូចឆ្នាំងតូច ហើយបង្កើតឆ្នាំងធំ
គ្រួសារធំ មហាគ្រួសារមហាថ្លៃប្រឌិតបដិវត្តន៍ខ្ពស់!

trou lèah bâng kruesa: to:ch chhnang to:ch haœy bânkaœt chnang thom
kruesa: thum moha: kruesa: moha: chney prâdit padévoat khpuh!

Renounce immediate family ties, the hearth's pot, and adopt the
big pot, the big family, the immense family;
have an extremely high revolutionary consciousness!

There were other significant modifications in the way the people were to address one another. Some words disappeared from the common vocabulary, such as the most used "Mr." and "Mrs.," and replaced by the inevitable *samamit*, or the shorter *mit*, "comrade." All forms of address for the clergy, as well as for high-ranking civil servants, were suppressed. All this is well known. Even the word "teacher," *lok kru*, or "professor," *sasracha*, no longer had currency and was replaced by *samamit vapathoa* or "comrade of culture."

353
ត្រូវបំបាត់ចោលគោលជំហរតំបន់និយម
អង្គភាពនិយម ផ្នែកនិយម ។ល។

trou bombat chaol ko:l chumho: dombânniyum
angkaphiepniyum phnaèk niyum - lak -

**You must absolutely wipe out regional stance,
team spirit, and individualism, etc.**

In the name of the collectivist ethos represented by the voice of the Party, every sense of solidarity at the regional level, the team level, together with individual thinking, had to be banished. This is just one more contradiction with socialist thought that is indicative of totalitarian ideology.

5—THE NEW ORDER

This new society, deprived of traditional religious holidays, without social classes save the proletariat, had to make a clean sweep of the past and enjoy a triumphant egalitarianism. More than any other revolutionary movement of the nineteenth or twentieth centuries, the Khmer Rouge, proclaiming themselves ardent patriots, dreamed of making the least amount of compromise with the country's historic past. In the iconoclastic storm of events, the duty to do away with the past helps to explain the Khmer Rouge's cruelty and contempt for human life. In killing humans, they felt that they were destroying not human beings, but the "feudalists," "capitalists," "compradors," or "lackeys of imperialism," etc.—a host of so-called injustices and blatant corruption instead of people made of flesh and blood.

354
កំទេចរបបចាស់ផ្លាស់យករបបថ្មី

kâmtéch robâ:p chah phlah yo:k robâ:p thmey

Destroy the old order, replace it with the new.

355
កែប្រែរបបចាស់ឱ្យទៅជារបបថ្មី
kaè praè robâ:p chah aoy tou chie robâ:p thmey
Transform the old order into the new order.

356 C
បំបាត់អាចាស់ ផ្លាស់អាថ្មី !
bâmbat a: chah phlah a: thmey
Abolish everything old, replace it with everything new.

The people took up this refrain to mock their executioners, and thereby, in saying it facetiously, ridiculed their destructive urges.

To deride the nonsensical policies of *Angkar* that forced the people to continuously relocate from the comfortable houses along the river banks to the poorer hinterland, and then into the uninhabited jungle, the people would say:

357 C
ជយោអង្គការដ៏រុងរឿង រុះផ្ទះក្បឿងទៅនៅផ្ទះស្បូវ
ជយោអង្គការដ៏ត្រឹមត្រូវ រុះផ្ទះស្បូវទៅនៅក្នុងព្រៃ
cheiyo: ângka: dâ: rong reueng, ruh phtéah kbŭeung tou nou phtéah sbou
cheiyo: ângka: treum trou, ruh phtéah sbou tou nou knong prey
Long live the glorious Angkar! Destroy houses with tiled roofs,
live in straw huts!
Long live the wise Angkar! Destroy straw huts and live in the forest!

358
មើលពីក្រោយហាំ មើលចំហេវ
mœ:l pi kraoy hâm mœ:l châmhév
From behind, all looks well; from the front, all is paltry.

This seemed to answer back the new masters of the country. This traditional saying is still used by young men today to describe the girls they tease: from the back, they seem pretty and attractive; from the front, they seem uninviting and cold.

359
តែម្នាក់ក៏ធ្វើបដិវត្តបានដែរ

taè mnéak kâ: thvœ: pdévoat ba:n daè
Even if you are alone, you can also make the revolution.

***

The Marxist conception of "proletarian" always was, in official phraseology, rendered as "worker-peasant." Workers, however, were rare, and constituted rather a privileged group, as we have seen. Only the poor peasants who were well educated in the eyes of the *Angkar* (that is, completely ignorant) were the base of this extreme revolution.

360
មានវណ្ណៈតែមួយគត់ គឺវណ្ណៈកសិករ

mien vannak taè muey kut keu: vannak kasékâ:
There is only one class—the peasant class.

361
គ្មានអ្នកមាន គ្មានអ្នកក្រ

kmien néak mien kmien néak krâ:
There are no longer any rich, there are no longer any poor.

Such are the type of declarations that peppered the *Angkar*'s official speeches, particularly at the beginning of the regime, to evoke in listeners a new, marvelous world about to be born, where the crying inequalities and injustices of Lon Nol's Republican government had been expelled.

The following slogan is in the same vein.

362
រស់នៅស្មើភាពគ្នា
ruh nou smaephiep knie
Let us all live in equality.

Signs of deference to superiors, and to the royal family especially, were obviously banished. Even the traditional gesture of greeting (សំពះ *sompéah*) found in most of Southeast Asia—a slight bow of the head with the two hands placed together—was considered a relic of the past. Yet, when Pol Pot was forced to receive his famous prisoner, Norodom Sihanouk, on 5 January 1979, the eve of Pol Pot's ignominious flight from Phnom Penh, in order to send the prince to the United Nations to defend the cause of Democratic Kampuchea against the Vietnamese invasion, the supreme Khmer Rouge leader demonstrated that he had not forgotten the traditional royal greeting used in the palace when he was young. Here is what Sihanouk has to say about the way Pol Pot welcomed him, in his *Prisoner of the Khmer Rouge:*

> It was the first time, since 1973—the time of my memorable trip to the liberated zone—that Pol Pot and I met. The dictator of Democratic Kampuchea awaited me, smiling, before the great palace door. Surprise: before the inevitable embrace, Pol Pot greeted me with a *sompéah*, the hands joined, with a small genuflection, as in the days of the "old society."

363
សមមិត្តការអង្វរករ វាហួសសម័យហើយ
samamit ka: ângvâ:kâ: vie hueh samay haœy
Comrade, bowing deeply is now out of date.

The black clothing and Ho Chi Minh rubber sandals, worn by all old people, then gradually, by all new people, was the visible sign of this frenzied egalitarianism.

364
សមមិត្តមានសិទ្ធិស្មើៗគ្នា សមមិត្តស្លៀកពាក់ខ្មៅ ស្បែកជើងខ្មៅ អង្គការក៍ពាក់ខ្មៅដែរ

samamit mien sit smae smae knie samamit sliek péak khmau
sbaèk chœ:ng khmau ângka: kâ: péak khmau daè

Comrades, you all have the same rights; comrades, you wear black clothing, black shoes; the *Angkar* also dresses in black.

365
ពាក់វែនតាខៀវឱ្យចំបើងសេះស៊ី

péak vaènta: khiev aoy châmbaœng sèh si:

Wearing sunglasses is like giving hay to horses.

This mocking remark might appear incomprehensible. In Cambodia, when plants begin to become scarce for animals to feed on, it is because heavy rains at the end of the rainy season have flooded the pastures in many areas of the country. It can also be because in the dry season, when cattle are fed with hay, horses are more frugal eaters, satisfied to graze on grass very close to the earth's surface. Feeding hay to a horse, would, in Khmer eyes, be seen as a horrible mistake—as useless as wearing sunglasses! The comparison is quite laughable! For the Khmer Rouge, wearing sunglasses was the height of decadence and here they have stigmatized this superfluous luxury.

6—THE END OF INDIVIDUAL PROPERTY

366
ត្រូវលះបង់ដាច់ខាតនូវកម្មសិទ្ធិសួនតួ

trou lèah bâng dach kha:t nou kamesit suentue

You must absolutely give up all personal property.

Here was a *sine qua non* of total collectivization. This injunction was one of the reasons for the complete evacuation of the towns. The *Angkar* had falsely promised the general population that they would be returning shortly to towns and cities, and that they could therefore leave without taking anything with them. In addition, during the retreat from towns, Khmer Rouge soldiers "invited" them to give up consumer goods to them, and during the first weeks and months of the regime, the "17 April" had to swap personal belongings—mostly clothing—with the *mulethans* for food. Furthermore, during the numerous deportations and movements, most were gradually stripped of the least bit of personal property.

However, in spite of this very harsh condition, some managed to keep personal papers or jewelry, because, if they were not taken to prison, there were never any body searches. According to Khmer tradition, the body was respected as sacred, even among the Khmer Rouge.

367
កំចាត់កម្មសិទ្ធិឯកជនកសាងកម្មសិទ្ធិសមូហភាព
kâmchat kamsit aèkchun kâ:sa:ng kamesit samu:haphiep
Away with individual private property; build collective property!

The same notion was usually found in a more striking formula:

368
កំទេចស្មូនត្ន កសាងស្មូនរួម !
kâmtéch suen tue, kâ:sa:ng suen ruem
Destroy individualism; build the collective spirit![13]

369
ស្មូនត្នូនិងស្មូនរួមវាទាក់ទងគ្នាដល់មូលធននិយម ដល់សង្គមនិយម
suen tue neng suen ruem vie téak to:ngknie dâl mulethuniyum dâl sangkumniyum
Individualism is to collectivism as capitalism to socialism.[14]

Selfishness corresponds to capitalism; if people are altruistic, they have a socialist attitude.

***

But the peasants found it very painful to turn over agricultural equipment, as well as animals, to the collective. Still, they had to abide by this:

370
របស់របរប្រើប្រាស់ដូចជា រទេះគោ រទេះសេះ
ជារបស់សមូហភាព
robâhrobâ: praœprah do:chchie rotèh ko: rotèh sèh
chie robâh samu:haphiep
All equipment, like cattle carts, horse-drawn carriages,
belong to the collective.

371
សត្វពាហនៈទាំងអស់ ត្រូវដាក់សហាករណ៍
ធ្វើជារបស់សមូហភាព
satpiehanak téang âh trou dak sahakâ: thvœ: chie robâh samu:haphiep
All domestic animals must be entrusted to the collective
to become collective property.

372
អ្វីក៏ដោយសុទ្ធតែជារបស់អង្គការ !
avey kâ: daoy sot taè chie robâh ângka:
Absolutely everything belongs to the *Angkar*.

No Cambodian could keep anything for himself. All property acquired during the former regimes had to be turned over to the authorities: bicycles, radios, clothing, save a spare pair of trousers and a shirt. Bank notes, as well, were destroyed. They were of no use in the new society. Let us say that in the new reality, the Khmer

Rouge leaders could amass any number of consumer goods (such as houses packed with radios), under the pretext that it did not belong to them but to the *Angkar*, which was the usual alibi!

This slogan indicated the complete collectivization of property, even the most personal. Of course, as we have already seen, everyone tried to hide gold and jewelry, which much later would become of great value when the Khmer Rouge society fell apart. The slogan takes on its significance when we know that in the name of this absolute principle, the fruit of millions of Cambodians' daily labor automatically became the *Angkar*'s, since all wages had been abolished.

To strip the new people of all the possessions they had been able to carry during the emptying of the towns, three methods were used. A Khmer Rouge soldier could ask that an item, like a watch, be handed over to him. In that case, the word used was ស្នើ (*snae*), "to ask, to propose." When this was formulated, force was implicit. Despite reluctance to comply with the request, one had to acquiesce; an outright refusal might have fatal consequences. A second method, mainly used in the first months of the regime, was barter: clothes or Western medicines were exchanged for food by the new people. The third method was more brutal. The following expression was used:

373
ជំរុះកំអែលសក្តិភូមិ
chumruh kâm aèl sakedèphu:m
Drop all the leftovers of feudalism.

Let us note that the word ជំរុះ (*chumruh*) is also used in the context of war, by soldiers who have to drop their weapons. The "17 April people" were indeed treated like prisoners of war. This more threatening injunction could be taken in the literal sense of shedding all items coming from the previous regimes, in the figurative sense, to mean that one had to embrace the revolutionary ideology and drop the old ones.

374
កាត់ផ្តាច់របបកម្មសិទ្ធិ
កម្ចាត់ចោលពាណិជ្ជកម្មចាស់ ហើយបង្កើតពាណិជ្ជកម្មថ្មី
kat phdach robâ:b kamaset
kâmchat chaol pienichkam chah haey bângkaet pienichkam thmey
Absolutely get rid of the property regime,
throw away the old trade and create a new trade.[15]

375
មិនបាច់លាក់របស់របរទេ ព្រោះអង្គការមានម៉ាស៊ីនឆ្លុះ
min bach léak robâh robâ: té prueh ângka: mien masi:ne chhloh
Useless to hide your own possessions,
the *Angkar* has magnifying glasses.

The word ឆ្លុះ (*chhloh*) could be any instrument that could enlarge or throw light on any object under investigation (looking-glass, microscope, torch, etc.). Such a declaration seems a joke, but alas, that was not the case. The new authorities, especially at the beginning of the regime, called upon all citizens to turn over consumer goods such as cassette players, and more to the point, radios—items that the more bold had already buried in plastic so that they could retrieve them later. Such a statement was so patently deceptive, since nowhere did the Khmer Rouge have any scientific equipment, but it could nevertheless frighten the less brave and make them give up these compromising objects.[16]

376
ថ្ងៃនេះអង្គការលើកទិសវាយកណ្ដុរ
thngay nih ângka: lœ:k teuh viey kândol
Today the *Angkar* has decided to attack rats.

It was not, as you might believe, a question of attacking, once more, hidden enemies of the revolution, but of searching houses or the edge of villages for the inhabitants' personal possessions: not only radios, but also books, paper, pens, etc.—all objects that could be used for subversive activities. As in *1984*, nothing is officially forbidden (except radios), but the possession of these objects could arouse suspicion. Teams were thus formed to search and verify that no one had them inside or outside the village.

377

មិត្តឯងធ្លាប់ស្រណុកធ្លាប់ស្រួល

mit aèng thloap srânok thloap sruel

Comrade, you have been used to a comfortable and easy life.

Of course, this was the Khmer Rouge talking to former town dwellers. Again, we have here a very common statement heard in speeches at the beginning of the regime. This betrayed a spirit of vengeance—in a certain way justified by the many who had benefited from corruption. However, we must not forget that the overwhelming majority of deportees were poor, or at best, from humble backgrounds.

***

With the disappearance of individual and private property and, at the same time, all markets, all human failings around the exchange of goods and commodities should have been crushed.

378

គ្មានលក់គ្មានដូរ គ្មានថ្ងៃគ្មានថូច
គ្មានលួច គ្មានប្លន់ គ្មានកំមុសិទ្ធិស៊ុនទូ

kmien luek kmien do: kmien thngo: kmien thguech

kmien luech kmien plân kmien kamesèt suen tue

Collectivism: The Dissolution of the Individual 281

> There are no more sales, no more exchanges,
> no more complaints,
> no more robberies, no more looting, no more individual property.

379
បដិវត្តន៍មិនមែនធ្វើតែភូមិនេះទេ គឺធ្វើទូទាំង
កម្ពុជា ដូចនេះអ្នកមិនត្រូវហូបផ្អែតតែឯងទេ
ត្រូវតែចែករំលែកឱ្យគេហូបផង

padévoat min mè:n thvœ: taè phu:m nih té keu: thvœ: tu:téang
kampuchie do:ch nih néak min trou ho:p châ'aèt taè aèng té,
trou taè chaèkrumlè:k aoy ké ho:p phâ:ng

> The revolution is not taking place in this village alone; it is taking
> place throughout all of Kampuchea; that is, do not stuff yourself
> with food—you must share with all the others.

Here again is another admirable expression of equality and justice. In reality, this was a complete fraud, for it is easy to imagine that little went to economically deprived zones. To receive aid, it was necessary to state that the goals of production had not been reached, thereby admitting that the collective farm had failed in its duty. This could have dangerous consequences. The radio only praised the most arid zones when, only with the strength of their hands and sweat of their brows, did the poorest have to meet, and go beyond, the plan's objectives. And, they were cited endlessly as models to follow, like, say, the province of Kompong Speu. In actual fact, food had to be shared with the People's Republic of China, irrespective of rats, since waste must have been so widespread in the absence of markets.

380
កម្មសិទ្ធិសមរម្យរបស់ប្រជាជនកម្ពុជា
គឺសំពាយ១ស្បោងតូច

kamesit sâmrum robâh prâchiechun kampuchie
keu: sâmpiey muey sbaong to:ch

> All that every Cambodian has the right to own
> is a small bundle he can carry on his back.

Admirable precept of monastic poverty, surely! Most Khmer Rouge soldiers, hardened by years of hard fighting and Spartan living conditions in the maquis, could easily adapt to it. According to eyewitnesses, this was definitely not the case for top leaders.

381 C
កម្មសិទ្ធិសមរម្យរបស់ប្រជាជនកម្ពុជា ពីក្នុងស្បោង១តូច

kamesit sâmrum robâh prâchiechun kampuchie
keu: ko:n sbaong muey to:ch
All that every Cambodian has the right to own is a small bundle.

The people gave the previous slogan a twist, to mock the Khmer Rouge. The small "bundle" thereby meant, derisively, "the stomach." No one received a salary and so had hardly enough to fill his own stomach.

***

Khmers, like all Asians, have always had a penchant for jewelry since time immemorial. We must however understand that in a climate where everything is perishable, gold and jewelry was a means of personal banking. All jewels were naturally forbidden during Pol Pot's time. The prudent thus hid everything that they could save from the frenzied days that followed 17 April 1975. Because body searches were not the rule, except when being thrown into prisons, Cambodians frequently managed to save their most precious belongings. They proved useful when the Khmer Rouge fled the country in 1979.

What did the Khmer Rouge rulers do with all this mass of wealth, and in particular, with the belongings of the numerous victims of extermination? They stored them in warehouses, and traded jewels for spare parts at the Thai border, as we noted. After the collapse of the revolutionary regime, some of those responsible for the numerous crimes against humanity arrived with pockets full in Thailand, and, after being able to pass themselves off as their own victims, they were welcomed as refugees in Western countries. It is certain that a large part was abandoned and taken as booty by the Vietnamese army.

382
មាសប្រាក់ ខ្សែក ខ្សែដែជាច្រវាក់ចងដែចងជើងសមមិត្ត
វាជាកត្តារាំងស្ទះក្នុងចលនាបដិវត្តន៍ ហាមប្រើដាច់ខាត !

mieh prak khsaèkâ: khsaèday chie chrâ:vak châ:ngday châ:ngchœ:ng samamit

viechie katta: réangstèah knong châlana: padévoat ha:mprœ dachkha:t

Gold, silver, necklaces, bracelets are chains
that bind your arms and legs.
Comrades, they shackle the revolutionary movement!
They are absolutely forbidden!

383 C
កន្សែងក្រហមសមនឹងអាវខ្មៅ ស៊ីនឹងឡេវអាវមួយកុងតូច

kânsaèng krâhâ:m sâm neung a:v khmau si:neung lèv a:v muey kong to:ch

The red krâma goes with a black shirt
adorned with a whole troop of buttons.

Kong to:ch, in Khmer Rouge parlance, designated a work team of some thirty individuals. The height of elegance for young workers, for whom all colored clothing had been banned, was to adorn their black shirt with as many buttons as possible, without forgetting to stitch some on the pockets. The white contrasted with the prevailing black garments in the sunlight. The difficulty was to find real buttons, and stylish younger people were led to carve pieces of plastic for lack of the real thing.

384
មាសប្រាក់ ស្រូវអង្ករទុកឱ្យល្អជូនអង្គការ
mieh prak srou ângkâ: tuk aoy lâ"â: chu:n ângka:
Gold, silver, paddy—turn over your belongings to the *Angkar*.[17]

This slogan echoed a traditional saying or *chpap proh*, typical of popular Khmer wisdom:

មាសប្រាក់ស្រូវអង្ករ ទុកអោយល្អកុំសប្បុរស
សំចៃកុំអោយអស់ មើលថែថ្លួនខ្លួនឯងណា
mieh prak srou ângkâ: tuk aoy lâ"â: kom sâborâh
sâmchay kom aoy âh mœ:l thaè thuen khluen aèng na:
Gold, silver, rice—take good care of them.
Do not be too generous.
Save and do not give all. Take good care of yourself.

7—THE SOCIALIST SOCIETY

385
ឰានកម្មសិទ្ធិឯកជនគឺ ធ្វើបដិវត្តសង្គមនិយមបានល្អ
kmien kamaset aèkechuen keu: tvœ: padévoat sângkumniyum ban lâ'â:
Once there is no individual property,
then we can work for a perfect revolutionary society.

386
ចង់ដើរអោយមានចលនាបដិវត្ត សង្គមនិយម
ត្រូវតែកំចាត់កម្មសិទ្ធិឯកជនអោយអស់ពីខ្លួន
chong dae aoy toan châlna padévoat sangkumniyum
trou taé komchat kamaset aèkechun aoy âh pi: khluen

If you want to join the socialist revolution,
you must totally disperse your own individual property.

387
គ្រប់សរសៃញាក់នៃសួនតួ និងសួនគ្រួ ត្រូវស្ថិតនៅក្រោមសួនរួមរបស់
ប្រជាជាតិ វណ្ណៈ ប្រជាជន និងបដិវត្តន៍ដាច់ខាត

krup sosaynhéak ney suen tue neng suen krue trou thet nou kraom suen
ruem robâh prochiechiet vannak prochiechun ning padévoat dach kha:t

The entire network of blood vessels vibrates
with individualism and family-ism, which must be placed beneath
the collectivism of the nation,
the proletariat, and the absolute revolution.

***

The people, fatalistic and with a sense of humor, saw that one of the permanent features of life, be it under a republican or revolutionary regime, was that everyone had a well-defined role and knew how to profit from the situation, or weather it, according to his abilities. This was an unchangeable societal trait under different forms of government, where the same attitudes prevailed. There are always profiteers and victims. This amused and fatalistic detachment is a telltale characteristic of the Khmer mentality.

388 C
អនាម័យពេទ្យ ស៊ីឆ្អែតសេដ្ឋកិច្ច វាយកំទេចយោធា វេទនាឈ្លប
លបៗនារសារ ហ៊ឺហាប្រធានកង ត្រូវដំបងប្រធានក្រុម
ក្រញេមក្រញ៉ូប្រធានពួក ដេកទ្រមក់សមាជិក

ana:may pét / si:chhâ'aèt sétekèch / viey kâmtéch yo:thie / vétenie chhlo:p /
lo:b lo:b nieresa: / heu:ha: prâtheien kâ:ng / trou dâmbâ:ng prâthien krom /
krânhémkrânhom prâthien puek / dék tromuek sama:chik.

Hygiene is for the health officer, food aplenty is the destiny of the quartermaster, attacking is the soldier's duty, a hard life is the lot of the militia, stalking is the way of the messenger, the battalion

*commander struts, the group leader bears the blame, the team
leader is indecisive, the members of the collective are all asleep.*

The *chhlop* played the role of municipal police or militia, as well as intelligence agent, throughout the country. But the exact definition of the word means stalking like a wolf, observing and listening to the people; in sum, they were spies. They were chosen among the healthiest adults and armed with rifles; soldiers carried heavier weapons. It was they who squatted in dark corners at night, under houses on stilts, to overhear intimate conversations and report them to the *Angkar*. It was they who closely watched the general population and carried out the hunt for "enemies." We might say that they were pitiable because they worked in the shadows and in the darkness of night.

To live with the Khmer Rouge, the people had to hearten and congratulate them for fulfilling different tasks. However, we should say that, as in the past, it was always those at the bottom of the social ladder who received the blows and blame, since they were forced to carry out a mad policy. The team leader, though the closest to the base, could be the most feared and loathed, for, at work, he was constantly watching the general population and was always threatening them.

389 C

អនាម័យពេទ្យ ស៊ុីផ្អែតកម្មាភិបាល ដាច់កបែកក្បាលប្រជាជន

ana:may pét si: chhâ:'aèt kama:phiba:ldach kâ: baèk kba:l prâchiechun

*Hygiene for health workers, a full stomach for the cadres,
slit throats and broken heads for the people*

390 C

អនាម័យពេទ្យ ស៊ុីផ្អែតសេដ្ឋកិច្ច
វាយកំទេចយោធា វែទនានារសារ ហ៊ុហាសិល្បៈ

ana:may pét si: chhâ:'aèt séthekèch

viey kâmtéch yo:thie vétenie nieresa: heu:ha: sèlepak

Health workers preach hygiene, the quartermaster eats to his heart's content, the soldier hits and destroys,
the messenger suffers [a hard life], the artist cuts a fine figure.

391 C
ប្រធានក្រុមធំជាងប្រធានភូមិ
prâ:thien krom thum chieng prâ:thien phu:m
The team leader is more powerful than the village chief.

Here is an ironical quip of the general population, who shielded itself from the abuse of power of group leaders who held sway over ten to fifteen people. Some would conduct themselves like true tyrants and overstep the orders of their superiors.

392
កុំបោះសន្ទូចរំលងភ្នំ
kom bâh sântu:ch rumlo:ng phnum
Don't cast the fishing line beyond the hill!

This traditional saw means that when one has a problem, it should be referred directly to one's own boss among local authorities, following the line of command. If one appeals directly to the higher authorities, it is a mistake. In Khmer Rouge society, one must first go to the *mekrom*, or team leader, then to the *mekong toch* or platoon leader, then to the *mekong thom* or company leader, then to the *mekong vireak* or battalion leader. If one addresses the battalion leader directly, the three others are displeased. The next slogan reiterates this.

393
ផ្លូវកាត់តែងមានបន្លា ត្រូវរាយការណ៍តាមលំដាប់
phlŏu kat taèng mien bânla: trou riey ka: ta:m lumdap
Shortcuts are always thorny paths; follow the line of command.

394
ទៅណាមកណាជាមួយអង្គភាព
tou na: mo:k na: chie muey ângkaphiep
Wherever you go, you must go with your unit.

Here, it is a question of small units, usually of three people. No one ever had the right to travel alone: in threes, one could watch the other two.

As far as it was possible, individual labor had been banished. The majority of the population was assembled in work groups, like an army of workers. The largest grouping corresponded to what was called *kong vireak* or "battalion." Composed of three hundred people, it was divided into groups of one hundred people (*kong thom,* large group), which were, in turn, subdivided into three groups of about thirty workers (*kong krom,* small groups), and each of these was divided into three groups of ten (*kong,* base teams), which consisted of *puok,* or small units of three people, if we ignore the head of the base groups. The only exceptions were, per haps, the children who minded animals, or those who went out to collect medicinal herbs and plants in the forest, and could go about freely as individuals—a very coveted and privileged task!

395
ត្រូវចេះហូបរួមធ្វើការរួម !
trou chèh ho:p ruem tvœ:ka: ruem
Learn to eat collectively, work collectively!

This general order, once more, was literally followed. Collective work and meals in the people's commune canteens marked the day's rhythm, almost from about the beginning of January 1976. The *Angkar* had succeeded in considerably restricting free time and private life.

396 C
ដានមនុស្សអាចម៍ជ្រូក

da:n monuh ach chru:k

Tracks of men, pigs' droppings

In the collective canteens, the people had to swallow feed usually given to swine, like rice husk or minced banana trunks. It is therefore not surprising that their excrement resembled that of pigs.

397
សេចក្ដីស្រេកឃ្លានជារោគមានអានុភាពជាងគេទាំងឡាយ

sékdey srék khlien chea ro:k mien anuphiep chieng ké téang lay

Hunger is the most effective disease.[20]

This verity was cynically repeated to the Khmer Rouge cadres to make them fully aware that starving people was the best way to both quell all rebellion and make the workers of the collectives the most docile servants of the *Angkar*. It is another piece of evidence that food shortages and famine were deliberate policies on the part of the leadership.

398
អនុវត្តឱ្យបានដាច់ខាតរបបស្បៀងអាហារដែលបក្សកំណត់ពីដើមដល់ចុងឆ្នាំ

a'nuvoat aoy ba:n dachkha:t robâ:b sbieng a:ha: daèl pah kâmnât pidaem dâl chong tchhnam

Absolutely carry out the orderly distribution of food determined by the Party from the beginning to the end of the year.[18]

This type of strict recommendation was given to the cadres by the top leadership. It is not only further evidence of the *Angkar*'s intentional use of food shortages, but also indicates that the responsibility for shortages would be shoved onto the local cadres who had been unable to apportion food allowances over the year. The leadership, once again, could wash its hands of the disastrous consequences of criminal decisions.

The Khmers followed ancestral customs of gathering and foraging for food to supplement their ever meager rations. This was done openly at the beginning of the regime in 1975 and in secret after the setting up of people's canteens—with a few exceptions in communes with more humane leaders. At the time, the following saying was heard:

399
ឆ្អើមមិនទាន់ឆ្អិន តែឆ្អិនលុនទាំងឆ្អឹង
chhâ'œm min toan chhâ'èn taè chhâ'èn lun téang chhâ'œng
You're disgusted with the raw food, but when it is cooked
you swallow it bones and all.

These words were spoken by Khmer Rouge leaders when they saw the people rush to swallow whole a hastily grilled frog or insect. It is a traditional saw that figuratively exemplifies the villagers' distrust of newcomers, which then turns to trust once the ice is broken.[20]

***

The people on the collective farms were no longer a group of individuals, but rather, in the eyes of the *Angkar*, a model anthill of workers.

400
ត្រូវខិតខំបង្កើន និងពង្រីក
កំលាំងមហាសាមគ្គីរួមធ្លុងតែមួយ
trou khèt khâm bângkaen ning pungri:k
kâmlang moha: sa:maki: ruem thlung taè muey
Let us strive to increase production
and strengthen the ties of close solidarity.

401
ត្រូវមានជនគំរូ ភូមិគំរូ ផ្ទះគំរូ !
trou mien chun kumru: phu:m kumru: phtèah kumru:
We need model people, model villages, model houses!

We have already seen how few were the model houses. As for the model Potemkin villages shown to foreign visitors, they were built in 1978, at the time that the country seemed to begin inviting select individuals to garner international sympathy in the fight against Vietnam.

402 C
សង្គមនិយមផ្ទះស្រាប់ ខោអាវស្រាប់
ម៉ាស៊ីនបញ្ចុកឈួសមុខដូចគ្នា
sângkumniyum phtèah srap khao a:v srap
ma:si:ne banhchok chhu:h mukh do:ch knie
Socialism is a house and clothes all set for you, a carpenter's plane to round rough faces, to make everyone identical.

The Cambodians displayed ironic ridicule at the pretensions of the Khmer Rouge, who insisted from the beginning of their rule that, henceforth, money was useless, since in a Socialist society everything was free. They were very quick to emphasize that the main goal of this totalitarian society was to transform people into clones of their fellow men.

***

Sarcastic protests against total collectivization must have been so numerous that some are even noted in cadre notebooks during their reeducation sessions. For instance, people in the collectives are reported to have been saying:

403 C

ពេលមុនសប្បាយ ពទូរនេះធ្វើបដិវត្តសង្គមនិយមអស់សប្បាយរលីង
pél mun sabay èlounih tvœ: sangkuniyum âh sabay roli:ng
Before, we were happy; with this society all happiness has totally disappeared.

A similar slogan was also reported:

404 C

កាលនៅជាឯកជនគោល្អាត់ស្កូមទេ
ឥឡូវដល់ពេលធ្វើបដិវត្តសង្គមនិយមគោទៅជាស្កូមវិញ
ka:l nou aèkechun kô lâ'â: ât sko:mté
èylou dâl pé:l tvœ: padévoat sângkumniyum ko: tou chie skomvinh
When there was private property, the cows were fine and fat; now that we have made the revolution, the cows have become scrawny.

405

ធ្វើសង្គមនិយមទាល់តែមាន
មនុស្សសង្គមនិយម
thvoe: sangkumniyum toal taè mien monuh sângkumniyum
You can build Socialism only if you have Socialist people.

This self-evident truth is said to have been first concocted by Ho Chi Minh himself in 1961, according to his biographer.[21] While the adage was launched by the top leadership of the Khmer Rouge, it shows that they borrowed much of their ideology from those who were to become their arch-enemies. The subsequent Heng Samrin Communist regime used a similar watchword:

406

មានតែប្រជាជនទេ ដែលអាចកសាងប្រវត្តិសាស្ត្រសកលលោក
min taè prochiechun té daèl a:ch kâ:sang provoatésah sakâl lo:k
Only the masses can construct the entire history of the world.

By contrast, this implies that individuals, and men of genius in particular, matter very little in human history.

407
ចង់កសាងសង្គមថ្មី ទាល់តែមានមនុស្សថ្មី

châng kâ:sa:ng sângkum thmey toal taè mien monuh thmey

To build the new society, there must be some new people.

In planning ahead for the 1980s, the Party had this program for a revolutionary utopia:

408
ចាប់ពីឆ្នាំ១៩៨០តទៅអង្គការរៀបចំរបបគំរូ ដែលពិភពលោកគ្មាន ហូបស្គាតមួយថ្ងៃបីពេល រស់នៅស្គាតស្រែដូចទីក្រុង គ្មានបែងចែកវណ្ណៈ

chap pi: chhnam muey poan pram buen ro:y paètsèp
tâ:tou ângka: riep châm robâ:p kumru:
daèl pi phup lo:k kmien ho:p sa'a:t muey thngay bey pél
ruh nou sa'a:t sraè do:ch ti: krong kmien baèng chaèk vannak.

Beginning in 1980, the *Angkar* will create a model society
that exists nowhere else in the world,
where everyone will eat his fill three times a day,
where everyone will live well, in villages and towns,
where there will be no more classes.[22]

8—THE END OF INDIVIDUAL LIBERTY

409
ត្រូវតែគោរពសមូហភាព !

trou taè ko:rup samu:haphiep

Respect the collective!

That was the fundamental law to follow.

410
ធ្វើការងារសមូហភាព !
thvœ: ka: ngie samu:haphiep
Carry out the collective's tasks!

This is a trivial watchword about daily life indicating that everyone had to take part in the slightest of collective duties: searching for firewood or water for the canteen, husking rice, sweeping, etc.

411
មតិភាគតិចត្រូវតាមពមតិភាគច្រើន
mèatè phiek tèch trou ko:rup mèatè phiek chraen
The minority has to give way to the majority.

This expressed, we would all agree, the basic rule of democratic society—the respect of the law of the majority. But for the Khmer Rouge, it was but an instrument to crush the will and desires of the individual in the name of the society. The local *Angkar* spokesman could very well turn this old maxim to his advantage—a sole individual tyrannized the group, since he always asserted his right to speak in the name of the popular will, by virtue of the sacrosanct Leninist principle of democratic centralism.

412
មិនត្រូវមានសតិអារម្មណ៍ស្ងួនត្ពូ !
min trou mien setè a:râm suen tue
Do not harbor private thoughts!

A person had to completely empty his mind, thereby abstaining from having personal ideas inherited from the old order. He had to have a clean, clear mind to welcome the new ideas the *Angkar* proclaimed. At the same time, he had no right to criticize the *Angkar*.

413
ចិត្តមិត្តមិនមែនដូចជាជង្គង់
ដែលគេបត់បែនបានដូចបំណងនោះទេ

chet met min mèn do:ch chie chungkung
daèl ké bâtbaèn ba:n do:ch bâmnâng nuh té
The heart, comrade, is not like the knee, which can bend at will.

From the mouth of Khieu Samphan, who was talking to Party cadres, this traditional saying meant that, once back in the collectives, they would find it a stiff task to reeducate the new people. Coercive methods will have to be drastic, the ultimate aim being to make everyone love the *Angkar* and consent to his own dehumanization.

414
កុំដើរហើរសេរី !

kom dae hae sérey
You are forbidden to travel freely!

The Khmer Rouge strictly forbade freedom of travel: this constituted an essential aspect of their policy. You could not move where you wished without written permission. This order was true even for Khmer Rouge leaders themselves, including high-ranking officials. Thus, Hu Nim, the minister of information and propaganda responsible for Radio Kampuchea, had to obtain official authorization for his own travel to the provinces.

This law was obviously aimed at those who tried to flee the regime for Thailand or Vietnam. Very few succeeded; most were arrested and brought to prison, or executed on the spot, along the many checkpoints set up throughout the country. Others managed to forge papers by themselves, which was difficult since people had access neither to paper nor pen. Still others succeeded in making false official stamps to give an official cachet to these forged documents! Once you had this precious document, it was relatively easy to go through checkpoints, for the vast majority of the inspectors could neither read nor write, and at best, vaguely knew how to make out a signature. Often they would look at the papers upside down, and ask, "Where are you going?" even though everything was plainly written on the paper they held before their eyes.

The principal reason for these restrictions was to squelch all opposition and to keep the discontented from uniting together. Thus, no one knew what happened or what was said in neighboring villages.

415 C
សំបុត្របើកផ្លូវ បាទត្រាត្រយូងចេក
sâmbot baek phlou bâh tra: trâyo:ng chék
Passes are stamped with banana buds.

To forge Khmer Rouge passes, the people used the big bud at the tip of banana bunches when in bloom. It is edible and when cut, it produces a purplish liquid of about the same color as the ink used by bureaucrats.

In the figurative meaning, ត្រយូងចេក *trâyu:ng chék* also means rocket launchers, as the shape is identical. In this case, it meant that, in flight, if one was well armed, the way was cleared.

416
មិត្តឯងសេរីណាស់ !
mit aèng sérey nah
Comrade, you are very free!

When the *Angkar* pointed an accusing finger and shouted these words, it was very dangerous indeed. It might mean immediate arrest; it might mean imminent death.

As Orwell warned us, in a totalitarian society the word "free" will only mean not restricted from a given condition, as in "a garden *free* from weeds." The word *seri* has always had negative connotations under Democratic Kampuchea. Thus, to be "free," to exercise one's free will and not to docilely and steadfastly obey the *Angkar*, was a sure sign that you were on the road to rebellion.

We should remember that during the time of the Sangkum, the *Khmer Serey*, what had remained of Son Ngoc Than's Democratic opposition, was already the number one enemy of the regime and liable to public condemnation at the bi-annual People's Congress, and to even public execution.[23]

417
សេរីភាពគឺគ្មានវិន័យ គ្មានសីលធម៌

séreyphiep keu: kmien viney kmien seylethoa

Liberty means the absence of discipline, the absence of morality.

This aphorism clearly shows that liberty was an absolute evil for the Khmer Rouge.

418
ត្រូវប្រយ័ត្នខាងសីលធម៌ ស្រីញីប្រុសឈ្មោល
កុំសេរីផ្ដេសផ្ដាសពាសវាលពាសកាល

trou proyat khang selathoa srey nhi: proh chhmô:l
kom sérey phdeh phdah pieh viel piehka:l

Women and men, be careful to follow this precept:
don't be carelessly free, doing as you please!

419
គោលជំហរចាត់តាំងអង្គការវិន័យខ្ពស់បំផុត
មិនសេរីនិយម មិនអត្តនោម័តនិយម មិនឯកចិត្តនិយម

ko:l chumhâ: chattang angka:viney khpuh bâmphot
min séreyniyum min attenaomatniyum min aèkchetniyum

The loftiest attitude is necessary to follow the strict discipline
of the *Angkar*: no freedom, no selfishness, no individualism.

The dictums were even more ominous:

420
បើចង់រស់នៅដោយសេរី អង្គការទុកដីឱ្យនៅមួយដុំ

bae châng ruh nou daoy sérey ângka: tuk dey aoy nou muey dom

If you wish to live exactly as you please,
the *Angkar* will put aside a small piece of land for you.

This clearly means that those who please themselves will see the *Angkar* keep a special spot to bury their bodies.

The threat was further clarified:

421
បើសេរីរឭំង ដាប់ពីតូចអោយហើយទៅល្អជាង

baœ sérey ènchœng ngoap pi : to:ch aoy haœy tou lâ'â: chieng

If you are free,
it would have been better that you had died young.

9—FORGING THE NEW MAN

422
ត្រូវចេះលត់ដំ !

trou chèh lut dâm

You must learn to steel yourself!

Every individual had to submit to a work routine as harsh as that of a smith putting the iron to the test of fire. This image is highly suggestive of the very harsh conditions of work and life that everyone had to accept uncomplainingly. It also suggests that one's character had to endure endless hardship in order to be shaped into the image of the new man. These words were spewed daily from the mouths of Khmer Rouge leaders, menacing anyone who did not shoulder the tasks with sufficient energy and enthusiasm or who somehow seemed to protest the harsh living conditions. These very conditions were supposed to forge the new man so dear to the ear of Communists, and especially to Maoists.

The same idea was similarly expressed in this way:

423
ត្រូវចេះហាត់ពត់លត់ដំ !
trou chèh hat put lut dâm
You must exercise yourself in order to steel yourself!

You had to become used to famine, to very harsh conditions of work and life. Some dared defy the authorities and revolts broke out because they could not endure such conditions. Misfortune fell on them and we have evidence that in prisons there were a few individuals who vociferously rebelled against the *Angkar* and poured a torrent of abuse at the regime before being massacred.

The phrase ហាត់ពត់លត់ដំ (*hat put lut dom*) expresses in a more forceful manner the notion of "reeducation" or "thought reform," which is usually translated from the Chinese as *rien so:t* (រៀនសូត្រ), "assiduous study" or *kâ:sang khluen* (កសាងខ្លួន), "the reconstruction of the self."[24]

424
មិត្តឯងត្រូវតែលត់ដំ ត្រូវតែកសាងខ្លួន !
mit aèng trou taè lut dâm trou taè kâ:sa:ng khluen
Comrade, you must steel yourself,
you have to reconstruct yourself!

The idea of "re-forming oneself" and "re-molding oneself" is found in Mao's *Little Red Book*.

But the people responded with skepticism:

425 C
ញញួរដំពន្លាក ពន្លាកដាប់ជ្រុញ
nhonhue dâm punlèak punlèak dab chrunh
The hammer strikes the wood chisel
and the chisel cuts out the carving board.

This traditional saying took on an entirely new meaning under the Khmer Rouge. In this hierarchical society, the orders were given at the top of the social ladder, and then transmitted quickly to the bottom, with the catastrophic consequences that we already know. No one made any errors; everyone blamed the man under him. He who found himself at the bottom of the heap had to take full responsibility. The Khmer Rouge leaders, at each echelon, always asserted this in order to exonerate themselves. How could it have been otherwise in this perfectly vertical society, where decisions taken at the top were carried out at all levels, always in great fear, for if they were not, one's personal safety would be in jeopardy.

The "hammer" symbolized the decision makers in Phnom Penh; the "sculptor's chisel" the entire Khmer Rouge hierarchy who could only follow the direction of its thrust downward on the wood to be shaped. It was labor on scorched earth, a country and people burnt alive.

This counter-slogan showed that the general population was not fooled; it knew how power served Pol Pot's regime. On this subject, we should realize that in a Communist country (and in one of a totalitarian regime's internal contradictions), the hierarchy was merely a transmission belt for orders and directions from a higher echelon to a lower one. This meant that when Pol Pot, surrounded by a very small number of the Standing Committee faithfuls, made a decision that was not only absurd but completely unreal, and indeed criminal, this same decision cascaded rapidly from one level to the next until it reached the bottom—and the people who had the duty to carry it out, no matter how much it went against the dictates of common sense. Pol Pot and his group, in return, must have had some indication of the difficulties their decisions were causing at the base level, even though they might have been surrounded by flatterers. But instead of changing their policies in the slightest, or blaming themselves, they put the responsibility of failure on the shoulders of their subordinates and the poor drones at the bottom of the social scale, fulminating always against the sabotage and conspiracy of the "enemies of the revolution."

10—THE MONARCHY IS ANACHRONISTIC

The monarchy is the antonym of collectivism.

426
ស្តេចមុន ស្តេចក្រោយ ចុះខ្សោយអង្គការ
sdach mun sdach kraoy choh khsaoy ângka:
Kings before, kings later; they cripple the *Angkar*.

427
ស្តេចអាចម៍ស្អុយដូចតែគ្នា
sdach ach sâ:"oy do:ch taè knie
The king's shit smells like everyone else's.

428
មិនចាំបាច់មានស្តេចឡើយព្រោះស្តេចអាចម៍ស្អុយដូចតែរាស្ត្រ
min chambach mien sdach laœy prueh sdach ach sâ:"oy do:ch taè rieh
A king is unnecessary,
for his shit stinks the same as his own people's.

Sihanouk played a historical role between 1970 and 1975. As he himself admitted, he had now been "spit out like a cherry pit."

Let us reiterate that Khmer Rouge expressions are, in their earthiness, in keeping with the tradition of Khmer sayings. Moreover, the *Angkar* repeated that under the monarchy, the people were subservient to the king. Now, everyone was equal—in theory, at least.

These assertions meant that, as far as the Khmer Rouge interpretation of Cambodian history was concerned, Norodom Sihanouk had ceased to play any historical role.

Reeducation classes

EPILOGUE

All the slogans in this collection constitute a cluster of supplementary proof that, on the *Angkar*'s part, there existed a deliberate policy of enslaving ever larger swaths of the population and ensnaring them in a repressive system that gradually spread throughout the entire country. This repression was not directed toward specific racial groups or ethnic minorities, but at social strata and political opponents, real or imaginary. The demographer Marek Sliwinski has scientifically established, based on a large sampling of families from all social classes, that perhaps a quarter of the population had been exterminated—almost two million out of eight—including 41.9 percent of the population living or having found refuge in Phnom Penh before 17 April 1975![1] These politically motivated mass killings reveal a deliberate policy of terror and extermination on the part of a small minority, seeking to hoist itself to the top, and then maintaining itself in power by violence and terror. It should be termed "politicide," rather than "genocide," for mass repression by the revolutionary state did not target any specific racial grouping—except the Vietnamese, who, let us say once again, had the good luck to be chased out of the country at the beginning of the regime.[2] For instance, I have not found a single slogan aimed at the Chams in particular, nor the Chinese, for that matter.

The people exterminated by Khmer Rouge executioners were first of all the "17 April," the new people. They made up some 40 percent of the population of the country. In the new regime, they had no rights at all and had to work without any compensation except food, the portions of which diminished over time. They did not have the right to vote in April 1976, when so-called legislative elections were held after the proclamation of the new constitution of Democratic Kampuchea on 5 January. It seemed for some that the only reason the lives of the "17 April" had been preserved was because they represented an immense, reserve army of free laborers. The revolution, wishing to triple rice production at one fell swoop, needed hands, millions of hands, since they had rejected the use, in this first period of transition and catching up, of all machines manufactured abroad.

As in all Socialist countries, the sacred ideal for the Khmer Rouge was Equality.

429
ឯកភាព សមភាព ភាតរភាព សមូហភាព សាមគ្គីភាព !
aèkaphiep samaphiep phietaraphiep samu:haphiep sa:maki:phiep
Unity, Equality, Fraternity, Collectivity, Solidarity!

These aspirations are admirable! Yet, we must notice that the notion of equality surpassed all others. Did that mean that people had to, above all, fuse their will with the *Angkar*'s? Would any and all deviation risk bringing the downfall of the entire Khmer Rouge edifice?

Let us also note that from the well-known motto of the French Revolution, "Liberty, Equality, Fraternity," the Khmer Rouge simply did away with "Liberty." How significant! On the other hand, they added three ideas reinforcing the notions of Equality and Fraternity. Without Liberty, all the other ideals are hollow words. Khmer Rouge thought proved, by the resulting massive crimes against humanity, that the way to Equality and Fraternity could only be along the road to Liberty. One cannot compel human beings to be good.

We should also remember that the fundamental principle of Communist revolutions, especially of the Maoist revolution, is that the end justifies the means. The end, according to this saying, is perhaps Fraternity, but first of all Equality. In Khmer society, with its centuries-old tradition of inequality, this goal was very laudable. But it justified, in the eyes of the all-powerful *Angkar*, the abolition of all liberties and the massive use of violence to proclaim Equality in one wave of a magic wand. Paradoxically, the Khmer Rouge only succeeded in reestablishing a system of castes and privileges more unequal than those that existed in the former regimes. It showed the French trinity of Liberty, Equality, Fraternity to be indivisible.

Peace is conspicuously absent from the Khmer Rouge pantheon. Peace was made synonymous with cowardice and betrayal of the motherland:

430
សន្តិភាពគឺចុះចាញ់ !
sântèphiep keu: choh chanh
Peace is surrender!

In addition, the Khmer Rouge violated human nature, since they sometimes pretended to make the general population carry out several tasks at the same time, in a mad frenzy of work without respite. It was not merely a question of progressing unruffled in the harsh pace of dull labor, but everyone had to advance at the same pace, at the same time! One had to move forward relentlessly, step by step, whatever his or her physical condition.

The next two catchwords are symbolical of the dire monotony of daily toil, the lot of all the Cambodians in people's communes and in collective public works projects.

431
ត្រូវជំរុញការងារអោយផុលផុសឡើងគ្រប់ជំហាន !
trou chumrunh ka:ngie aoy pholphoh laeng krup chumhien
Give an impetus to your work and rush headlong at each step!

432
ទោះជាអស់កំលាំងយ៉ាងណាក៏ដោយ ត្រូវតែទៅមុខជានិច្ច !
tueh chie âh kâmlang ya:ng na: kâ: daoy trou taè tou mukh chie nich
In spite of exhaustion, you must always move forward!

"Move forward" can also be taken in a concrete sense, for, during the many relocations, almost all on foot without water or food, the same watchword was heard to goad people onward. "Where are we going?" "Right ahead of you!" Never did they really know where the *Angkar* was leading them.

Once their bodies had been used to the limits of human resistance, the poor workers would die on the spot:

433
ស្លាប់នៅលើការដ្ឋាន !
slap nou lœ: ka:rotha:n
On the work site until death!

The process of dehumanization was being achieved: Cambodians had become, every one of them, a small cog in a gigantic machine that crushed them. They were all identical, in perpetual motion to make what Marx would have called "surplus value" for the *Angkar*. In the name of world revolution, Cambodians were expected to give up their souls. They gave up their last breath in the mud of the monsoon rains or in the dust of the dry season. Unrelentingly, everything had been accomplished—according to the will of the *Angkar*.

GLOSSARY

Angkar Padevoat The revolutionary organization.
bâbâ Very thin rice soup, with barely any fish or meat. Associated with starvation in the minds of the population.
chhlop Local militia in the *sahakor* in charge of surveillance of the civilian population.
khamaphibal Revolutionary cadre.
kâsang khluen "The reconstruction of the self," meaning reeducation.
Khmer Rouge Name given by Sihanouk to the communist revolutionaries he harshly repressed in the 1960s. They never referred to themselves in this way, but called themselves "revolutionaries" ("Communists" between themselves) and called their regime and faction "Democratic Kampuchea."
khnoh Fetter, in the shape of a semi-circular iron ring, with a smaller ring at each end, through which a long iron bar is threaded. Usually several prisoners are shackled to the same bar, which is locked at both ends.
komtech "To crush to bits," the fate of both external and internal enemies of the Khmer Rouge.

krâma	The multipurpose checkered red and white Khmer scarf. *Kamaphibal* and *Angkar* leaders always wore one to look more peasant-like. It could be used for tying the hands of a prisoner behind his back or for blindfolding a person before hitting him to death on the nape of the neck.
mondolkoma	Special camps where young children were educated away from their parents.
Mulethan	"Base people," i.e. those who found themselves in the outer regions of Cambodia that were under Khmer Rouge control during most of the civil war (1970–75).
niredey	Khmer Rouge cadres from the Southeast region under the leadership of Ta Mok. They had the reputation of being very cruel.
prâhok	A form of fermented, salty fish paste. Rich in protein, it constitutes the primary seasoning in Cambodian cooking, principally in the countryside.
rien so:t	"Assiduous study, learning by heart," for reeducation.
sahakor	"People's communes," "state farms," or "collectives" where people lived collectively and performed slave labor.
samamit	"Comrade" in Khmer Rouge parlance (*mit*, for short).
sompéah	A slight bow of the head with both palms placed together as a gesture of greeting and respect. Found in most Southeast Asian countries.
yothea	A Khmer Rouge soldier (or soldiers).

NOTES

INTRODUCTION

1. *Les aventures de la liberté* (Paris: Grasset, 1991), ch. "Dans ce Phnom Penh désert … (La preuve par le Cambodge)," p. 384.

2. *Sangkum Reastr Niyum,* or the People's Socialist Community, the regime set up by the prince after stepping down from the throne and leading his paternalistic regime from 1955 to 1970.

3. Article from *Le Monde,* 5 July 1979; quoted by Patrick Seriot in his *Analyse du discours politique soviétique* (Paris, Institut d'Etudes slaves, 1985), p. 29.

4. A. Besançon, *Présent soviétique et passé russe* (Paris: Livre de Poche, 1980); cited by Patrick Seriot, *Analyse,* p. 37.

5. Saveros Pou, *Guirlande de cpap* (Paris: CEDORECK, 1988).

6. Ibid., p. 337. See also Karen Fisher-Nguyen, "Khmer Proverbs: Images and Rules," in *Cambodian Culture since 1975: Homeland and Exile,* ed. May M. Ebihara, Carol A. Mortland, and Judy Ledgerwood (Ithaca, NY: Cornell University Press, 1994), p. 91ff.

7. Saveros Pou, ibid., p. 338.

8. S-21 is the code number of the regime's central prison-interrogation center, now turned into the Museum of Genocidal Crimes and renamed Tuol Sleng.

9. Stephen Heder, with Brian Littlemore, *Seven Candidates for Prosecution: Accountability for the Crimes of the Khmer Rouge* (American University, Washington College of Law, War Crimes Office, June 2001), p. 45.

10. Ibid., pp. 45, 53.

11. For the full account of the fate of returnees in the reeducation camps of Ieng Sary from 1976 to 1979. See Ong Thong Hœung, *J'ai cru aux Khmers rouge* (Paris: Buchet-Chastel, 2003).

12. Heder, *Seven Candidates*, p. 80.

13. *Les faits véritables sur le pouvoir dictatorial de Pol Pot: 1975–1978*, Center for Research and Documentation of the Democratic Movement for National Unity (DMNU), 8 September 1996, [Pailin and Phnom Malay], Cambodia,

14. A *krâma* is an all-purpose checkered (red and white, or blue and white) scarf worn by the Khmer peasants and promoted as a revolutionary insignia of true proletarian-ship by the Khmer Rouge.

15. See *The Journal of Communist Studies*, vol. 3, no. 1, March 1987.

16. Michael Vickery, *Cambodia 1975–1982* (Boston MA: South End Press, 1984), p. 81.

17. Ibid., p. 182.

18. See the booklet printed by the Documentation Center of Cambodia entitled *The Khmer Rouge Notebooks: 1970–1978, Poems, Slogans, Songs, Part I*, September 1998, 67 pp. Sayings collected from a Khmer Rouge Notebook, numbered 29 by the Documentation Center.

19. See explanation, slogan no. 271.

20. See explanation, slogan no. 153.

21. See explanation, slogan no. 233.

22. See explanation, slogan no. 243.

23. See explanation, slogan no. 413.

24. In an interview with Philip Short, a British researcher and author, Khieu Samphan strongly denied being the author of slogans collected by the Document Center of Cambodia (DCCam) and used by Craig Etcheson in a November 1998 article published in the *Phnom Penh Post* of 27 November–11 December 1998. Khieu Samphan repeated those strong denials to me when I interviewed him on 24 October 2003.

25. See Krang Ta Chan incomplete prison archives 1977–78 preserved at Tuol Sleng Museum. Uncatalogued.

26. *Front National de Libération Populaire du Kampuchéa*, or National Liberal Front of Kampuchea, created by Son Sann (1911–2001). Son Sann was founder of the National Bank of Cambodia in 1955, prime minister in 1967–68, and privy councilor.

27. *Front Uni National pour un Cambodge Indépendant, Neutre, Pacifique et Coopératif,* the royalist party.

28. See Esméralda Luciolli, *Le mur de bambous: le Cambodge après Pol Pot,* ed. by Régine Desforges and Médecins Sans Frontières (Paris: Médecins Sans Frontières, 1988).

29. King Norodom Sihanouk himself admitted this in his memoir, *Prisonnier des Khmers rouges*. He exclaimed in front of Khieu Samphan

who was threatening him: "... *I who have been your fellow traveller and have helped you as much as I could and using all my prestige to defeat the enemy and seize power...*", November 1976 (Paris: Hachette, 1986), p. 141.

30. See also on the subject Kate Frieson's excellent study, "Revolution and Rural Response in Cambodia, 1970–75," in *Genocide and Democracy in Cambodia, the Khmer Rouge, the United Nations and the International Community*, Monograph Series 41/Yale University Southeast Asian Studies, 1993, pp. 33–55.

31. Quoted by Justin Cornfield, *Khmers Stand Up! A History of the Cambodian Government 1970–1975* (Melbourne, Monash Papers on Southeast Asia, no. 32, Center of Southeast Asian Studies, Monash University, 1994), p. 98, in interview for TV documentary, *Vietnam: The 1000 Day War*, episode 9 [undated].

32. *Gouvernement Royal d'Union Nationale Khmer*, Khmer Royal Government of National Unity.

33. Read the description of Comrade Thep detailing what happened during the civil war in villages captured by the revolutionaries in *The Gate* (London: Harvill Press, 2003), pp. 54–6.

I IN PRAISE OF THE REGIME

1. I identified one *munty* (office) in 1994, hidden away in the forest of Bokeo district. I was told by many sources that Saloth Sar, (then identified as Ta Pouk), Ieng Sary, Son Sen, Tiv Ol, Ney Saran, and their consorts—the core of Angkar under Vietminh protection—moved from one secret base or *munty 100* to another for security reasons.

2. The most likely version of his untimely death was that it had been engineered by his entourage, who gave him an overdose of his own medicines. Pol Pot was about to be caught by an American special forces unit and dispatched to Canada where the legal system would allow him to be tried for his crimes against humanity. His Thai protectors had at long last yielded to US pressure. The emblematic figure of the revolutionary movement would then have been at risk of revealing many details of surviving Khmer Rouge in positions of authority, or protected by the powers that be, which they would never have allowed to come to light. The Chinese Communist Party might also have been incriminated. Ta Mok, for instance, had been for many years in close relationship with Bangkok's Chinese embassy.

3. Foreign Broadcast Information Service (FBIS), transcripts: Asia-Pacific *Daily Reports*, 4 Oct. 1977, H 25 and 26.

4. See ch. 5, "La société polpotienne," in *Prisonnier de l'Angkar*, Mœung Sonn and Henri Locard (Paris: Fayard, 1993), pp. 97–115.

5. See Sihanouk, *Prisonnier des Khmers rouges* (Paris: Hachette, 1986).

6. Memorized by Hem Borith in 1994.

7. Sihanouk, *Prisonnier des Khmers rouges*, pp. 50–51.

8. *Les faits véritables sur le pouvoir dictatorial de Pol Pot: 1975–1978*, Center for Research and Documentation of the Democratic Movement for National Unity (DMNU), 8 September 1996, [Pailin and Phnom Malay], Cambodia, p. 79.

9. "Allegedly" because there are two branches in the tiny Khmer Communist movement: one pro-Vietnamese, and one more pro-Chinese. In their continuous rewriting of history, Pol Pot and his group dated the creation of the Revolutionary People's Party, later to become the CPK, to a secret party Congress at the Phnom Penh railway station on 30 September 1960. In so doing, he disowned March 1951, when the Khmer Communist Party was created by the Vietnamese Communists. In fact, Chea Sim and Hun Sen, present secretary and assistant secretary of the ex-Pracheachon or Cambodian People's Party (CPP) celebrated with great pomp, in March 1996, the forty-fifth anniversary of its foundation, and in March 2001, its fiftieth anniversary.

10. The name of Saigon in the days when it was part of Cambodian territory.

11. The transliteration "Kampuchea" has been adopted rather than the accepted name of "Cambodia," to conform to Khmer Rouge jargon.

12. FBIS, 20 Sept. 1977, H 1.

13. FBIS, 19 Jan. 1978, H 12.

14. FBIS, 13 Sept. 1978, H 5. Another report of the visit on Democratic Kampuchea radio says: "After viewing the Angkor temples, artistic pieces, stone inscriptions and various sculptures, the delegation of the Marxist-Leninist Communist Party of France remarked that the Kampuchean people are people who have performed sacred feats which completely disprove the slanderous propaganda of imperialists, old and new colonialists and the international expansionists." FBIS, 19 Sept. 1978, H5. One may hope that such reasoning on the revolutionary radio must be attributed to Khmer Rouge propaganda and could never have been voiced by the French visitors.

15. Christophe Bourseiller, *Les Maoïstes: la folle histoire des Gardes rouges français* (Paris, Plon, 1996), p. 299.

16. Ibid., p. 137.

17. We can note, as an example of the misunderstanding and ignorance on the part of France about the true nature of Maoism at the time, Valéry Giscard d'Estaing's declaration at the death of Mao in September 1976: "with the death of Mao, a beacon of humanity has gone out." Giscard was then president of the French Republic.

18. *The Provençal* of 7 October 1978, quoted in Bourseiller, *Les Maoïstes,* p. 287.

19. FBIS, 5 Jan. 1979, H 3.

20. Read, for instance, how E. P. Thompson solved the issue in his classic Marxist interpretation of England's social and economic history in *The Making of the English Working Class* (London: Pelican Books, 1963), at the time of the Industrial Revolution. There he proposed to demonstrate (quite unconvincingly, though) that, in the early decades of the nineteenth century, the various social groups that were shamelessly exploited by the new entrepreneurial class were first disunited. But, because of that ruthless exploitation, they joined ranks under the flag of the Chartist movement to form one single "working" or "proletariat" class.

II MAOIST-INSPIRED SLOGANS

1. Read, on this subject, Thomas Engelbert's and Christopher E. Goscha's study based on Vietnamese sources: *Falling out of Touch: A Study on Vietnamese Communist Policy towards an Emerging Communist Movement, 1930–1975* (Melbourne: Monash University, 1995).

2. FBIS, 10 Sept. 1976, H 2.

3. FBIS, 20 Sept. 1976, H 4.

4. FBIS, 3 Oct. 1977, H 5–6.

5. Charles Meyer, *Derrière le Sourire khmer* (Paris: Plon, 1971), pp. 232–3.

6. Prince Norodom Sihanouk with Bernard Krisher, *Prince Sihanouk Reminisces: World Leaders I Have Known* (Bangkok, Editions Duang Kamol, 1990), p. 108.

7. Ibid., p. 111.

8. 1 May 1979, "'*Squandered Chinese aid' spelt Pol Pot's ruin.*"

9. I am indebted to Tom Fawthorp for having pointed this revealing article out to me.

10. Documentation Center of Cambodia, (DCCam), Cadre notebook, 053 KHN.

11. In the 2002 growing season, it was only between 1.6 and 1.9 tons per hectare, among the lowest yields in the world.

12. FBIS, 16 April 1976, H 6 and 7.

13. Khieu Samphan, in his 15 April 1976 speech, FBIS, 16 April 1976, H 3.

14. Elizabeth Becker, *When the War Was Over: Cambodia's Revolution and the Voices of Its People* (New York: Simon and Schuster, 1987), p. 414.

15. *Le petit livre rouge: les citations du Président Mao* (Paris: Le Seuil, 1967), p. 111.

16. This slogan is quoted by Ben Kiernan in *The Pol Pot Regime: Race, Power and Genocide in Cambodia* (New Haven: Yale University Press, 1996) and applied to the Chinese community, "*Dig up the grass, dig up the roots,*" p. 288.

17. *Le petit livre rouge*, ch. 21, p. 117–121.

18. FBIS, H 2.

19. See Mœung Sonn's account in Mœung Sonn and Henri Locard, *Prisonnier de l'Angkar*, pp. 199–210.

20. *Le petit livre rouge*, p. 153.

21. Ibid., p. 114–115; see the whole of ch. 20.

22. FBIS, 29 Dec. 1977, H 4.

23. FBIS, 15 Jan 1976, H 1.

24. See, for instance, Boua Chantou, Ben Kiernan, and David Chandler, *Pol Pot Plans the Future: Confidential Leadership Documents from Democratic Kampuchea* (New Haven: Yale University Press, 1988). The chapter introduced by David Chandler is entitled "The Five Year Plan."

25. For more slogans on reeducation, see the following chapter "The *Angkar* and Its Tactics," particularly slogans 132 to 136.

26. *Le petit livre rouge*, ch. 27, "Criticism and Self-criticism."

27. The word here is *samathi*, which refers to Buddhist meditation.

28. Ch. 22, "Methods of Thought and Work," in *Le petit livre rouge*.

29. See Y Phandara, *Retour à Phnom Penh* (Paris: Métailié, 1982), p. 153: "We often heard the following sentence: 'You want to hold a pen? Take a hoe, it is your pen. The soil will be your paper. Go and sign as much as you wish!'"

30. FBIS, 4 Oct. 1977, H 26 and 34.

31. *Le petit livre rouge,* p. 121 (11 June 1945).

32. See *Searching for the Truth*, Magazine of the Documentation Center of Cambodia, no. 12, December 2000, p. 18.

III THE *ANGKAR* AND ITS TACTICS

1. Documentation Center of Cambodia (DCCam), catalogue no. DO1266, with a somewhat different translation.

2. Francois Godement, *La renaissance de l'Asie* (Paris: Odile Jacob Editions, 1993), p. 148.

3. Quoted by John Marston, "Metaphors of the Khmer Rouge," in *Cambodian Culture since 1975: Homeland and Exile,* ed. Ebihara, et al. (Ithaca and London: Cornell University Press, 1994), p. 110.

4. Sombat, aged 61, interviewed in 2001 at Kep by Fabienne Luco. See: *Entre le tigre et le crocodile, approche anthropologique sur les pratiques traditionnelles et nouvelles de traitement des conflits au Cambodge* (Phnom Penh, UNESCO, 2002), p. 58.

5. FBIS, 4 Oct. 1977, H 37.

6. Becker, *When the War Was Over*, p. 406.

7. FBIS, 29 Dec. 1977, H 2.

8. This is a literal translation of the Khmer យើង ខ្ញុំ "We-I" signifies the complete fusion of the individual into the group.

9. Y Phandara, *Retour à Phnom Penh*.

10. François Ponchaud, *Cambodia Year Zero,* 2nd ed. (New York: Holt, Rinehart, Winston) p. 113, quoted from a refugee, the watchword: "The people are the brain of the *Angkar*."

11. Becker, *When the War Was Over*, p. 414.

12. See *Revolutionary Immortality: Mao Tse-Tung and the Chinese Cultural Revolution* (New York, Vintage Books, 1968), a book in which Robert Jay Lifton could be regarded as having anticipated all the founding principles of Pol Pot-ism—no wonder, as they ape Maoism.

13. Notebook from meetings, kept in the Tuol Sleng archives. Uncatalogued. It is signed by Duch (Kaing Kek Ieu), the director of the institution.

14. Quoted by Laura Summers in *The Journal of Communist Studies*, London, vol. 3, no.1 (March 1987), p. 27.

15. David Chandler, *The Tragedy of Cambodian History* (New Haven and London: Yale University Press, 1991), p. 247.

16. FBIS, 6 Oct. 1978, H 15.

17. FBIS, 4 Oct. 1977, H 28.

18. See Jean-Luc Domenach, *Chine: l'archipel oublié* (Paris: Fayard, 1992).

19. See, for instance, the confession of de Hu Nim, "Planning the Past," in Boua et al., eds., *Pol Pot Plans the Future,* pp. 227– 317.

20. Read Ong Thong Hœung, *J'ai cru aux Khmers rouges: Le Récit d'une Illusion* (Paris: Buchet-Chastel, 2003).

21. Chuon Meng, *Let Us Look at the World of the Khmers* (Phnom Penh, printed by the Ministry of Information and Culture, 1980), p. 30 (in Khmer). *Author's note*: The Pol Pot-ist "teacher" usually grilled small children, in order to get information about their fathers and mothers, or neighbors. He questioned them about their parents' trade or profession, or that of uncles and acquaintances during the Republican regime. Then the "teachers" would report what they had learned to the heads of the people's communes or the *Angkar Loeu* (superior authority), so that arrests could be made.

22. In Tam was a famous opponent to the Khmer Rouge, slated for execution by the revolutionaries. He was governor of Battambang province at the time of the takeover and, contrary to all Cambodian leaders, did not surrender to the Khmer Rouge, but fled into the maquis on the Thai border, where he started a Free Khmer resistance movement at Phnom Malay. He soon had to give up the fight for lack of international support. He has been the only so-called "super-traitor" who survived Democratic Kampuchea. See Mœung and Locard, *Prisonnier de l'Angkar*, p. 233–234.

23. Interview of P. H., born in 1951, carried out in Phnom Penh in July 1995.

24. See Dr. Zhisui Li, "The Death of Mao," ch. 1, in *The Private Life of Chairman Mao: The Inside Story of the Man Who Made Modern China* (London, Chatto and Windus, 1994).

25. FBIS, 19 Oct 1977, H 2.

26. Ponchaud, *Cambodia Year Zero*, p. 117–118.

27. According to P. H., born in 1951, interviewed in Phnom Penh in July 1995.

28. Interview of B. C., born in 1937, an ethnic Prou from Ratanakiri, on 12 January 1994.

29. Given by an ex-Khmer Rouge from Koh Kong province.

30. Given by an ex-Khmer Rouge from the Svay Rieng province.

IV THE HUNT FOR "ENEMIES OF THE PEOPLE"

1. FBIS, 28 Dec. 1977, H 1.
2. FBIS, 6 Oct. 1977, H 1.
3. FBIS, 21 Sept. 1976, H 1.
4. Ch. 3, "Socialism and Communism," in *Le petit livre rouge*.

5. FBIS, 3 Oct. 1977, H 6.
6. FBIS, 18 April 1977, H 3.
7. See Marek Sliwinski, *Le génocide Khmer rouge: une analyse démographique* (Paris: L'Harmattan, 1995).
8. FBIS, 28 Sept. 1977, H 5.
9. DCCam, Cadre Notebook 9.
10. FBIS, 4 Jan. 1977, H 1.
11. FBIS, 28 Dec. 1977, H 6.

12. Charnel houses, or small wooden structures, were set up in which human bones were collected during the Heng Samrin regime or the People's Republic of Kampuchea regime (1979–1989) as memorials to remind the local inhabitants of the horrors of what was called at the time "Pol Pot-ism."

13. This pagoda has been identified by Kan Khun as that of Wat Kâr, Kompong Sima village, south of the town of Battambang, in his autobiography, *De la dictature des Khmers rouges à l'occupation vietnamienne, Cambodge, 1975–1979* (Paris: L'Harmattan, 1994), p. 86.

14. See, in particular, Maurice Eisenbuch, "The Ritual Space of Patients and Traditional Healers in Cambodia," *Bulletin de l'Ecole française d'Extrême Orient*, 79 (2), Paris, 1992.

15. Interview of Y. H., born in 1950, in Pursat on 16 August 1994.

16. This very complex problem deserves long study. We might object to the statement that it already exists in Nayan Chanda's excellent study, *Brother Enemy: The War after the War. A History of Indochina since the Fall of Saigon* (New York: Harcourt Brace Jovanovich, 1986). However, he looks at the matter from a geopolitical and diplomatic angle. In addition, his point of view is close to the Vietnamese, and consequently, he did not carry out an exhaustive study of the very intricate relationship between the two revolutions. More recently, the study quoted above by Thomas Engelbert and Christopher E. Goscha, which precisely analyzes the relationships between the two Communist parties, is based almost exclusively on Vietnamese sources, on the one hand, and stops in 1975, on the other.

See Steve Heder's *Cambodian Communism and the Vietnamese Model, vol. 1: Imitation and Independence (1930–1975)* (Bangkok: White Lotus). It is based on a mass of Communist archives from the two neighboring countries and demonstrates how close the two parties have been in their Maoist strategy, disagreeing simply about tactics and about who should lead the revolution in Cambodia.

17. Sliwinski, *Le génocide,* p. 77.
18. See, for example, the well-documented study of those minorities by

Gerald Cannon Hickey, *Free in the Forest: Ethnohistory of the Vietnamese Central Highlands, 1954–1976* (New Haven and London: Yale University Press, 1982). According to this study, "The Vietnamese penchant for taking land earned them the name 'the land eaters' among local Jarai," p. 226.

19. *Black Paper: Facts and Evidences of the Acts of Aggressions and Annexation of Vietnam against Kampuchea,* Department of Press and Information of the Ministry of Foreign Affairs of Democratic Kampuchea, Phnom Penh, September 1978.

20. Interview of K. S. (born in 1958), in Kompong Thom, on 31 January 1994

21. David Chandler, *Brother Number One: A Political Biography of Pol Pot,* rev. ed. (Chiang Mai, Thailand: Silkworm Books, 1999).

22. FBIS, 4 Oct 1977, H 18.

23. This atmosphere is evoked in Molyda Szymusiak's book, *The Stones Cry Out: A Cambodian Childhood, 1975–1980,* trans. Linda Coverdale (London: Sphere, 1987).

24. See Sliwinski, *Le génocide,* pp. 43 and 48.

25. See Anthony Reid's study, *Southeast Asia in the Age of Commerce, 1450–1680: Vol. I, The Lands below the Winds* (New Haven: Yale University Press, 1988).

26. Read, in particular, Haing Ngor, with Roger Warner, *Surviving the Killing Fields: The Cambodian Odyssey of Haing Ngor* (London: Chatto and Windus, 1988).

27. Quoted in Kèn Khun, *De la dictature des Khmers rouges à l'occupation vietnamienne, Cambodge 1975–1979* (Paris: l'Harmattan, 1994), p. 80.

28. See, for instance, Mœung Sonn and Henri Locard, *Prisonnier de l'Angkar,* ch. 13.

29. Quoted by Doctor Zhisui Li, *The Private Life of Chairman Mao* (London: Chatto and Windus, 1994), p. 125.

30. See "Planning the Past ... The Forced Confession of Hu Nim," in *Pol Pot Plans the Future,* ed. Boua et al., p. 246.

31. FBIS, 14 April 1978, H 3–5.

32. See the definition of "crime against humanity" given by André Frossard in *Le crime contre l'humanité* (Paris: Robert Laffont, 1987).

33. These last two slogans were found by the Documentation Center of Cambodia in a cadre notebook (TSL C177) and published in *Searching for the Truth,* no. 22, October 2001. Translation by Sour Bunsou.

34. Boua, Chandler, and Kiernan, *Pol Pot Plans the Future,* p. 189.

35. Pierre Brocheux, *Hô Chi Minh* (Paris: Presses des Sciences Politiques, 2000), p. 199.

36. *Au-dalà du ciel: cinq ans chez les Khmers rouges* (Paris: Bernard Barrault, 1984).

37. Interview in the *Phnom Penh Post*, 4–17 October 1996, p. 8.

38. Kiernan, *The Pol Pot Regime,* p. 324.

39. Quoted in Karen Fisher-Nguyen, "Khmer Proverbs: Images and Rules," in *Cambodian Culture since 1975, Homeland and Exile,* ed. Ebihara, Mortland, and Ledgerwood (Ithaca, NY: Cornell University Press, 1994), p. 97, and translated *"An evil heart, but an angel's mouth,"* with the commentary *"sweet words mask an evil heart."*

40. Quoted by Sliwinski, *Le génocide*, p. 86.

41. Interview of M. S., on 20 November 1995.

42. Interview of I. C., in Phnom Penh, October 1995.

43. Slogan found in Kompong Thom province. Explanations given by H. N.

44. See Doan Van Toai, *Le Goulag vietnamien*, (Paris: Robert Laffont, 1980), p. 284.

45. Quoted by François Ponchaud, *Cambodia Year Zero*, p. 67, and translated "Nothing to gain by keeping them alive, nothing to lose by doing away with them."

46. Translated from French edition, *Cambodge année zéro* (Paris: Juliard, 1977), p. 97.

47. See end of chapter, "The Calvary of a People," in Ponchaud, *Cambodia Year Zero*.

48. *Le petit livre rouge*, p. 19 (from 1957).

49. Ibid., p. 166 (from 1964).

50. FBIS, 19 Jan. 1977, H 2.

V LABOR

1. Chapter 9 of the 1976 constitution.

2. See slogans 46 to 50.

3. FBIS, 19 April 1977, H 4.

4. This is based on testimonies of local inhabitants who saw trains loaded with the precious grain.

5. See *Le petit livre rouge*, ch. 21.

6. FBIS, 19 April 1977, H 4.

7. FBIS, 18 April 1977, H 6–7.

8. FBIS, 16 April 1976, H 10, from a speech by Hou Nim, "Minister of Information and Propaganda," on the occasion of the first anniversary of "the victory of 17 April."

9. FBIS, 1 Feb. 1977, H 4.

10. Given in Mondolkiri, on 17 July 1994.

11. Boua et al., eds., *Pol Pot Plans the Future*, p. 51.

12. FBIS, 19 Jan. 1977, H 5.

13. Boua et al., eds., *Pol Pot Plans the Future*, pp. 193–194.

14. A supporter of the Khmer Rouge revolution, he was mysteriously assassinated in Phnom Penh in December 1978, during the night preceding his planned departure. See Elizabeth Becker, *When the War Was Over*. Read also Malcolm Caldwell's "The Role of the Peasantry in Revolution" in *Journal of Contemporary Asia*, vol. 1, no. 1 (Autumn 1970).

15. See David P. Chandler, *Brother Number One: A Political Biography of Pol Pot* (Boulder, CO: Westview Press, 1992), p. 122.

16. FBIS, 19 Jan. 1978, H 18. Production was supposed to reach 6 tons, of course, wherever irrigation made it possible to grow two crops.

17. This watchword is close to slogan 22.

18. FBIS, 29 Sept. 1978, H 10.

VI COLLECTIVISM: THE DISSOLUTION OF THE INDIVIDUAL

1. FBIS, 4 Oct. 1977, H 30.

2. FBIS, 15 March 1978, H 1 and 2.

3. See ch. 3, "Sihanouk Unopposed," and in particular, "Communism in Cambodia, 1955–1963," pp. 107–121, in David Chandler, *The Tragedy of Cambodian History* (New Haven: Yale University Press, 1991). See also Thomas Engelbert and Christopher E. Goscha, *Falling out of Touch: A Study on Vietnamese Policy towards an Emerging Cambodian Communist Movement, 1930–1975* (Melbourne: Monash University, 1995), p. 58ff. Also see Steve Heder, *Vietnamese Communism and the Khmer Rouge (1930–1975)* (Bangkok: White Lotus, forthcoming).

4. Pol Pot, *Black Book* (Phnom Penh: CPK, 1978), p. 29–31.

5. See for instance Panh Rithy's documentary film, *Bophana*, which recounts a heart-rending love story between a junior cadre and a girl from his village, which did not have the approval of the Party.

6. See in ch. 3 above, section 3, "Watchwords for Soldiers and Civilians," Ponchaud's listing of the twelve commandments of Angkar.

7. See Mœung Sonn and Henri Locard, *Prisonnier de l'Angkar*, pp. 160–162, testimony from Taney prison, near Kompong Som.

8. Interview of P. H., born in 1951, in Phnom Penh in July 1995.

9. See Chandler, *Brother Number One*, p. 137.

10. Moeung Sonn and Henri Locard, *Prisonnier de l'Angkar,* pp. 263–264.

11. I owe much of this information to a personal communication from Peggy Levine who has made an extensive study of marriages under Democratic Kampuchea.

12. As reported by Keo Kunthirat who, in 1977, was married at nineteen to a Jarai soldier guarding Préah Vihear temple, in Rovieng, Preah Vihear Province. Interviewed 24/01/04.

13. These last two slogans are quoted by John Marston in "*Metaphors of the Khmer Rouge,*" ch. 8 of *Cambodian Culture since 1975*, p. 113–114, 1994. The translation here is somewhat different.

14. *Searching for the Truth,* no. 10, October 2000, p. 52.

15. Ibid., p. 56.

16. See slogan 99, ch. 3: "Angkar has the many eyes of the pineapple."

17. Provided by Hem Borith, 23 August 1994.

18. *Searching for the Truth,* no. 5 May 2000.

19. *Searching for the Truth*, no. 21 September 2001.

20. Given by Hem Borith.

21. Pierre Brocheux, *Hô Chi Minh*, (Paris: Presses des Sciences politiques, 2000), p. 203.

22. Provided by Hem Borith in July 1995.

23. See David Chandler, *The Tragedy of Cambodian History*, describing the bloody repression of the *Khmer Serei,* pp. 130–141.

24. See slogan 132.

EPILOGUE

1. Sliwinski, *Le génocide Khmer rouge.*

2. See Barbara Harff and Ted Robert Gurr, "Toward Empirical Theory of Genocides and Politicides: Identification and Measurement of Cases since 1945," *International Studies Quarterly* 32 (1988), pp. 359–371.

SELECT BIBLIOGRAPHY ON
DEMOCRATIC KAMPUCHEA, 1975–1979

I – PUBLISHED EYEWITNESS ACCOUNTS

BIZOT François. *Le portail*. Préface de John Le Carré. Paris: La Table Ronde, 2000. Translated by Euan Cameron as *The Gate,* foreword by John Le Carré (London: The Harvill Press, 2003).
CHAN Rany. *L'Enfer où Dieu prenait soin de nous, ou quatre ans sous Pol Pot*. Paris: Fayard, 1995.
EA Meng-Try and Sorya SIM. *Victims and Perpetrators? Testimony of Young Khmer Rouge Comrades*. Phnom Penh: Documentation Center of Cambodia, Series No. 1, 2001.
FENTON James. *Cambodia Witness: The Autobiography of Someth May*. London: Faber and Faber, 1986–1988.
HIM Chanrithy. *When the Broken Glass Floats*. New York: W. W. Norton, 2000.
HUDSON Christopher. *The Killing Fields*. London: Pan Books, 1984.
MŒUNG Sonn and Henri LOCARD. *Prisonnier de l'Angkar*. Paris: Fayard, 1993.
NGOR Haing S. and Roger WARNER. *A Cambodian Odyssey*. New York: Macmillan, 1987.
———. *Surviving the Killing Fields: the Cambodian Odyssey of Haing S. Ngor*. New York: Bantam Books, 1988; London: Pan Books, 1989.
NORODOM Sihanouk. *War and Hope: The Case for Cambodia*, New York: Pantheon Books, 1980; New York: Random House, 1980.
———. *Souvenirs doux et amers*. Paris: Hachette, 1981.
———. *Prisonnier des Khmers rouges*. Paris: Hachette, 1986.
ONG Thong Hœung. *J'ai cru aux Khmers rouges: retour sur une illusion*. Paris: Buchet-Chastel, 2003.

PICQ Laurence. *Beyond the Horizon: Five Years with the Khmer Rouge.* New York: St. Martin's Press, 1989.

PIN Yathay. *Stay Alive, My Son.* New York: Free Press, 1987; Simon and Schuster, 1988; with John Man, London: Arrow, 1989.

SCHANBERG Sydney H. *The Death and Life of Dith Pran.* London: Penguin Books, 1980. Film script of *The Killing Fields.*

SHEEHY Gail. *Spirit of Survival.* New York: William Morrow, 1986.

SOR Sisavang. *L'Enfant de la rizière rouge.* Paris: Fayard, 1990.

SZYMUSIAK Molyda. *The Stones Cry Out: A Cambodian Childhood, (1975–1980).* London: Sphere, 1987.

TEEDA Butt Mam and Joan D. CRIDDLE. *To Destroy You is No Loss: The Odyssey of a Cambodian Family.* New York: Anchor Books, Doubleday, 1989.

UNG Bunhaeng and Martin STUART-FOX. *The Murderous Revolution: Life and Death in Pol Pot's Kampuchea.* Chippendale: Alternative Publishing Cooperative, 1985; Bangkok: Tamarind Press, 1986.

UNG Loung. *First, They Killed My Father.* New York: Harper Collins, 2000.

VANN Nath. *A Cambodian Portrait: One Year in the Khmer Rouge's S-21.* Translated by Moeun Chhean Nariddh. Bangkok: White Lotus Press, 1998.

II – BOOKS ON DEMOCRATIC KAMPUCHEA

BECKER Elizabeth. *When the War Was Over: The Voices of Cambodia's Revolution and Its People.* New York: Simon and Schuster, 1986.

BOUA Chanthou, Ben KIERNAN, and David CHANDLER, eds. *Pol Pot Plans the Future: Confidential Leadership Documents from Democratic Kampuchea, 1976–1977.* New Haven: Yale University Southeast Asian Studies Council Monograph, no. 33, 1988.

CHANDA Nayan. *Brother Enemy: The War after the War. A History of Indochina since the Fall of Saigon.* New York: Harcourt Brace Jovanovich, 1986.

CHANDLER David. *A History of Cambodia.* Boulder, CO: Westview Press, 1983, 1992; Chiang Mai, Thailand: Silkworm Books, 1993.

———. *The Tragedy of Cambodian History: Politics, War, and Revolution.* New Haven, Connecticut: Yale University Press, 1991.

———. *Voices from S-21: Terror and History in Pol Pot's Secret Prison.* Berkeley: University of California Press, 1999.

———. *Brother Number One: A Political Biography of Pol Pot*. Rev. ed. Chiang Mai, Thailand: Silkworm Books, 2000.

CORNFIELD J. Cornfield. *Khmers Stand Up! A History of the Cambodian Government, 1970–1975*. Melbourne: Monash University Papers on Southeast Asia, no. 32, 1994.

ENGLEBERT Thomas and Christopher E. GOSCHA. *Falling out of Touch: A Study on Vietnamese Communist Policy towards an Emerging Cambodian Communist Movement, 1930–1975*. Melbourne: Monash University, 1995.

ETCHESON Craig. *The Rise and Demise of Democratic Kampuchea*. Boulder, CO: Westview Press; London: Frances Pinter, 1984.

HEDER Stephen R. *Cambodian Communism and the Vietnamese Model, Vol. 1: Imitation and Independence (1930–1975)*. Bangkok: White Lotus, 2004.

JACKSON Karl D. *Cambodia 1975–1978: Rendezvous with Death*. Princeton: Princeton University Press, 1989.

KAMM Henry. *Cambodia: Report from a Stricken Land*. New York: Arcade Publishing, 1998.

KIERNAN Ben. *The Pol Pot Regime: Race, Power, and Genocide in Cambodia under the Khmer Rouge, 1975–79*. New Haven: Yale University Press, 1996.

MARTIN Marie-Alexandrine. *Le mal cambodgien: histoire d'une société traditionnelle face à ses leaders politiques, 1946–1987*. Paris: Hachette, 1989.

OSBORNE Milton. *Sihanouk, Prince of Light, Prince of Darkness*. Chiang Mai, Thailand: Silkworm Books, 1994.

PONCHAUD François. *Cambodia Year Zero*. New York: Holt, Rinehart, Winston, 1977.

SHAWCROSS William. *The Quality of Mercy: Cambodia, Holocaust and Modern Conscience*. New York: Simon and Schuster, 1984.

SLIWINSKI Marek. *Le génocide Khmer rouge: une analyse démographique*. Paris: L'Harmattan, 1995.

VICKERY Michael. *Cambodia: 1975-1982*. Boston: South End Press, 1984.

YSA Osman. *Oukoubah, Justice for the Cham Muslims under the Democratic Kampuchea Regime*. Phnom Penh: Documentation Center of Cambodia Series No. 2, 2002.

GENERAL INDEX

absolute power, 1, 6, 10, 31, 61, 99, 158, 270
adolescents, 6, 30, 41, 69
adultery, 257, 264, 265
agriculture, 15, 53, 70, 86, 89, 163, 168, 195, 215, 218, 234–236, 239–50, 277
America, 12, 13, 27, 85, 86, 112, 157, 161, 168, 170, 177, 256, 311
  bombings, 108, 129, 130
Amin Dada, Idi, 49
Angkar, passim
Angkor, 26, 28, 31, 32, 41, 65, 73, 223
Anlong Veng, 8, 32
army, 9, 33, 34, 44, 47, 50, 52, 89, 108, 127, 143, 144–153, 164, 232
arrests, 34, 56
ASEAN, 49

bâbâ, 72
Ba Phnom, 138
Bandung Conference, (1955), 49, 65, 78
Banteay Meanchey, 138
Banteay Srey, 28
Battambang, 54, 87, 130, 138, 170, 205, 231, 238, 317
Becker, Elizabeth, 74, 75, 103
Beijing. *See* China
Besançon Alain, 3
Bizot, François, 30

Boeung Trabek, 16, 108, 133, 147
Bokassa, Jean Bedel, 49
Bokor, 216
Bourseiller, Christophe, 51
Buddhism, 41, 78, 79, 87, 93, 104, 121, 148, 151, 169–175
burials, 81

cadres, 1, 7, 8, 9, 16–19, 21, 26, 32, 33, 55, 93, 127, 130, 141, 289
Caldwell, Malcolm, 74, 103, 236, 320
capitalism, 156, 271
Cardamoms, 237
Ceauçescu, Nicolae, 49
celebrations, 14, 33–5, 44, 45, 46–7, 50, 55, 65, 68, 71, 123, 254, 255, 257, 262–9
Central Intelligence Service, (CIA), 126, 140–141, 147, 200, 258
Chamcar Loeu, 29
Chams. *See* ethnic minorities
Chandler, David, xvi, 240
chastity, 103, 146, 257
chauvinism, 73, 80, 105
Chhbar Ampeou, 147
children, 6, 43-4, 77, 81, 89, 107, 124–125, 142–144, 148, 182, 226, 316
China, xiv, 8, 35, 85
  Chinese influence, xiv, 5, 8, 13–14, 20, 21, 27–29, 51, 52, 53, 58, 61–98, 177, 180, 215, 236, 245, 255, 281

ethnic Chinese in Cambodia, 179, 303
Chinese advisors, xiv, 11, 65, 68–9, 127, 157, 180, 347
Gang of Four, 64
Chou En-lai, 13, 65
Christianity, 3, 14, 79, 103, 112, 121, 144
Chuon Meng, 133, 316
citizenship, 161, 162, 184
classes, 157
Cochinchina, 179
clothing, 11, 27, 282, 283
collectives, 3, 13, 14, 15, 19, 29, 34, 46, 55, 75, 135, 152, 200, 251
collectivization, 14, 15, 23, 182, 194, 228, 251–306
communal eating, 183
communes. *See* collectives
Communism, 13, 22, 23, 149, 212
  Cambodia, 5–7, 19, 28, 32, 35, 37, 41, 44, 51, 56–60, 103, *passim*
  China, 28, 44, 61–6, 68–71, 75–98
  France, 37, 180
  Soviet Union, 1, 44, 62, 69, 70
  Vietnam, 8, 28
Communists, 1, 2, 166, 176, 209, 211, 263
Communist Party of Kampuchea (CPK), xiv, 1, 7, 8, 11, 27, 28, 34, 39, 44, 46, 52, 61, 62, 65, 75, 160, 215. *See also* Standing Committee,
concentration camps, 185. *See also* collectives
constitution of DK, (Jan. 1976), 11, 39, 54–5, 91, 147
cooperatives, 3, 195. *See also* collectives
counterrevolution 126, 159, 162, 194
culture and society, xiii, xv, 1, 2, 3–4, 18, 32, 47, 253
Cultural Revolution. *See* Mao

Danish Marxist-Leninist Party, 125, 126
Degeyter, Adolphe, 35
Deng Tsiao-ping, 63, 158
Dey Krahom, 16, 133, 147
deportation. *See* relocation
Documentation Center of Cambodia (DC-Cam) 17
Duch (Kaing Khek Ieuv), 136, 147, 202
Dudman, Richard, 103

École Miche, 103, 121, 144
École Polytechnique, 74
education, 1, 3, 8, 13, 22, 66, 75, 97, 107, 194, 253. *See also* reeducation, schools
egalitarianism, 271
enemies, 15, 56, 125, 126, 151, 153, 155–213, 221, 253, 261
Engels, Friedrich, 58, 61, 63
ethnic minorities, 7, 13–14, 22, 34, 44, 124
  Chams, 14, 176, 303
  Chinese. *See* China
  Khmer *Loeu,* (Jarai, Kroeung, Tampuon, etc.) 7, 37, 148, 150, 181, 233, 234, 249
  Vietnamese, 13, 175–181
evacuations, 15, 23, 37, 126, 127, 129, 163, 184, 186
executions, 13, 20, 56, 87, 91, 151, 158, 162, 184, 187, 195, 201, 209, 210, 271, 303
  mass exterminations, 153, 155, 179, 204
  mass graves, 170, 174
escape, 162, 295, 296
extermination. *See* executions

family relations, 106, 107–108, 136–137, 160, 251, 252, 257, 264–271. *See also* adultery, chastity, children, rapes
  marriages, 257, 258, 265–269

General Index

factories, 168, 222
famine. *See* hunger
fertilizers, 89, 107, 204
flee. *See* escape
food, 14, 15, 33, 72, 83, 129, 182, 183, 190, 191, 217, 221, 222, 234, 235, 238, 239, 241, 243, 258, 288, 289, 290. *See also* hunger
France, 39, 41, 43, 50, 58, 122, 180
freedom, 18, 56, 57, 293–298
FUNCINPEC, 23
FLNPK (*Front de Libération Nationale Khmer*), 23
FUNK, (*Front National Uni du Kampuchéa*) 30, 49

genocide, 179–180, 303
Godement, François, 101
Great Leap Forward. *See* Mao
GRUNK *Gouvernement d'Union Nationale Populaire du Kampuchéa*, 29
guerrillas. *See* maquis

Hanoi. *See* Vietnam
health, 127, 157, 151, 152
 in hospitals, 191, 192
 of patients, 186–193
Heder, Steve, 317
Heller, Michel, 2
Heng Samrin, 123, 124, 292, 317
Hitlerism, 2
Ho Chi Minh, 27, 86 182, 199, 274, 292
holidays. *See* festivals
Hou Youn, 28, 29, 33, 95
Hu Nim, 28, 29, 33, 78, 95, 194, 295
Hua Guofeng, 63–64, 103, 240
humor, 6, 285–287, 291
hunger, 14, 15, 20, 33, 34, 35, 81, 118, 152–153, 182, 204, 241, 289. *See also* food
Hun Sen, 312

ideology, 5, 8, 151, 179, 194, 199, 201, 210
imperialism, 45, 77, 108, 125, 126, 156, 161, 168, 175, 177, 271
Ieng Sary, xv, 8, 9, 27, 43, 44, 66–7, 95, 144, 147, 159
In Tam, 139 316
indoctrination, 1, 8, 107. *See also* re-education
industry, 54, 58, 70, 86, 227
informing, 114, 137, 142, 206
Institute of Scientific Training and Information (*previously Institut Khméro-soviétique, now* Institute of Technology of Cambodia, ITC), 74
L'Internationale, 35–39
irrigation, 15, 31–2, 70, 73, 73, 82, 164, 240, 241, 247, 248

Jarais, 37, 225, 321. *See also* ethnic minorities
jewelry, 88, 116, 276, 278, 282, 283
Jurquet, Jacques, 50–1, 312

Kaè Pauk, 9, 66, 159
Kampot, 216
Kandal, 240
Kang Sheng, 51
KGB, 126, 140–141, 147, 200
Khieu Ponnary, xv, 159
Khieu Thirit, xv, 159
Khieu Samphan, xv, 8, 9, 16–17, 18, 19, 28, 29, 33, 66, 71, 109, 143, 159, 160, 161, 203, 242, 260, 295, 310, 311
Khmer *Loeu*. *See* ethnic minorities
Khmer Rouge, *passim*
khnoh, 207, 307
Kiernan, Ben, 200
Kim Il-sung, 78, 79, 82, 119, 159
Koh Kong, 216
Komping Puey, 54, 231
Kompong Cham, 29, 65, 133, 242

Kompong Chhnang, 62, 157, 240
Kompong Som, 86, 217
Kompong Speu, 240, 281
Kompong Thom, 67, 165, 240
Kompong Trabek, 143
kong chalat. See work/front-line brigades
Koy Thuon, 141, 258
krâma, 11, 87, 206, 307
Krang Leou, 62, 157
Kratié, 107, 129
Krisher, Bernard, 66
Kroeung, 37. *See also* ethnic minorities
Kuomintang, 157, 200

labor. *See* work
Lenin, Vladimir Ilyich, 1, 35, 63, 103, 125, 189
Lévy, Bernard-Henri, 1
Lévy, Beny 51
liberty. *See* freedom
Lifton, Robert Jay, 112
Lin Piao, 63, 158
Liu Shao shi, 63, 158
Lon Nol, 9, 124
Luco, Fabienne, 315

Machiavellianism, 3, 22, 61, 205, 261
Mao Zedong, xiv–xv, 1, 10, 13, 35, 44, 47, 68, 71, 73, 76, 78–98 *passim* 99, 103, 125, 131, 134, 135, 141, 149, 156, 157, 158, 180, 212, 216, 222, 237, 256, 258, 299
  Cultural Revolution, 20, 22, 63, 66, 76, 94–98, 140, 156, 158, 197, 198, 222, 263
  Great Leap Forward, xiv, 63, 70–1, 73, 82, 156, 193, 197, 215, 217, 224, 242
  Maoism, 5, 21, 194, 216
  Maoist, 2, 132, 166, 197, 225, 298, 305
maquis, 12, 17, 25–26, 27, 40, 65, 85, 163, 197, 225, 298, 305

Marseillaise (La), 39
markets. *See* money
marriages. *See* family
Marx, Karl, 58, 61, 63, 103, 211, 306
  Marxist, 2, 120, 168, 169, 233
  Marxism, 35, 58–59
mass graves. *See* executions
Mat Ly, 12
Mekong, 27, 53
model, 291
Mœung Sonn, 139
Mondolkiri, 73, 249
money, (trade, barter, currency, markets) 33, 107, 145, 163, 237, 278, 281
Monique, Princess, 27–28
Montagnards. See Khmer *Loeu*
mulethans (base people), 11, 13, 72, 245, 255, 276, 308
Myrdal, Jan, 235

National Museum, 86
new people. *See* "17 April people"
Ne Win, 49
Ney Saran, 9
Nhiek Tioulong, 44
niredey, 9, 88, 107, 142, 147, 308

Norodom Phurissara, Prince, 29
Norodom Sihanouk, 1, 8, 12, 13, 25, 26–30, 33, 39, 41, 54, 59, 65–66, 95, 127, 169, 173, 177, 274, 301, 311
North Korea, (Pyongyang) 39, 78, 119, 159, 160, 236, 247
  advisors, 127
  juche, 78
  Workers' Party of Korea, 160
Nuon Chea, 7, 9, 34, 41, 55, 66, 95, 125, 126, 159, 173, 212, 234, 256, 260, 261

Orwell, George, 10, 18, 113
  Big Brother, 10, 113
  "doublethink," 266
  "newspeak," 2
  1984, 18, 113, 135
  Orwellian, 3, 266

Paris Agreement (21 Oct. 1991), 20
Parti Communiste Marxiste-Léniniste (PCMLF) 50–1
Penn Nouth, 41
people's communes. *See* collectives
Phnom Kulen, 27, 28
Phnom Penh, 9, 32, 34, 39, 41, 46, 50–1, 53, 59, 63, 65, 67, 68, 74, 75, 86, 104, 107, 129, 132, 133, 157, 160, 163, 168, 184, 212, 235, 255, 300
Phnom Srok, 87, 138
Picq, Laurence, 260
Pol Pot (Saloth Sar), xv, 5, 7, 9–10, 13–14, 28, 29, 32, 34, 35–44, 46–47, 50, 51, 65–69, 75, 79, 95, 97, 101, 102, 104, 111, 113, 120, 123, 144, 154, 158, 159, 160, 161, 177, 180, 181, 184, 194, 199, 212, 225, 235, 252, 253, 255, 256, 259, 261, 274, 300, 311
  democracy according to Pol Pot, 260–262, 294
  Office 870, 7, 101
  Pol Pot-ism, 6, 112, 233
politburo. *See Angkar*
Pochentong, 147
Ponchaud, François, 145, 210
population statistics, 8, 234, 235, 303
Pottier, Eugène, 35
Prey Nokor (Saigon), 45
Prey Nup, 139
Prey Veng, 138, 143
prisons, 6, 51, 87, 102, 132, 135, 138, 148, 160, 162, 168, 169, 170, 206–210, 222, 223, 257
  S-21, (Tuol Sleng*)*, 6, 118, 132, 134, 136, 147, 160, 177, 194, 202, 242

khnoh, 307
private property, 32, 33, 194, 275–284
production, 70, 155, 166, 215
proletariat, 141–142, 181, 194, 261, 273
propaganda, 1, 2, 97
purges, 9, 62, 64, 88, 119, 142
purity, 109, 182

racism, 87, 106
Radio Democratic Kampuchea, 17, 33, 39, 65, 126
Ramayana, 236
rapes, 115, 116, 258
Ratanakiri, 8, 43, 44, 144, 181, 249
reeducation, 1, 8, 16 17–18, 55, 90–94, 131–135, 159, 162, 183, 195, 201, 295, 298, 299, 302
religion, 169–175
relocation, 62, 69, 73, 185, 186, 216, 272, 306
repression, 99, 108, 115, 130, 163, 167, 305
resistance. *See* maquis
revolution, *passim*
Revolutionary Flag (newspaper), 1
S-21 (Tuol Sleng). *See* prisons
rice. *See* agriculture
ruralization. *See* relocation
Russey Keo Vocational School, 67

sahakor. *See* collectives
Saloth Nhiap, 67
Saloth Sar. *See* Pol Pot
Saloth Suon, 67
Sangkum Reastr, Niyum, 1, 16–17, 29, 44, 65, 297, 309
Saveros Pou, 3, 4, 5
schools, xv, 95, 96–97, 107, 170, 222, 226
Sao Phim, 9, 147
self-criticism. *See* reeducation
self-sufficiency, 85

"17 April people", 11–12, 13, 115, 128, 135, 183–186, 187, 188, 193, 203, 238, 245, 257, 276, 278, 303
Siemreap, 65
Sisowath High School, 67
Sliwinski, Marek, 303
social classes, 11–13, 54, 58–60, 184
socialism, 253, 284–293
soldiers. *See* army
Son Ngoc Than, 297
Son Sen, xv, 7–8, 9, 44, 63, 66, 67, 95, 101, 120, 144, 189
songs (revolutionary), 1, 9, 20, 33, 37, 106, 107, 263, 267
Soth Polin, 102
Soviet Union, 2, 36, 135, 140, 141, 149, 156, 223
Sraè Cham, 139
Stalin, Joseph, 61, 63, 113, 125, 241
Standing Committee, 6, 7–8, 15, 16, 19, 34, 64, 147, 197, 242, 260
Stung Treng, 27
suicides, 268
Summers, Laura, 315
Sun Hao, 14, 154, 157, 158, 217, 240
Svay Rieng, 178

Takeo, 20, 175, 178, 205, 240
Ta Mok, 8, 9, 66, 142, 311
Tampuons, 37, 225
teams. *See* work
Technological Institute of Cambodia
Teng Ying-chao, 240
terror, 3, 41, 49, 102, 130, 159, 229
Thailand, 33, 88, 127, 295, 311
Thala Bariwatt, 27
Thiounn Mumm, 74, 95
Thompson, E. P., 313
Ton Si Yoeun, 68
Tonle Sap, 53
torture, 56, 117, 132, 134, 135, 137, 151, 152, 162, 177, 202, 242, 258, 261

totalitarianism, 2–3, 5, 10, 18, 31, 33, 54–55, 101–102, 116, 131, 156, 162, 253, 261, 291
Tou Samouth, 7, 256
trade. *See* money
Tramkâk, 20, 175
Tuol Sleng. *See* S-21

United Nations Transitory Authority in Cambodia (UNTAC), 20
USA. *See* America
utopia, 35, 37, 182, 184, 244, 249, 293

vegetables, 223, 237
Vickery, Michael, 13
Vietnam, 9, 13, 28–30, 33, 52, 53, 61, 111, 127, 290, 295
  Hanoi, 140, 156, 168, 177, 236
  Vietminh, 8, 116, 130, 146, 180, 208
  Vietnamese, 2, 11, 122, 126, 140, 151, 157, 168, 175–181, 256, 274, 303, 312
  war booty, 33, 86, 283
Vorn Vet, xv, 9

weapons, 157, 164
work, 91, 155, 163, 164, 187, 215–250, 305, 306
  front line brigades, 150
  work sites, 215
  work teams 226, 228, 286–288,

Y Phandara, 108
yothea. *See* army
Yun Yat, xv, 8

SLOGAN INDEX

Note: Numbers refer to slogans

American(s), 8, 65, 97, 129, 130
anger, 167, 290, 291
Angkar, 1, 7, 11, 22, 36, 43, 65, 72, 82, 84–152, 195, 196, 214, 241, 244, 248, 251–253, 297, 346, 357, 364, 372, 375, 376, 384, 408, 419, 420
Angkor, 40
annihilate, 235, 240
answer, 142, 144
apes, 1
arm, 260-262, 382
arrest, 255, 257
ashes, 3, 294
assignments, 108, 112, 116
attack, 158, 176, 179–181, 200, 290, 293, 298, 301, 388

bâbâ, 39, 276, 315–317
baby, 5. *See also* newborn
battlefield, 287-289, 302
belongings, 67, 351, 384
blood, 5, 161, 300, 387
body, 157, 202, 203, 226, 233
brain 95, 203
brother, 90, 119, 129, 131, 275, 320
bundle, 380, 382

canals, 81, 302, 315
capitalism (lists), 174, 175, 178, 369
celebrate, 337, 338
cement, 187, 188

children 89, 91, 151, 156, 190, 286
Central Intelligence Agency (CIA) 147, 148, 235
classes, 31, 88, 167, 360, 408
clean, 28, 227
clear-sighted, 7, 12, 42, 43, 97, 98
clothes, 233, 364, 402
collectives 158, 316, 350, 367, 368, 370, 371, 388, 395, 409, 410
collectivism, 369, 387
collectivity, 333, 429
Communist Party of Kampuchea, (CPK), 12
corpse, 245
corruption, 27, 28
criticize, criticism, 71, 72
crush, 197, 198, 261, 263, 264, 313

dams, 81, 302, 327
death, 347, 433
destiny, 18, 56, 57, 388
destroy, 49, 51, 167, 174, 181, 187, 234, 239, 354, 357, 368, 390
development, 40, 208
die, 159, 259, 421
dikes, 302, 315, 325
disease, 218, 220, 397
discipline, 73, 110, 111, 346, 417, 419
do, 80, 83, 114, 116, 171, 286
dog, 191, 311
duck, 118, 275

earth, 22, 25, 161, 326
easy, 273, 274, 377
eat, 53, 223, 229, 315-317, 390, 395
enemies, 158, 159, 163, 165, 167–169, 173, 180, 181, 194, 205–207, 229, 231, 234, 235, 239, 240, 245, 248, 256, 277, 290, 291, 293
equality, 362, 429

family, 350-352, 387
father, 89, 90, 275, 320, 351
fault, 205, 248
ferocious, 121, 122
feudal (-ism), 46, 48, 65, 174, 175, 178, 179, 373
fields, 271, 302, 315, 316, 321, 322, 325
fight, 160, 259, 294, 295, 300, 311
fish, 157, 193
food, 191, 229, 246, 320, 331, 338, 379, 388, 398, 399
forbidden, 382, 414
free, 31, 32, 154, 324, 414, 416, 418, 421
freedom, 419

genii, 192, 196
ghosts, 193, 195, 339, 345
give up, 273, 351, 366
glorious, 6, 10, 15, 19, 26, 63, 320, 357
gnaw, 235, 241
god, 195, 196

hand, 170, 276, 284, 303, 306
head, 58, 118, 201, 202, 389
health, 289, 388-390
heart, 244, 413
hectare, 312–314, 322
hide, 139, 233
history, 261–264, 406
hit, 51, 390
hoe, 170, 171
houses, 401, 402

hunger, 223, 397
hungry, 246
hygiene, 388–390

ill, 217, 219, 222
imperialism, 8, 46, 47, 49, 65, 97, 167, 176, 180, 244
independence, 19, 29, 31
individualism, 181, 353, 368, 369, 387, 419
industries, 24, 288
innocent, 256, 257

joy, 6, 24

KGB, 147, 148, 235
king, 426-428

lazy 213, 215, 220
leap forward, 32, 36–39, 41, 43
learn, 242, 303
leg, 219, 247, 260–262, 382
liberate, 31
liberty, 31, 32, 417
lips, 156, 157
live, 267, 357, 362, 408
Lon Nol, 12
love, 86–88, 347
loyal, 133, 136, 141

masses, 26, 232
master, 18, 22-25, 56, 280, 323, 324
meetings, 82, 132
messenger, 388, 389
militia, 156, 388
mistake, 59, 155, 255, 256
model, 73, 401, 408
monks, 185, 186, 190
mother, 5, 89, 90, 275, 320, 351
motherland, 18, 32, 85, 299

nature, 323, 330, 331
neck, 155, 163

Slogan Index

neutrality, 19, 29
new, 303, 354–356, 407
new born, 154

obedience, 119
obey, 111,112, 346
old, 179, 182, 355, 356
opiate 184
order, 109, 111, 113, 115, 354, 355

parasites, 185
parasitic, 209
parents, 91, 150
Party, 227, 229, 260, 275, 333, 335, 398
peace, 19, 29, 430
peasant, 25, 26, 33
people, 10, 61, 95, 155, 157, 166, 168, 173, 175, 229, 232, 241, 303, 307, 329, 333, 341, 389, 401, 407, 428
personal, 351, 366
pineapple, 99–101
plan, 93, 288, 289
pot, 201, 222, 352
prahok, 37, 236
prisons, 252, 254
prisoners, 212
private 412
private (individual, personal) property, 366, 367, 378, 385, 386, 404
property, 61, 371, 374
production, 169, 283, 298, 301, 303, 313, 332, 400
protest, 245
pure, 28, 92

question, 141, 142, 144, 145

rabbit, 222, 225
reactionary, 46, 49, 175
reconstruction, 132, 424
religion, 184
replace, 354, 356
report, 102, 150
respect, 108, 112, 119, 158, 409

responsible, 282, 334
responsibility, 249
revolution (-ary), 5, 7, 14, 18, 20, 21, 26, 45, 63, 83, 84, 164, 166, 167, 226, 227, 242, 282, 299, 303, 317, 333, 349, 352, 359, 379, 382, 385, 386, 387, 404
rice, 61, 64, 79, 207, 222, 304, 305, 308–319, 321, 322, 325
rifle, 170, 171, 303
roots, 50, 165
running dogs, 9, 178

Samdech Euv (Norodom Sihanouk), 2–4
save, 64, 275
scatter, 180, 200
schools, 82
secrecy, 127, 128
secret, 103, 140, 207, 232
see, 80, 101, 105
self-criticism, 71
shackle(s), 251, 382
shit, 53, 210, 316, 427
silver, 382, 384
sisters, 90, 119, 275, 320
sky, 322, 324
smash, 4, 199, 292
socialism, 369, 402, 405
socialist, 385
society, 1, 65, 186, 217, 218, 235, 303, 337–339, 385, 407, 408
soldiers, 69, 155, 156, 160, 348, 349, 388, 390
solidarity, 156, 400, 429
soul, 84, 85, 157
speak, 94, 105, 230, 244
spirit, 60, 368
steel, 423, 424
stomach, 210, 389
strength, 52, 53
strike, 167, 169, 179, 292, 313
struggle, 164, 289, 340
study, 132, 289, 346

sun, 265, 301
tail, 303, 311, 329
task, 115, 278
teachers, 131, 285
team, 353, 388, 391
tears, 5, 39
theory, 704, 76
tons 312, 313, 322
torture, 163
towns, 279, 408

unity, 33, 429

vanquish, 35, 165, 211, 212
vermin, 200
victims, 30, 216
Vietnamese, 197–202
village, 391, 401, 408

war, 166, 211, 212, 305
water, 22, 23, 25, 74, 118, 157, 201, 228, 236, 305, 314, 316, 317
weed out, 258
wheel, 261–264
wise, 7, 11,
work, 5, 41, 230, 266, 269, 274–276, 281, 284, 285, 290, 291, 294, 296, 297, 299, 301, 321, 323, 324, 395, 431
workers, 236, 237
work sites, 287, 433
worms, 236, 237